Fly Fishing California

A No Nonsense Guide to Top Waters

Ken Hanley & Friends

Stealthy approach for wily mountain trout.
Photo by Ken Hanley.

NO NONSENSE
Tucson, Arizona

Fly Fishing California

A No Nonsense Guide to Top Waters
ISBN-10 1-892469-10-3
ISBN-13 978-1-892469-10-6

© 2007 No Nonsense
Fly Fishing Guidebooks

Published by:
No Nonsense Fly Fishing Guidebooks
P.O. Box 91858
Tucson, AZ 85752-1858
(520) 547-2462
www.nononsenseguides.com
12345 10 09 08 07
Printed in China

Editors: Howard Fisher, David Banks
Maps, Illustrations, Design & Production:
Pete Chadwell, Dynamic Arts
Cover Photos by John Sherman

No part of this book may be reproduced, stored in a retrieval system or transmitted in any form, or by any means, electronic, mechanical, photocopying or otherwise, without the prior permission of the publisher. You may reproduce segments of this book when using brief excerpts in critical reviews and articles, with appropriate credit.

The staff at No Nonsense Fly Fishing Guidebooks has made every effort to ensure that all references to placenames, roads and water bodies were accurate at the time this book was printed. However, such things do change occasionally.

Dedication

I dedicate this work to Leon Berthiume, Dennis Johnson, and Steve Yool. They fueled my fire for sunrises and sunsets atop the Sierra crest. I also dedicate this guide to teachers past. They gave me the gift to ask questions and the tools to discover answers.

Acknowledgments

I'd like to show my gratitude to a few of my colleagues. Their talents and unselfish expertise are an integral part of this guide. Andy Burk and Scott Saiki are two of the most credible fly fishers plying our northern waters. Their daily ventures afield offer the latest fly fishing news. Jeff Solis, Peter Piconi, Bill Calhoun, and Gary Bulla have a fine grasp on the southern intricacies of California. They are my "Pipeline" to Santa Barbara and beyond. My partner Jay Murakoshi, Sandy Watts, Woody Woodland, and Mike Mercer were always available to discuss fly selection and design.

A very special thanks to Jeff Solis, Dave Stanley, Kate Howe, Bob Zeller, and Cheryl Hoey for their valuable contributions to this project.

I appreciate the fine photography of John Sherman, Brian O'Keefe, and others for their support.

This guidebook received advance review and improvements from fly fishers: Ernie Kinzli owner of Ernie's Casting Pond, Kurt Lemons owner of Upstream Flyfishing, Bill Kiene, Alan Barnard and Andy Guibord of Kiene's Fly Shop, Ed Digardi of San Jose Fly Shop, and again, Andy Burk of The Reno Fly Shop. Thank you so much—your additions will help everyone enjoy fly fishing in The Great Golden State.

Finally, special thanks to Pete Chadwell and David Banks for taking my chicken scratches and turning them into a fine guidebook.

Author with striped bass.
Photo by Andy Guibord.

About the Author

Ken Hanley, a California and Pacific Coast fly fishing expert, has been conducting fishing and adventure specialty programs since 1970. More than 14,000 students have taken advantage of Ken's varied programs both in the field and on the water. His award-winning instructional programs are well respected throughout the adventure industry. He's a founding member of the Pacific Pro Surf Association.

Ken was chosen as the 2005 inductee into the NCCFFF Fly Fishing Hall of Fame. For more than twenty years The Hall of Fame award has been presented to the individual who has made outstanding contributions to the sport of fly fishing. The criteria for this distinction include the improvement of the art, science, literature, techniques, enjoyment and conservation of fly fishing and the resource.

While Ken's home waters of California are what he knows best, his extensive field experience spans the globe from the highest peaks in Tibet and the Himalaya, to the remote wilderness regions of Asia, New Zealand, Mexico, Europe, and North America. In all, he's caught more than 90 different species of fresh and saltwater gamefish.

In addition to authoring fly fishing guidebooks, Ken writes and photographs for national and regional publications in the outdoor industry. Ken's other fly fishing titles include *Fly Fishing the Pacific Inshore*, *Fly Fishing Afoot in the Surf Zone*, *Fly Fishing Afoot for Western Bass*, *California Fly Tying and Fishing Guide*, and *Mexico: Blue Ribbon Fly Fishing Guide*.

Table of Contents

Photo by Brian O'Keefe.

Photo by John Sherman.

Photo by John Sherman.

Photo by Don Vachini.

Photo by Brian O'Keefe.

4

Photo by John Sherman

Photo by John Sherman

Photo by John Sherman

5

Stalking trout on Hot Creek.
Photo by John Sherman.

California Fly-O-Matic

You would do well engaging in a little homework before hitting the road. Use this guide, and then dial up one of the contact numbers in the Resources section. A simple phone call can give you some scouting info that's the ticket to your field success. Fly shops, guides, clubs, and park services, all provide timely details concerning local waters. Their information is generally very accurate and should help in your decision-making process.

Don't be intimidated by the vastness of California. Rather, take a logical approach to observing the basics of exploring this state with a fly rod in hand. Start by asking yourself if you prefer river or still water environments? How about the saltwater experience inside calm estuaries? Do you like largemouth bass or albacore tuna? My point is to first have you narrow down the playing field. Then you can begin concentrating on the specifics of species or habitat.

At any rate, to assist in getting your adventures on the proper path, the following tips will help any angler in their quest of the Golden State Fly Fishing Experience.

Game Fish & Their Habitat

California literally presents you with dozens-upon-dozens of species to engage. With such a diverse offering you would do well by adopting these categories to define our game fish habitats first: Freshwater/Coldwater (streams, rivers, lakes), Freshwater/Warmwater (lakes, ponds, reservoirs, delta), Inshore Saltwater (rocky shoreline, estuary, sandy beach, harbor, inner bay), Offshore Saltwater (open ocean). By using this system you'll effectively target a specific range of game fish in each arena. Having narrowed the playing field, your final choice of game fish becomes much easier.

Weather

California has terrific conditions most of the year... however... it does rain, it does snow, and it does become very windy at times! Coastal locations can be pretty cold during many summer mornings, while the Sierra Nevada Mountains can be fairly hot during August and September. The weather is dynamic, constantly evolving. The most volatile months anywhere in the state are November, December, and January. The most stable times, and prolific angling months, would include May through October.

Hazards

There are really just a few I'd like to mention in this guidebook.

Those of you scouting our streams and rivers should be aware of rattlesnakes. Be especially careful around dry snags and fallen timber. Waterways like the Merced River and Kings River come to mind in particular.

Respect altitude! Many folks traveling from sea level into the High Sierra don't take the time to acclimatize properly. Travel slowly. Enjoy a few extra hours rest at altitude (or an extra night if need be) before hiking and exerting yourself. Learn about the symptoms and first aid techniques for altitude sickness before venturing above 5,000 feet in elevation.

Saltwater anglers will need to be aware of the changing tide cycle. It certainly affects access and safety procedures. Anyone exploring the surf zone should note the intensity of those breaking waves. It doesn't take much to get knocked down and disoriented. I always travel with a partner when fly fishing the surf scene.

Fly Selection & Hatches

This guide doesn't pretend to be a Western entomology or baitfish cycle authority. Those subjects can fill volumes of encyclopedias. The hatches and baitfish mentioned in this guide are a basic reference to help you assemble your tackle. These are what I would consider cornerstone hatches (and miscellaneous prey populations) for all of California. There is no question that more categories exist, but you can feel confident with these as a foundation to your collection. You can always choose your own favorite fly design, however these basic food categories are essential to address:

Trout Rivers/Streams: mayflies (blue-winged olive, callibaetis, green drake), caddis (Western sedge, micro caddis), stoneflies (black, little yellow stone), midge, sculpin, ant, grasshopper.

Trout Still Waters: midge (chironomid), damselfly (nymph and adult), dragonfly (nymph), trout fry, mayfly (callibaetis), ant, grasshopper, snail.

Bass Still Waters: deer hair popper, panfish fry, threadfin shad, smelt, leech, dragonfly and damselfly (nymph and adult), bass fry, crawdad.

Inshore Saltwater: ghost shrimp, rock crab, anchovy, marine worms, mole crab, perch fry, sculpin.

Offshore Saltwater: anchovy, sardine, mackerel.

Rods

Those of you targeting smaller intimate freshwater trout habitat would do fine with 3- and 4-weight outfits. The larger 5- and 6-weight classes will provide you with the best "all-around" performance on most

A great assortment of flies for delta stripers.
Photo by John Sherman.

California waters.

If you're pursuing shad, steelhead, bass, and light saltwater species, consider 7- and 8-weight designs. They can provide the necessary power to handle heavier current, strong winds, heavy (or large) flies, and a wide selection of specialty lines.

Striped bass anglers would benefit from 8- through 10-weight outfits. These rods afford great lifting and leveraging power. The most popular outfits are the 9- or 10-weight class.

Inshore saltwater anglers can ply the coast with 7- through 10-weight designs. The 8-weight outfit is a terrific choice for most outings.

Offshore saltwater adventurers would do best with 10- through 12-weight outfits. These rods are needed to handle extreme conditions.

Reels

Standard "click and pawl" drag systems are fine for most freshwater pursuits. If you choose to target game fish like steelhead or salmon, then perhaps a disk drag design would be a better choice. The disk drag option is certainly a benefit for anyone working in the saltwater arena.

If you find yourself drawn to chasing species that can rip line off your spool, consider using a large arbor design. The benefits include a rapid retrieve rate, relaxed line that improves castability, and protecting your tippet from an overpowering drag setting. The only possible drawback of the large arbor might be the capacity for your backing and line combination. Speak with the professionals at your local fly shop (or attend one of the terrific trade shows around California). I'm sure they can offer you assistance with this issue.

Lines

A floating line is the perfect choice for most river and stream outfits. However, it would behoove you to add a second line that is a sinking option as well. That way you can cover everything from topwater presentations to bouncing streamers along the bottom. The two lines I enjoy working with are WF (weight forward) floating and type-2 sink tip designs.

Still water anglers should consider "the stealth factor" when choosing a line. The newer clear lines provide a nice advantage under extreme conditions. Again, I like the WF designs for this application. My second choice for negotiating still waters, is actually a full sinking line. It helps me to stay in a deeper retrieve path, maximizing my time in a specific strike zone. In this case, a type-2 class is very efficient.

The saltwater scene provides some unique challenges. I've found that a "shooting head" system, and/or modified sink tip with intermediate running line design, is integral to the field experience. I typically use a head (or sink tip option) that cuts quickly through current and depth requirements. Two of my favorite shooting heads are 30' of LC-13 (lead core 13), and a type-4 sinker. I also enjoy working with the sink tip/full line options in grain weights of 200 to 350. Companies such as RIO, Airflo, Teeny, and Cortland can provide you with specialty designs for exploring the saltwater game. Full floating lines can often be used while working around harbors and estuaries.

Wading Gear

You have to love that Gore-Tex® material! Man is that stuff comfortable to work with. Be sure to wear the appropriate combination of undergarments to address seasonal water temperatures. Stocking-foot waders (of any material design) are the "go to" choice for many fly fishers around California. For maximum flotation, though, you still can't beat neoprene. Wader designs are really your own choice. Be smart with whatever you wear, and don't get too aggressive once you're in the water. Watch the current, watch your footing, and watch out for fatigue. I highly recommend using a wading belt or pullover jacket that seals your waders. Wading staffs are also indispensable safety items.

Private Fly Fishing Waters

California, like many states, has some terrific pay-for-fly-fishing opportunities. These locations can provide you with a high degree of solitude and quality angling time. Their inclusion here, however, in no way implies an endorsement. Fee-fishing is a popular, time tested and growing way to enjoy fly fishing. Opportunities of this type bear mentioning in a guidebook such as this. You'll find a variety of these resources listed throughout the book.

Guides

A qualified guide will steer you towards the best fishery in places that match your field skills, preferences, and conditioning. You can find some of the best guides in our state listed in the Resources section of this guidebook.

Crowding

There are hundreds of fishable streams and rivers throughout California, and over a million acres of still water habitat to explore. Our coastline stretches nearly a thousand miles and the delta systems have over a thousand miles of navigable waterways to explore! There's absolutely no reason to feel crowded, just go find another piece of the puzzle to enjoy. The point is, move around. I try not to fish the most popular sites on weekends, and stay away from them on most holidays as well. It does take an adjustment, but the rewards are worth the extra effort you'll make to participate in our collective fly fishing experience.

Switching locations also helps with angling conservation. Rotating your destinations reduces or minimizes your impact on any single resource. It's

Heading out of San Diego.
Photo by John Sherman.

a "win/win" deal. You'll experience the joys of new waters while giving your favorite locations a chance to recover.

Ratings

How do you rate your last fly fishing experience? You consider the weather, the company, access, game fish, a great cast and presentation, almost everything. When retelling your experience, aside from where you had lunch, the three most helpful comments for others include access, game fish, and water quality.

The 1 to 10 rating scale in this guide employs these considerations. Anything rated an "8" or above represents the highest quality water and is a "must" for any fly fisher in the Golden State. A "1" rating would be atrocious. I haven't even considered these waters for this guidebook.

All the locations in this book rate a "5" or better. Keep in mind that the scale is a stepping-stone of sorts. Develop your own ratings the day you're on the water!

Common California Game Fish

Illustrations by Joseph R. Tomelleri.

Rainbow Trout

Steelhead Trout

Brown Trout

Brook Trout

Cutthroat Trout

Chinook Salmon

Coho Salmon

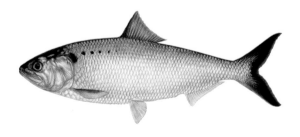

American Shad

Largemouth Bass

Smallmouth Bass

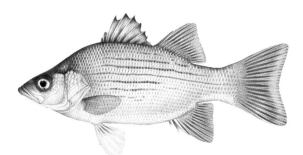

White Bass

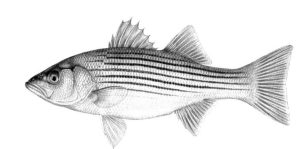

Striped Bass

Spotted Bass

Black Crappie

Yellow Perch

Bluegill

Prospecting for steelhead on the Smith River.
Photo by John Sherman.

Flies to Use in California

Adams

Parachute Adams

Blue Winged Olive Cripple

Pale Morning Dun Cripple

Callibaetis Cripple

Elk Hair Caddis

Hexagenia May

Humpy

Little Yellow Stonefly

Adult Foam Damsel

Stimulator

Royal Stimulator

Sofa Pillow

Madam X

Whitlock's Hopper

Black Fur Ant

Adult Midge

Serendipity

Photos by Pete Chadwell.

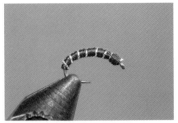

Giant Blood Midge

Disco Midge

Suspended Midge

Timberline Emerger

Bird's Nest

Hunched Back Infrequens

Bead Head Prince

Bead Head Pheasant Tail

Bead Head Hare's Ear

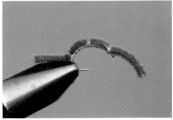

San Juan Worm

Zug Bug

Marabou Damsel

Sheep Creek Special

Woolly Bugger

Dragon Bugger

Carey Special

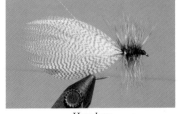

Hornberg

Zonker

Photos by Pete Chadwell.

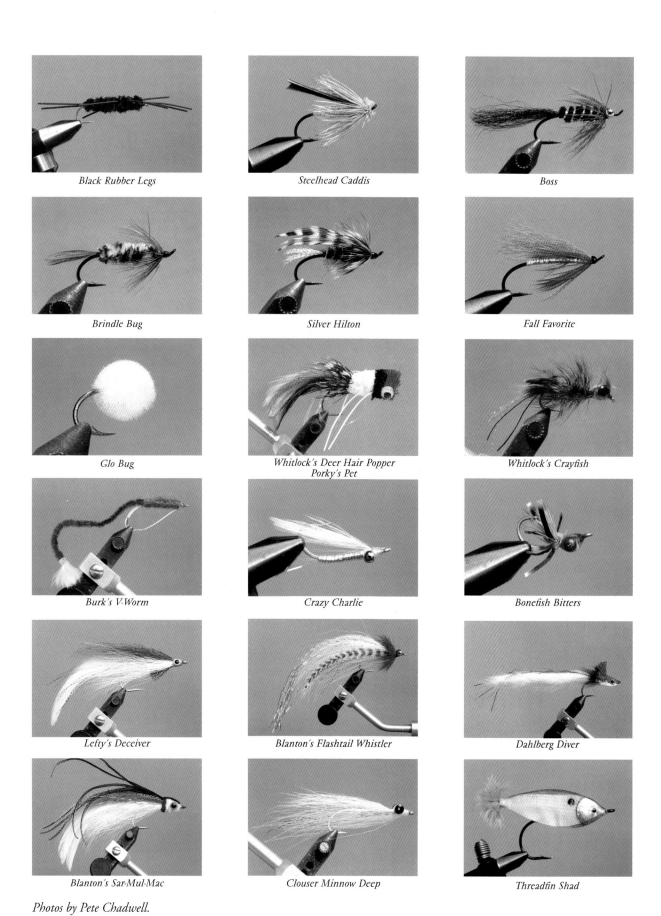

Black Rubber Legs

Steelhead Caddis

Boss

Brindle Bug

Silver Hilton

Fall Favorite

Glo Bug

Whitlock's Deer Hair Popper
Porky's Pet

Whitlock's Crayfish

Burk's V-Worm

Crazy Charlie

Bonefish Bitters

Lefty's Deceiver

Blanton's Flashtail Whistler

Dahlberg Diver

Blanton's Sar-Mul-Mac

Clouser Minnow Deep

Threadfin Shad

Photos by Pete Chadwell.

A great day on the Klamath River.
Photo by John Sherman.

Top California Fly Fishing Waters

Feather River. Photo by John Sherman.

Spotted Bass. Photo by Ken Hanley.

Lower Sacramento River. Photo by John Sherman.

Smith River. Photo by John Sherman.

Feather River. Photo by John Sherman.

American River. Photo by Ken Hanley.

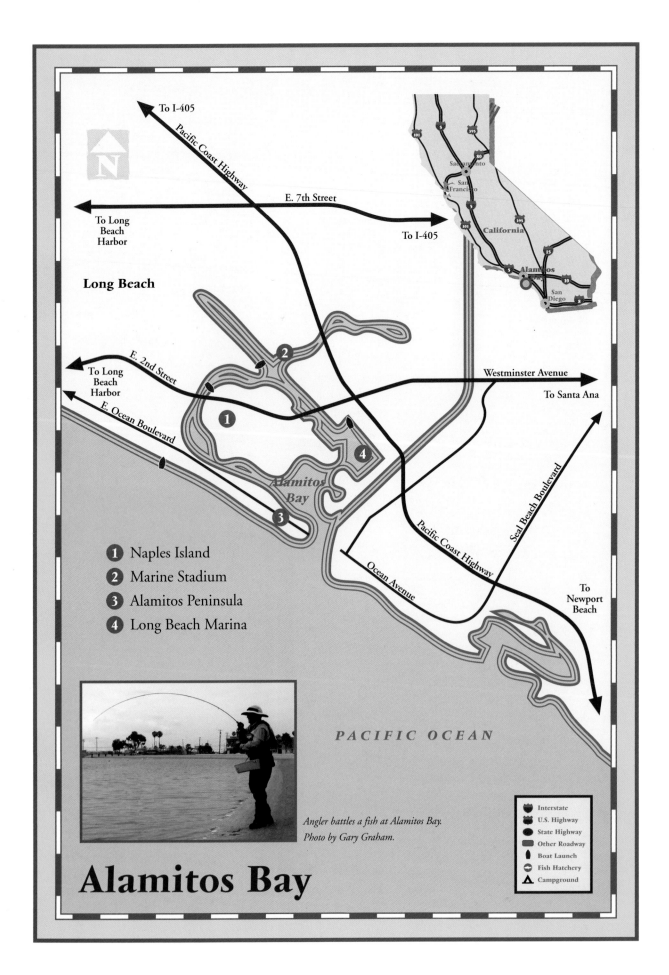

To I-405

Pacific Coast Highway

E. 7th Street

To Long
Beach
Harbor

To I-405

Long Beach

California

Alamitos

San
Diego

E. 2nd Street

To Long
Beach
Harbor

Westminster Avenue

To Santa Ana

E. Ocean Boulevard

1

4

*Alamitos
Bay*

Seal Beach Boulevard

3

Pacific Coast Highway

Ocean Avenue

1 Naples Island

2 Marine Stadium

3 Alamitos Peninsula

4 Long Beach Marina

To
Newport
Beach

PACIFIC OCEAN

Angler battles a fish at Alamitos Bay.
Photo by Gary Graham.

Interstate
U.S. Highway
State Highway
Other Roadway
Boat Launch
Fish Hatchery
Campground

Alamitos Bay

Alamitos Bay Region

If you're looking for a classic small saltwater experience in the Los Angeles area, Alamitos Bay is it. The place is intimate, the game fish are plentiful, and only lightweight tackle is needed. This is a perfect combination for anyone. First-time explorers and experienced salty fly rodders alike will find a wonderful fishery that challenges their skills on many levels. I also like the wide choice of habitat.

The area we refer to here includes Alamitos Bay proper, Naples Island, Long Beach Marina, the Marine Stadium and Park areas, and the Alamitos Peninsula. The outer shoreline of the peninsula affords access to the Pacific surf zone and jetty environs. The inner peninsula and Bayshore Walk provide direct contact to the protected waters inside Alamitos Bay. To the delight of the foot patrol, there are beaches all around this productive complex. Boaters also enjoy the easy navigation in the bay's quiet backwaters.

The variety of habitats includes eelgrass beds, sandy beaches, flats, and cover such as docks and pilings, jetties and, of course, boating channels. The baitfish and food chain are extremely healthy in these parts. All of these combine to present you with year-round game fish action.

Pacific Coast Highway is your direct artery into Long Beach and the Alamitos Bay region. Surface roads including Westminster Avenue, Marina Drive, Appian Way, Bay Shore Avenue, and Ocean Boulevard provide access to specific locations around the bay complex.

Author with barred surfperch.
Photo by Glenn Kishi.

Types of Fish
Spotted sand bass, barred sand bass, barracuda, corbina, croaker, halibut, surfperch, and jacksmelt.

Known Baitfish
Anchovy, mackerel, smelt, squid, shrimp, and crabs.

Equipment to Use
Rods: 6–9 weight, 9 feet in length.
Reels: Large arbor and disk drag design.
Lines: WF floating, intermediate, type-4 or type-6 sinking shooting heads, modified sink tip 200 to 300 grains.
Leaders: 1X to 5X, 4–7 feet in length in general, some prefer up to 15 feet in length in extreme calm or clear conditions.
Wading: Wet-wade or use lightweight waders and booties for sandy beaches.

Flies to Use
Streamers: ALF Baitfish, Popovic's Surf Candy and Jiggy #2, Squid Fly #1/0, Rusty Squirrel Clouser #4, 10-40 Sandworm, Ruffy #4, Clouser Minnows #2–6, Salt Bugger (bleeding anchovy) #4, Sea Habit Bucktail (white knight) #2/0, Sar Mul Mac Anchovy #3/0.
Topwater & Subsurface: Gurgler #2/0–#2.

When to Fish
Bass: June through September; prime time is August.
Barracuda: All year; prime time is late July through September.
Corbina: Summer.
Croaker: Prime times are summer and fall.
Halibut: June through September.
Surfperch: All year; prime time is May through September.

Seasons & Limits
Varying restrictions on tackle, access, and limits apply. Consult the California Department of Fish & Game booklet and call local shops for updates.

Accommodations & Services
Find marinas, launch ramps, and hoists in Long Beach and Marine Stadium environs. Supplies and lodging abound around Long Beach.

Rating
A big 8.5. For wading and small-craft anglers, this is one of the best saltwater fly fishing places in California.

Editor's note: For more excellent information about fly fishing West Coast bays and shoreline habitat, consult Ken's other fine books, *Fly Fishing Afoot in the Surf Zone* and *Fly Fishing the Pacific Inshore.*

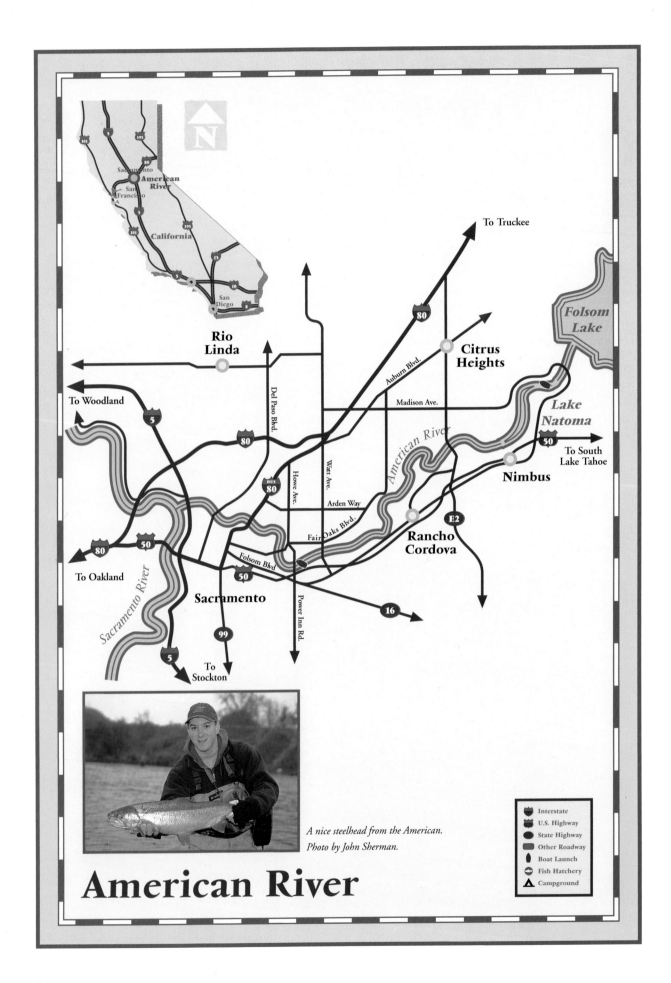

To Truckee

Folsom Lake

Rio Linda

To Woodland

Del Paso Blvd.

Auburn Blvd.

Citrus Heights

Madison Ave.

Lake Natoma

American River

To South Lake Tahoe

Wyatt Ave.

Howe Ave.

Nimbus

Arden Way

Fair Oaks Blvd.

Rancho Cordova

E2

Folsom Blvd.

Sacramento River

To Oakland

Sacramento

Power Inn Rd.

To Stockton

16

A nice steelhead from the American.
Photo by John Sherman.

American River

	Interstate
	U.S. Highway
	State Highway
	Other Roadway
	Boat Launch
	Fish Hatchery
	Campground

American River
Lower Section

A wonderful 22-mile tailwater fishery flows right through the heart of California's state capital and into the Sacramento River. And believe it or not, the lower American River gets less overall pressure than a place such as Fall River during peak season! Keep in mind, however, that there are millions of potential anglers near this stretch of river. The lower American is urban fly fishing, but it's worth the adventure.

The American doesn't have trout, but it does have a variety of hearty and challenging game fish. Combining resident and anadromous species, the river offers a chance to try for fish ranging from 1 to 30 or more pounds.

Boaters tend to get the most from this river. Anyone with a canoe, pram, or small skiff will enjoy the many easy-to-get-to access points. Boat traffic and snags present hazards that float tube users should heed. Many tubers find a way to anchor themselves when they find high-quality fly fishing locations. Bank anglers gain access around Discovery and Goethe parks, the California State Exposition (Cal Expo), Arden Way, Howe Avenue and Watt Avenue bridges, and Sunrise Blvd. It's good to call ahead to check the levels of the dam-regulated river flows. The Sacramento-area fly shops listed in the back of this guide will help.

The easiest way to get to this section of river is to take U.S. Route 50 to either of the suburbs of Fair Oaks or Rancho Cordova. From here many surface streets lead to the river.

American River Striper. Photo by John Sherman.

Types of Fish
Smallmouth and striped bass, American shad, steelhead, salmon (chinook), plus panfish and catfish.

Known Baitfish
Threadfin shad, game fish fry, crayfish.

Equipment to Use
Rods: 6–8 weight, 8–9 feet in length. Some folks enjoy 7–8 weight Spey outfits.
Reels: Mechanical or palm drag. I prefer disk drag systems and large arbors with at least 75 yards of backing.
Lines: For deepwater nymphs and streamers, use modified sink tips in 200 to 300 grain weights, type-4 density uniform sinking line, or shooting head system with type-4 or type-6 sinking head. Use a floating WF line for poppers and shallow streamer work.
Leaders: 1X to 5X, 6–9 feet in length (varies with river conditions).
Wading: Chest-high waders and boots (cleats aren't usually necessary).

Flies to Use
Streamers: Sea Habit Bucktail (White Knight) #1/0, Chartreuse Deceiver #1/0 and #3/0, Bullet Head #6, Black and Olive Beaded Krystal Bugger #2–10, Olive or Tan Clouser Minnow #2–6, assorted Shad Flies #6, Poxybou Crayfish #4–8.
Topwater & Subsurface: Gurgler #2, Blue Crease Fly #1/0, Madam X #6, Whitlock's Hopper #8.

When to Fish
Smallmouth Bass: All year, prime times are spring and fall.
Striped Bass: All year, prime time is July through October.
American Shad: Mid-spring through June.
Steelhead: September through March.
Salmon: August through October.
Panfish: Summer months are prime.
Catfish: All year, but summer is prime.

Boat Access
Sailor Bar Park, Sunrise, El Manto, Rosmore, Ancile Hoffman Park, Gristmill, Watt Avenue, Howe Avenue, Discovery Park (mouth).

Seasons & Limits
Restrictions on dates, tackle, and harvest vary per species and sections of the river. Consult the California Department of Fish & Game regulations or a local fly shop.

Accommodations & Services
All lodging and supplies are available in Sacramento.

Rating
I love this place. Overall, a solid 7.5. At times it can be a 9!

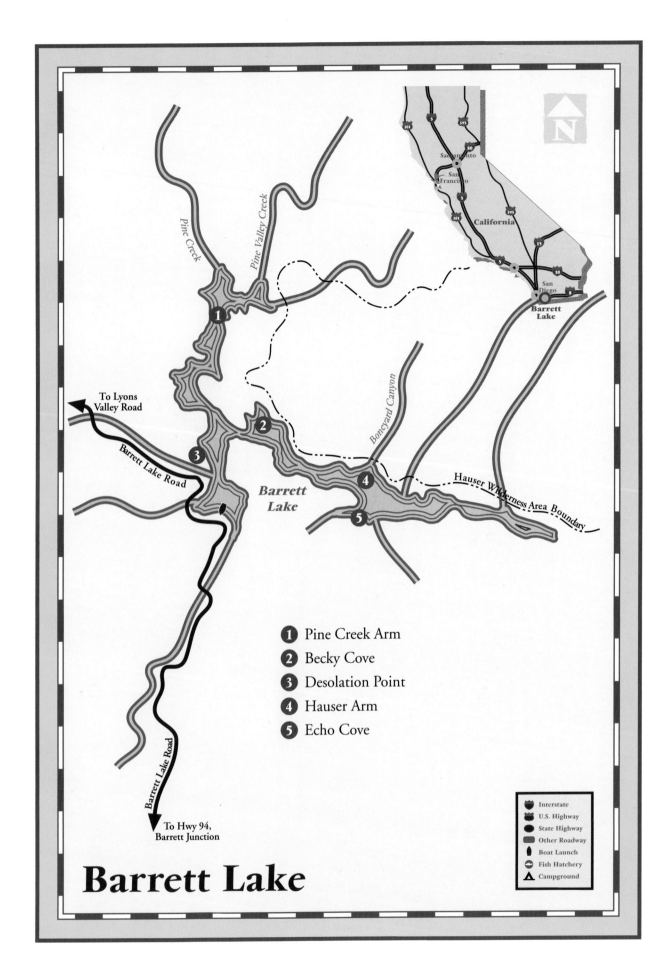

N

To Lyons
Valley Road

Pine Creek

Pine Valley Creek

Barrett Lake Road

Barrett
Lake

Boneyard Canyon

Hauser Wilderness Area Boundary

San Diego

Barrett
Lake

California

Sacramento

San Francisco

To Hwy 94,
Barrett Junction

1 Pine Creek Arm
2 Becky Cove
3 Desolation Point
4 Hauser Arm
5 Echo Cove

Interstate
U.S. Highway
State Highway
Other Roadway
Boat Launch
Fish Hatchery
Campground

Barrett Lake

Barrett Lake

by Jeff Solis

A good-sized impoundment surrounded by chaparral-covered hills, Barrett Lake is home to the only pure-strain northern largemouth bass in San Diego County. This fact, combined with the reservoir's strictly limited fishing access (by reservation only), creates the likelihood of a once-in-a-lifetime encounter with bass on the fly. The average catch is between 10 and 25 bass caught and released per day, with a 10-fish day being "just okay" fishing.

There are a variety of ways to fish for the beautiful bass of Barrett Lake. Your best bet is to travel by boat to one of the many arms of the reservoir, then get out and use a float tube or wade. Concentrate your efforts on one of the many large areas of flats containing structure such as submerged boulders and deadfall. If you're content to cast surface poppers all day, you'll catch fish. If you're seeking bigger fish, work streamer patterns such as Clouser Minnows or Lefty's Deceivers close to or through deadfalls, stick-ups, or other fish-attracting structure.

If you're lucky enough to gain access, this terrific fishery is the place where you're likely to catch more bass on a fly rod than ever before in your life. Directions to Barrett Lake will be furnished when you make your reservations.

Largemouth bass are the main attraction.
Photo by John Sherman.

Type of Fish
Northern largemouth bass, smallmouth bass, bluegill, and crappie.

Known Hatches & Baitfish
Threadfin shad is the predominant baitfish, plus leeches, frogs, and bass fry.

Equipment to Use
Rods: 7–8 weight, 8–9 feet in length.
Reels: Standard click or disk drag.
Lines: WF or floating intermediate.
Leaders: 1X to 3X, 5–8 feet in length.
Wading: Wading can be very productive, but boating is best.

Flies to Use
Nymphs: Dragonfly, Damselfly, and Carey Special.
Streamers: Dave's Crayfish, Woolly Bugger, Clouser Minnow, Lefty's Deceiver #4.
Topwater & Subsurface: Adult Dragon or Damselfly, Shad or Frog Deer Hair Popper #4–6, Gurgler #2.

When to Fish
All day.

Seasons & Limits
Call City of San Diego Fish line 619-465-3474 or visit the City's website at www.sandiego.gov. Reservations required as noted below. Open April through September. Strictly catch and release. Barbless hooks and lures only. No bait.

Accommodations & Services
Boat rentals are available, but no private craft are allowed.

Reservations
Weekends and Wednesdays only during the season. Contact Ticketmaster locations throughout California or www.ticketmaster.com. Current permit costs are $50 plus $7.50 service charge includes boat and motor. 1-4 anglers per boat, plus $10 per person at lake. Cash only, no credit cards or checks. California fishing license also required for ages 16 and older. No concessions or drinking water at lake. Consult web site for all rules and regulations. Advance reservations required. From San Diego take I-8 east to Japatul Road. Head south to Lyons Valley Road. Gate is past milepost #12 from this direction, or take Highway 94 east to Honey Springs Road to Lyons Valley Road, turn right, 1.7 miles to gate. Parking is extremely limited.

Rating
Barrett Lake is a 9.5 in my book.

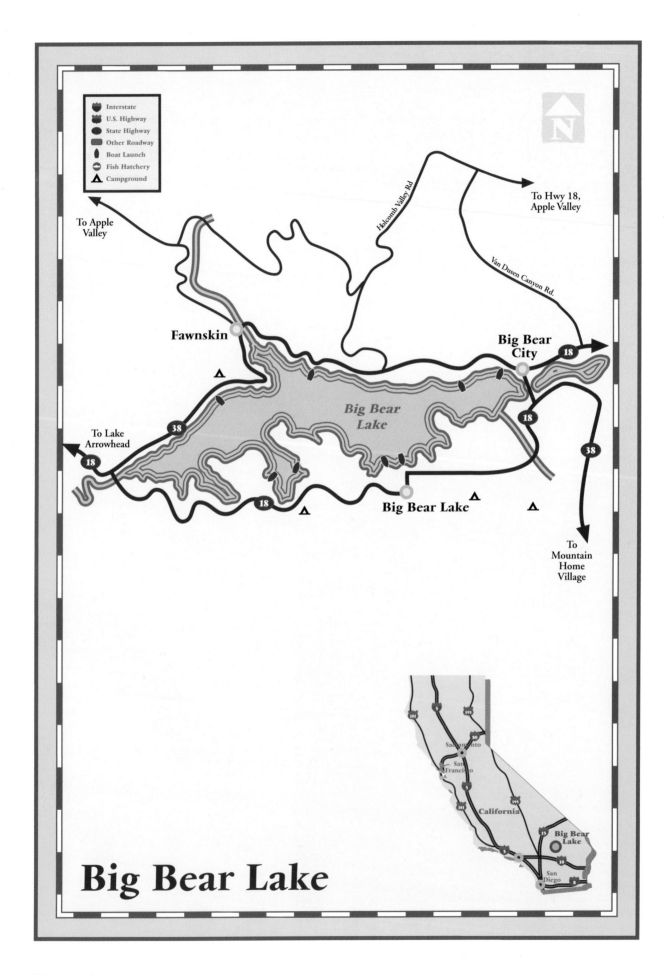

Big Bear Lake

Big Bear Lake

by Jeff Solis

Located in the heart of the San Bernardino Mountains, Big Bear Lake offers some of the best early- and late-season trout fishing in Southern California. Summer still produces some fast and furious trout fishing but also throws three- to five-pound bass into the mix.

At 3,015 surface acres, Big Bear has approximately 70 miles of rocky shoreline, points, and coves. Using a float tube is the best way to cover the most water, with a full sink or sink tip line to get your streamer pattern or beadhead nymph down. If you're looking to take trout on dry flies and emerger patterns, the east end of the lake is the best place to be in the spring. As the water warms, try some of the sheltered bays, such as Boulder Bay or the area near the dam.

Big Bear Lake also has numerous areas distinguished for their grassy shorelines, lily pads, submerged logs, and other fish-attracting structures favored by the lake's bass population. The walking or wading angler can easily access these spots, and a well-presented leech pattern or surface popper will often result in a jolting strike.

To reach Big Bear Lake, take Interstate 10 east from San Bernardino to Highway 30. Go north on 30 until it forks with Highway 330. Continue north on 330 until it ends at Highway 18, turn right, and proceed to the lake.

The city of Big Bear Lake has grown steadily over the last 30 years and is now a destination for hunters, hikers, skiers, horseback riders, and golfers, as well as anglers. With all of these attractive activities, Big Bear Lake is a great place for anglers to spend a weekend with the whole family!

Healthy rainbows abound.
Photo by John Sherman.

Types of Fish
Trout, bass, catfish, crappie, and bluegill.

Known Hatches & Baitfish
Midges, mayflies, damselflies, game fish fry, and shad.

Equipment to Use
Rods: 5–7 weight, 8–9 feet in length.
Reels: Standard click or disk drag.
Lines: WF double-taper floating for dries. Full sink or sink tip for streamers and nymphs.
Leaders: 4X to 6X, 7–9 feet in length.
Wading: Can be very productive. Wear chest-high waders and boots.

Flies to Use
Dries: Renegade #14–18, Parachute Adams, Adams #14–20, Griffith's Gnat #16–20, Roy's Special Emerger #18–20, Looping Callibaetis #16.
Nymphs: Beadhead Pheasant Tail, Beadhead Hare's Ear, Beadhead Prince #10–18, Brassie #12–20.
Streamers & Poppers: Woolly Worm or Bugger #2–12, Zonker #6–10, Matuka, Muddler Minnow #4–10, Light Spruce Fly #6–12, foam or deer hair poppers #2–10, Clouser Minnow #1/0–6, assorted dragonfly and leech patterns #2–8.

When to Fish
Spring, summer, and fall.

Seasons & Limits
Open year-round. There is no limit on bluegill, and you can keep 25 crappie, 5 trout, and 5 bass at least 12 inches in length. Check current regulations for other limits and restrictions.

Nearby Fly Fishing
Santa Ana River and Bear Creek.

Accommodations & Services
Plenty of camping can be found around the lake, and numerous motels are in the area. There are many stores on the north and south shores, including some that rent fishing boats, canoes, ski boats, and jet skis.

Rating
With a variety of cover to explore, Big Bear Lake rates an 8.

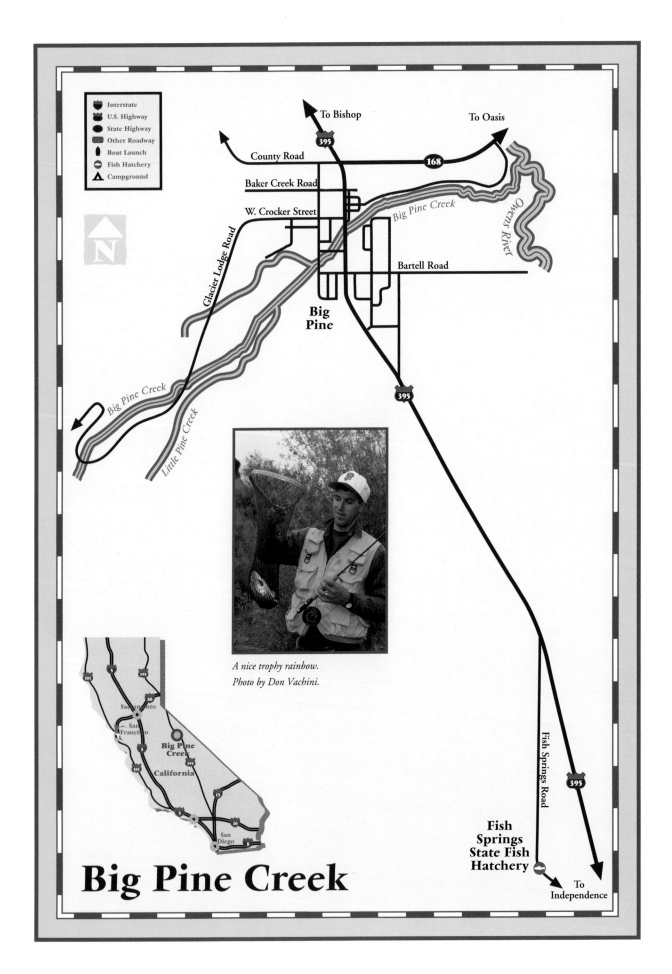

Legend:
- Interstate
- U.S. Highway
- State Highway
- Other Roadway
- Boat Launch
- Fish Hatchery
- Campground

N

To Bishop

To Oasis

County Road

395

168

Baker Creek Road

W. Crocker Street

Big Pine Creek

Owens River

Glacier Lodge Road

Bartell Road

Big Pine

Big Pine Creek

Little Pine Creek

395

A nice trophy rainbow.
Photo by Don Vachini.

101
5
395
80
Sacramento
San Francisco
5
Big Pine Creek
California
101
395
15
5
10
San Diego
8

Fish Springs Road

Fish Springs State Fish Hatchery

395

To Independence

Big Pine Creek

Big Pine Creek

by Kate Howe

Fly tyer and all-around international angler Kate Howe used to live in these parts and provided the information here. She was particularly fond of this small water because of the constant fly fishing challenge and because it always made her want to come back for more. Big Pine Creek's glacier-fed waters wind 15 miles from lakes at the foot of Palisade Glacier to the creek's confluence with the Owens River. The creek's upper reaches are full of Ice Age cobblestone, with waters of a glacial blue-green tint. Down the mountain, small freestone rocks and sand replace the cobblestones. On the valley floor the creek becomes a high-desert meadow stream with undercut banks and a sand-and-rock bottom.

The brown trout of Big Pine Creek are wild and live up to that reputation. Most average around 8 to 12 inches. Daily, some angler is surprised with a 16-inch or better brown. Stocked rainbows and Alpers trout also add to the mix in the creek.

Dry fly fishing on Big Pine Creek can be nonstop in summer, after spring runoff when the water temperature has risen and the hatches stabilize. Nymphing always produces trout and, depending on water depth and cover, usually the bigger fish of the day. A dry fly fished with a dropper is an awesome combination and streamer fishing can be fantastic, giving the angler an opportunity to probe deep pools and undercuts for dominant fish in prime holding water.

Navigating the creek can be tough, with lots of brush to negotiate and rocks to climb over. These areas, however, can produce the best action, since many anglers don't take the time to investigate them. For the less athletic, there are also easily accessible areas just a short hike from the parking areas.

The town of Big Pine is five hours north of Los Angeles on Highway 395. The fishing starts right in town, with more access on Glacier Lodge Road (going west). Access to the eastern section of the creek is via a dirt road off Highway 168.

Tumbling section of Big Pine Creek.
Photo by Don Vachini.

Types of Fish
Wild brown trout and stocked rainbows.

Known Hatches & Baitfish
The standard Sierra smorgasbord of caddis, mayflies, stoneflies, terrestrials, and trout parr.

Equipment to Use
Rods: 2–5 weight, 7–9 feet in length.
Reels: Click or disk to match the rod.
Lines: WF or double-taper floating lines.
Leaders: 5X or 6X, tapered to 10 feet in length.
Wading: Wet-wade in the summer, but wear long pants to protect your legs from the brush. In cold weather, use hip boots or chest waders. Cleated, felt-soled boots are suggested.

Flies to Use
Dries: Elk Hair Caddis, Palisade Special, PMD #14–22.
Nymphs: Gold Ribbed Hare's Ear, Pheasant Tail, and Caddis Pupa #12–22 are all the nymphs you need.
Streamers: Midnight Special, Woolly Bugger, Leeches #8–10.

When to Fish
Fishing is good all day and into the evening.

Seasons & Limits
The general trout season from the last Saturday in April through November 15. Check current California regulations.

Nearby Fly Fishing
Baker Creek offers another quality small-water experience. For bigger water, try the Owens River for browns, rainbows, and bass.

Accommodations & Services
Big Pine has lodging, gas, groceries, and two campgrounds. Fly shops are found in Lee Vining, Bridgeport, Yosemite, and Mammoth Lakes. For area guide service contact Trout Scouts of Sierra Guide Group (760) 872-9836, www.sierraguidegroup.com. Pine Creek Pack Station (800) 962-0775 is available for access to the back country.

Rating
For the small-stream angler, Big Pine Creek rates an 8.

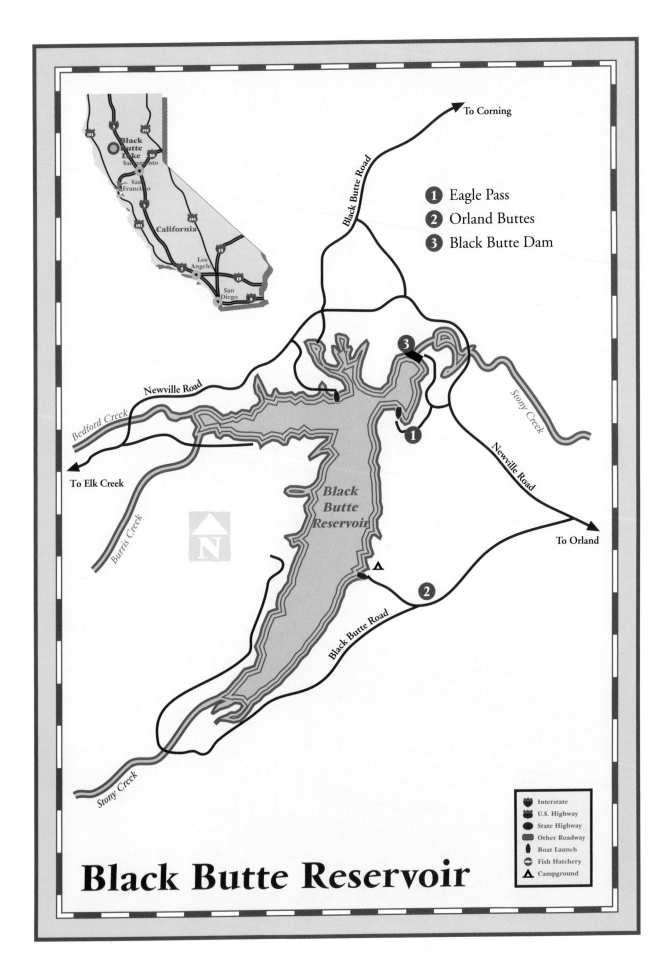

To Corning

1 Eagle Pass
2 Orland Buttes
3 Black Butte Dam

Black Butte Road

Newville Road

Bedford Creek

Stony Creek

To Elk Creek

Burris Creek

Black Butte Reservoir

Newville Road

To Orland

Black Butte Road

Stony Creek

Interstate
U.S. Highway
State Highway
Other Roadway
Boat Launch
Fish Hatchery
Campground

Black Butte Reservoir

Black Butte Reservoir

This popular lake, the result of an Army Corps of Engineers project, provides a cool place for outdoor recreation and is a fine bass fishery. The winter months in particular provide excellent fly fishing opportunities. There are three boat ramps and some 40 miles of shoreline to explore. All this, plus other handy facilities and an easy 12-mile drive off Interstate 5, make this lake a fun fly rod adventure.

Black Butte Reservoir is best known for its spring crappie populations. These fish grow to two pounds or more! Largemouth bass up to six pounds are also popular game fish around the reservoir. The black bass population is hit pretty hard during the peak spring angling months. Consider midweek adventures to increase your chance of a quality outing. Try small, protected coves on the western shore for the most consistent action. Stumps, rocky cover, and tapering points of land are the best features to explore.

To get to Black Butte Reservoir, take Interstate 5 to the farming town of Orland, about 40 miles south of Red Bluff. Exit west on Black Butte Lake Road. Then go 12 miles on Newville Road.

Types of Fish
Largemouth bass, crappie, bluegill, and catfish.

Known Baitfish
Crayfish and minnows.

Equipment to Use
Rods: 5–7 weight, 8½–9 feet in length.
Reels: Palm or mechanical drag.
Lines: Floating, intermediate, or sink tip type-3.
Leaders: 1X to 5X, 5–9 feet in length.
Wading: Wear hip boots for fishing from the bank. Use a float tube for fishing along the shore and in coves.

Flies to Use
Nymphs: Jansen Callibaetis, Zug Bug #14, Pheasant Tail #16.
Streamers: Hot Flash Minnow, Clouser Minnow, Whitlock Near Nuff Sculpin, Zonker #6, Burk's V-Worm #10, Whitlock Softshell Crayfish #8, Poxybou Crayfish #4–8.
Topwater: Gurgler #2, Deer Hair Mouse, Dave's Hopper #6, Gaines Bluegill Popper #12.

When to Fish
Fish for bass all year, prime time is spring. For panfish, especially crappie, fish spring and fall.

Seasons & Limits
General season all year, consult local fly shops or the California Department of Fish & Game regulations booklet.

Accommodations & Services
Three launch ramps, a supply store, marina, boat rentals, and a variety of campsites are at the lake. Lodging and gas are available in Orland.

Rating
A lot of boats, like warm water, can put the fish down; otherwise, a good 6.

Great spring crappie fishing!
Photo by John Sherman.

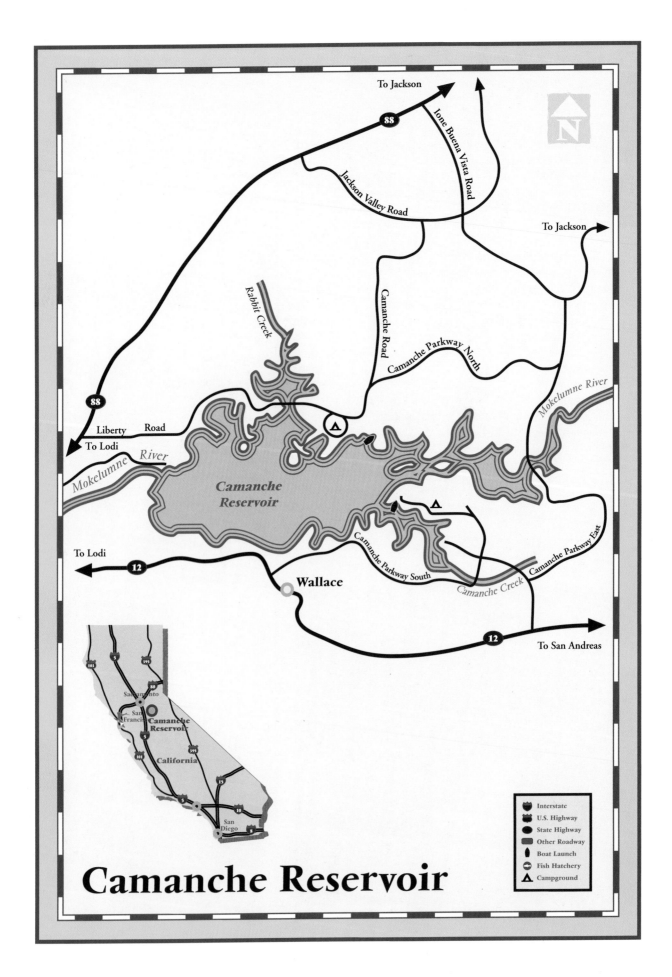

Camanche Reservoir

Camanche Reservoir

This reservoir is in a classic California foothills location, in the heart of the Sierra Nevada's Mother Lode Country. The site abounds with rocky shoreline, points, and coves. Canoes, kayaks, prams, pontoons, and tubes all gain considerable access to excellent fly fishing. Anglers afoot can enjoy some pretty nice action as well, particularly during first and last light. Night fishing for crappie can be extremely productive.

The shoreline winds approximately 60 miles around the lake. Bank angling is best around the south and north shores. Camanche provides you with 7,500 surface acres to explore, so a boat of some kind is helpful. Expect significant boat traffic during the summer months, as Camanche is also a popular water-skiing destination.

Fortunately for the fly fishing community, the better angling takes place during the cooler weather of spring, and the place is busting with game fish at this time! To catch the warmwater species, try crayfish patterns with hints of red, brown, blue, and orange. Anything that slithers or crawls through bassy cover is sure to draw interest. For the stocked trout or kokanee, fish down around 10 to 20 feet, or try to find the 50F to 55F temperature zone.

If topwater is your game, fish in the early morning and evening. When the heat hits the water, most of the game fish go deep. Deep-water tactics with heavy sinking lines and streamers will keep you in the game.

Camanche is about 30 miles east of the Central Valley city of Stockton. Drive east on Highway 88 through Clements. Turn off on Highway 12 to reach the south shore region. Or stay on Highway 88 to Liberty Road (east) for north shore access.

Camanche shoreline. Photo by Brian Sak.

Types of Fish
Rainbow trout, kokanee salmon, smallmouth, largemouth, spotted bass, crappie, and panfish.

Known Hatches & Baitfish
Trout: Callibaetis mayflies, tan or yellow caddis, damselfly nymphs, and shad streamers.
Bass: Threadfin shad, bluegill, game fish fry, crayfish, leeches, and frogs.
Panfish: Small jigs, nymphs, and sponge spiders.

Equipment to Use
Rods: 5–7 weight, 8½–10 feet in length.
Reels: Palm or mechanical drag.
Lines: Intermediate, sink tip type-4, modified sink tips of 130 to 200 grains, or shooting heads type-4 or type-6.
Leaders: 1X to 6X, 6–12 feet in length.
Wading: Felt-soled boots, hip boots, or chest waders are okay, but the reservoir is best worked from a boat or inflatable if possible.

Flies to Use
Nymphs: Putnam's & Bug Eye Damselfly, Black AP #12, Kaufman's Dragonfly #8, Poxyback Callibaetis #16, Black Ant, Prince #14, Gold Bead Prince #10–16.
Streamers: Sea Habit Bucktail #1/0, Flashtail Clouser #1/0–2, Purple Eelworm #6, Burk's V-Worm #10, Hot Flash Minnow, Whitlock's Near Nuff Sculpin, Purple Eelworm, Bullet Head, Whitlock Near Nuff Sculpin #6, Poxybou Crayfish #4–8, Black Woolly Bugger #4, Blanton's Flash Tail series #6–8.
Topwater & Subsurface: Gurgler #2, Swimming Frog, Loudmouth Shad #6, Gaines Bluegill Popper #12, Sponge Spider #10–12, Bett's Micro Popper #8–10, Elk Hair Caddis #10–14.

When to Fish
Trout & Kokanee: November through April; prime months are January through April.
Bass: March through November; prime months are April to May and October to November.
Panfish: All year, prime times are spring and fall.

Seasons & Limits
Fish all year and plan on general state regulations and limits. Check at a fly shop or the Camanche store, or consult the California Department of Fish & Game regulation booklet for more exact information.

Accommodations & Services
Camping, public launches, a marina, boat rentals, a store, and supplies are available at the lake.

Rating
I really enjoy this lake and the great boating opportunities. Overall at least a 6.5.

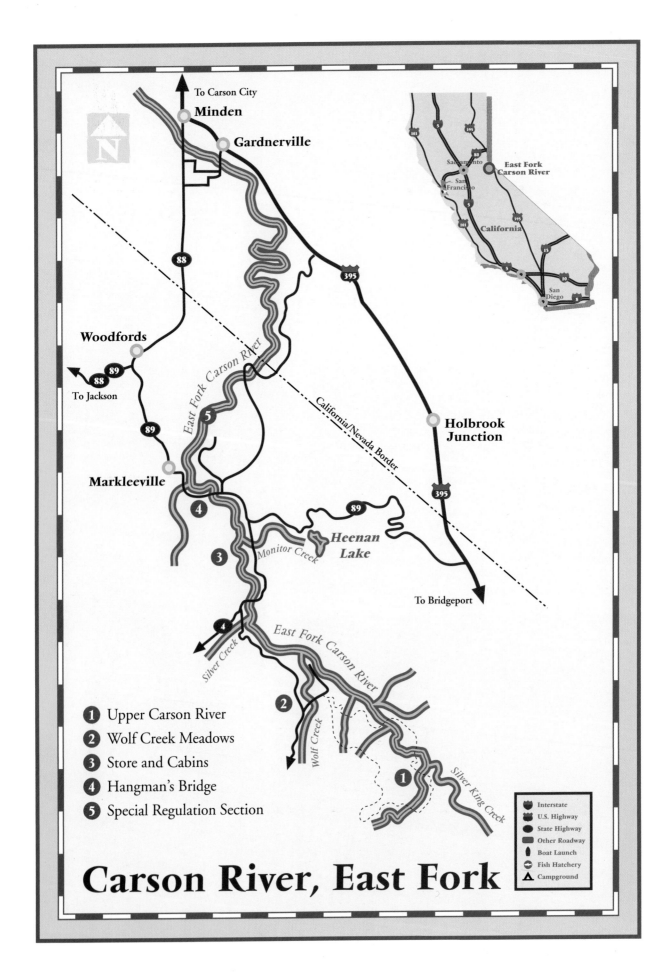

To Carson City

Minden

Gardnerville

88

395

Woodfords

88 89

To Jackson

89

East Fork Carson River

5

California/Nevada Border

Holbrook Junction

395

Markleeville

4

89

3

Heenan Lake

Monitor Creek

To Bridgeport

4

Silver Creek

East Fork Carson River

2

Wolf Creek

1

Silver King Creek

1 Upper Carson River
2 Wolf Creek Meadows
3 Store and Cabins
4 Hangman's Bridge
5 Special Regulation Section

Interstate
U.S. Highway
State Highway
Other Roadway
Boat Launch
Fish Hatchery
Campground

East Fork Carson River

California

San Diego

Sacramento

San Francisco

Carson River, East Fork

Carson River

East Fork

by Dave Stanley

This is a classic freestone stream with lots of riffles, rapids, deep runs, and pools. These conditions create excellent habitat for stoneflies, caddisflies, and some species of mayflies, all found throughout the Carson drainage. The upper river provides many different experiences, access being one. Above Wolf Creek the narrow, fast-flowing waters are accessible by a rough 4WD trail, on horseback, or by foot.

As is typical on this type of water, nymph and wet-fly fishing methods produce fish throughout the season. Usually late on summer evenings there is excellent dry-fly fishing. The large numbers of baitfish also mean success is likely for skilled streamer anglers.

The river from Wolf Creek down to Hangman's Bridge (just outside of Markleeville) has several inflow tributaries that make the river grow dramatically. Here, less adventuresome anglers have relatively easy access off Highway 89 and Highway 4.

Hangman's Bridge to the Nevada state line is a special regulation river section, accessible only by 4WD, on foot, or in good water years, by raft or pontoon boat. Large fish are consistently taken in this stretch.

The river remains a viable trout fishery where it enters Nevada and passes through the Gardnerville area. The river then changes primarily to a warmwater fishery as it flows toward Lahontan Reservoir, although trout can still be found here and there.

To get to the East Fork of the Carson from the California side, take Interstate 50 past Lake Tahoe to Highway 89 south. After about 12 miles Highways 88 and 89 merge; follow the signs to Markleeville. The river parallels the highway.

From Reno, take U.S. Route 395 south to Minden, Nevada. Take Highway 88 west to Woodfords, California, and the junction of Highways 88, 89, and 4.

Angler below riffles on the East Fork of the Carson River.
Photo by Don Vachini.

Types of Fish
Rainbow, cutthroat, and brown trout, and mountain whitefish. Brook trout in tributaries.

Known Hatches
Like the Truckee and Walker rivers, caddis are prolific here. Mayflies appear in March, hatching sporadically through late September and early October. Golden stones hatch in March and April prior to or just at the beginning of runoff, and little yellow stones appear from June through August.

Equipment to Use
Rods: 5–6 weight, 9 feet in length.
Reels: Standard trout reels are fine.
Lines: Floating, occasionally sink tips for deep water.
Leaders: 3X to 6X, 7½–10 feet in length.
Wading: Felt-soled boots, or chest-high neoprene or breathable waders.

Flies to Use
Dries: Elk Hair Caddis, Adams, Humpy, Royal Wulff, Parachute Hare's Ear, other parachute patterns in various colors, Little Yellow Stones, Stimulators, Ants, and Hoppers.
Nymphs: Bird's Nest, Gold Ribbed Hare's Ear, Prince, Zug Bug, or any of these with beadhead. Green Rockworm, Golden Stone, Little Yellow Stone, Western Coachman, Soft Hackles, Caddis Pupa and Emergers.
Streamers: Muddler Minnow, Woolly Bugger, Hornberg, Zonker, Matuka.

When to Fish
Depending on runoff, June and July and September and October usually have the best dry fly action. Fish with nymphs throughout the season. Streamers work well in the cooler waters of spring and fall.

Seasons & Limits
California: From Hangman's Bridge to Nevada State line; last Saturday in April to November 15, artificial lures and barbless hooks only. From Carson Falls to Hangman's Bridge; Last Saturday in April to Nevmber 15. Above Carson falls; closed all year.
Nevada: Open all year.
There are special regulations in California. Check the appropriate state regulations!

Accommodations & Services
All services are readily available in larger towns like Gardnerville and Carson City, Nevada, and Markleeville, California.

Rating
Good dry fly, nymph, and streamer fishing. If solitude in mountain splendor is what you like, Dave Stanley rates the East Fork of the Carson a solid 8.

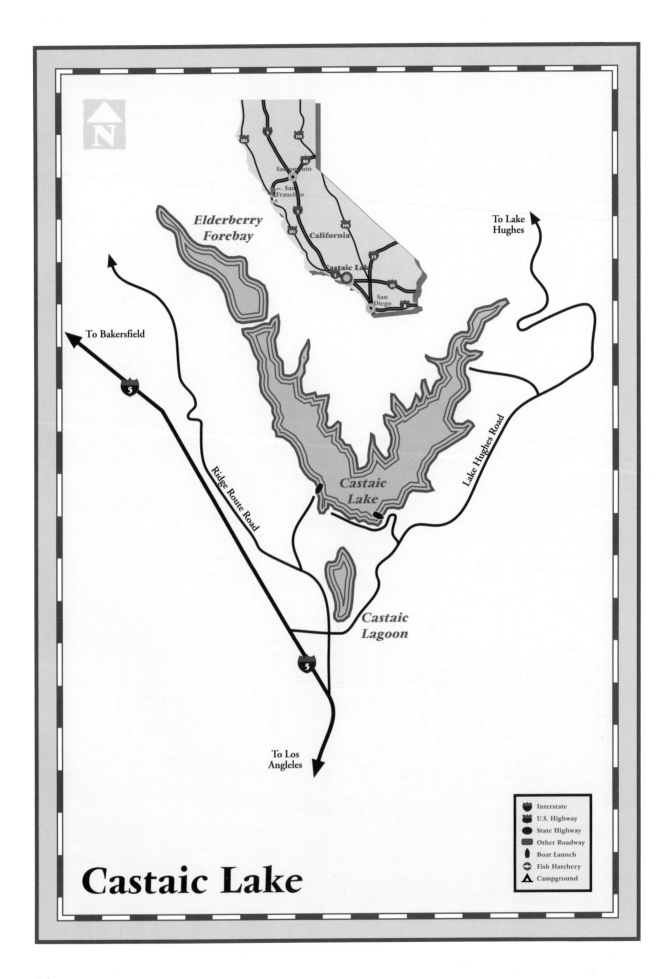

Elderberry Forebay

To Lake Hughes

To Bakersfield

Ridge Route Road

Lake Hughes Road

Castaic Lake

Castaic Lagoon

To Los Angleles

	Interstate
	U.S. Highway
	State Highway
	Other Roadway
	Boat Launch
	Fish Hatchery
	Campground

Castaic Lake

Castaic Lake

by Bob Zeller

Southern California has a world-class bass fishery at Castaic Lake, where a 22-pound largemouth bass was caught and released in 1991. It was four ounces shy of a world record, and many believe the next record will come from this water. As of this writing the current state record bass, a 21-pound, 12-ounce giant came from this lake too (also 1991). Striped bass are also making their way to Castaic. The water is one hour north of LAX airport off Interstate 5, just north of the little village of Castaic.

Local anglers suggest fishing near the west launch ramp, across the lake and away from the congestion of the main boat ramp. The water drops off at a rock wall there, and you can see cruising bass. There is plenty of casting room and several docks from which to fish. Many at the rock wall take fish with plastic worms. Fly anglers can try to reach the bottom with a Rabbit Fur Leech or a Deer Hair Minnow then jig it slowly along the rock wall.

Another way fly rodders can approach Castaic is to rent a boat and fish the shoreline with a Popping Bug. One can also take the boat to the reservoir's eastern arm, the fishing side, where there is less pleasure-boat traffic. Generally, look for points, coves, and rocky cover that bass like.

Lake Castaic Lagoon, below the dam, holds planted trout. Try this water if you aren't interested in catching monster bass on a fly rod. The lagoon also produces some big bass but, unfortunately, the shore is lined with small trees and is not fly rod friendly.

Castaic is well known for its large and abundant stripers and largemouth bass. Photo by John Sherman.

Types of Fish
Largemouth, smallmouth, striped bass, rainbow trout, catfish, and bluegill.

Known Hatches & Baitfish
Schools of shad abound.

Equipment to Use
Rods: 4–7 weight, 8 ½–9½ feet in length.
Reels: Disk drag is fine.
Lines: Floating, sinking, or sink tip.
Leaders: For bass, 1X to 4X, 5–9 feet in length. For trout, 4X to 7X, 7 ½–10 feet in length.
Wading: Shore fishing is possible, but boats and float tubes are best.

Flies to Use
Bass: Wiggle Bug, Rabbit Leech #2–6, Woolly Bugger #4–12, Carey Bugger #4–6, Matuka #8–10, also Boilermaker, Chugger, Deer Hair Popper; Deceivers and Sar Mul Mac for stripers.
Trout: Adams Parachute #12–18, Black Gnat #18–24, Midge Adult #18–24, Callibaetis #14–16, Pheasant Tail, Hare's Ear #10–18, Woolly Worm #10–12, Zug Bug #10–16.

Seasons & Limits
Open all year. March through September for bass. November through May for trout. Check current California Deparment of Fish and Game regularions booklet, or call a fly shop or marina for specific information. The lake is managed by the L.A. County Department of Parks and Recreation and is open from sunrise to sunset. It offers boating, fishing, boat rentals, swimming, and picnicking. A parking fee of $6.00 is charged per vehicle. Trailers, boats and jet skis are an additional $6.00. Call (661) 257-4050 for more information.

Nearby Fly Fishing
Try Lake Piru, Piru Creek, Sespe Creek, Santa Clara River, and Lake Casitas.

Accommodations & Services
Hotels are available in Castaic; bait, groceries, boat rentals at the lake.

Rating
If you and your fly rod are looking for big bass, Bob Zeller (along with others) rate Castaic Lake a 7.

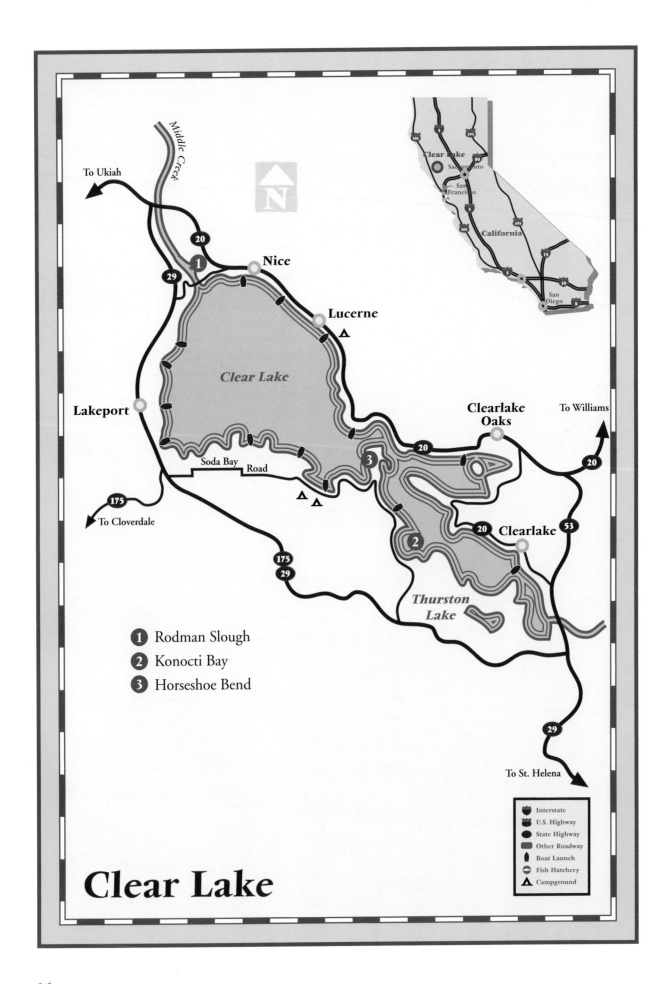

Clear Lake

Middle Creek

To Ukiah

1 Nice

2 9

Clear Lake

Lucerne

Lakeport

To Williams

Clearlake
Oaks

20

Soda Bay Road

175

To Cloverdale

175
29

3 Horseshoe

20

20

20 Clearlake 53

2

Thurston
Lake

29

1 Rodman Slough

2 Konocti Bay

3 Horseshoe Bend

To St. Helena

	Interstate
	U.S. Highway
	State Highway
	Other Roadway
	Boat Launch
	Fish Hatchery
△	Campground

Clear Lake

If you love the bass game, then this lake is one of the best destinations in northern California, if not the state—bar none! Why such a bold statement? It's simple: an outstanding population of game fish, terrific variety of cover and structure, super-active food chain, easy access, and all necessary supplies and resources located right on the lake. Clear Lake is not a pristine wilderness experience, but it is a solid fish-catching experience throughout most of the year.

Clear Lake is actually green, despite being one of the largest natural freshwater lakes in California. The game fish in this water have it all, and on a silver platter: built and natural cover, abundant baitfish and insect life, even carpets of algae to gaze through! Everything is in place for a trophy fishery.

The lake is best fly fished from the 100 miles of shoreline. Stick to the tule-lined sections that harbor bass and panfish. Clear Lake's numerous pilings are another magnet for trophy bass and black crappie. These human-built structures are havens for ambush predators that crash on schools of baitfish. When the bite is on (and you have to be there to believe it), Clear Lake is a hog hunter's delight.

Access is available all year, 24 hours a day! Try working the night bite at least once in your life. It's spooky, but it's awesome fishing when huge and aggressive bass are out prowling during this time. Lights on most of the docks will aid your adventure. Boaters need to be extra careful and slow their progress through congested areas.

In spring, the bass spawning activity around Horseshoe Bend can provide red-hot fly fishing. In the fall, even when the surface becomes slimy, toss poppers into the soup and chug away for explosive reactions from hungry, or territorial, largemouth.

Clear Lake is 110 miles north of the San Francisco Bay Area, through the wine country on scenic Highway 29. Or, from Interstate 5, go north to Williams and head west on Highway 20.

Clear Lake is the largest natural lake in the state with 100 miles of shoreline. Photo by Brian Sak.

Types of Fish
Largemouth bass, crappie, catfish, and bluegill.

Known Hatches & Baitfish
Threadfin shad, silverside smelt, game fish fry, crayfish, frogs, worms & grubs. Damselflies and dragonflies.

Equipment to Use
Rods: 5–9 weight, 8½–10 feet in length.
Reels: Palm or mechanical drag.
Lines: Intermediate, full sinking, type-4 or type-6 sinking shooting heads, or modified sink tips of 130 to 200 grains. WF floating on occasion.
Leaders: 1X to 6X, 5–10 feet in length.
Wading: Excellent bank angling around docks and tule patches. A terrific lake for inflatables, canoes, kayaks, and prams.

Flies to Use
Nymphs: Burk's Damsel, Putnam's Damsel #12, Kaufman's Dragonfly #6, Prince or Hare's Ear Aggravator #6.
Streamers: Whitlock Near Nuff Sculpin, Jansen's Threadfin Shad, Hot Flash Minnow, Bellied Newt, Purple Eelworm #6, Poxybou Crayfish #4, Tan or White Flashtail Clouser #2, Sea Habit Bucktail (White Knight) #2–1/0, Burk's V-Worm #10, Crystal Rubber Bugger #4.
Topwater: Swimming Frog, Andy's Loudmouth Shad #6, Gurgler #2–1/0, Deer Hair Mouse #4, Chartreuse Diver, Gaines Bluegill Popper #12.

When to Fish
Fish for bass all year, with prime times being spring and fall. Summer is best for panfish and catfish.

Accommodations & Services
Everything is right around the lake: resorts, marinas, ramps, stores, and gas stations.

Season & Limits
You can fish for something just about every month of the year. Check current California Department of Fish & Game regulations booklet, or call a fly shop or marina for specific information.

Rating
Certainly one of the state's top five bass locations, with the undoubted potential for a 9 during fall and spring. A 7.5 minimum throughout the year.

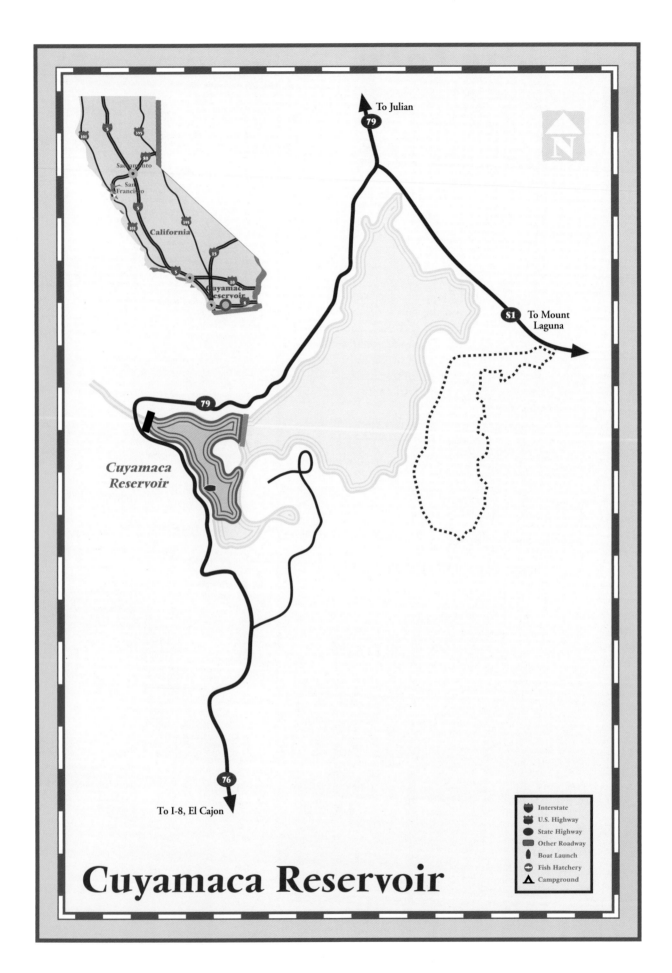

To Julian

79

S1 To Mount Laguna

79

*Cuyamaca
Reservoir*

76

To I-8, El Cajon

Cuyamaca Reservoir

Interstate
U.S. Highway
State Highway
Other Roadway
Boat Launch
Fish Hatchery
Campground

Cuyamaca Reservoir

by Jeff Solis

Near the remote town of Julian, find Cuyamaca Reservoir, one of Southern California's premier fly fishing still waters. With trout, small- and largemouth bass, and panfish willing and able to eat your fly most of the year, Cuyamaca Reservoir offers the most consistent fishing in San Diego County. This area was badly burned in the fall 2003 Julian wildfire and is now recovering.

The lake is nestled in a 4,600-foot-high mountain meadow, surrounded by oak and pine. Deer and wild turkey frequent the area, and snow is not uncommon during the winter. Yes, this is in San Diego County so crowding may be a consideration. On Wednesdays, many members of the San Diego Fly Fishing Club are not at work, but fishing here. On weekends and holidays float tubes are limited to the last three hours of the fishing day.

Cuyamaca Reservoir is relatively shallow, with a maximum depth of about 15 feet. This is enough for big rainbow trout, however, and some up to 14 pounds have been taken here on a fly. The first and last hours of daylight are often the best times for great dry fly action. During the day, nymphs and Woolly Buggers fished slowly on the bottom are the best producers. Use a sink tip line for this technique.

To reach Cuyamaca Reservoir from San Diego, take Interstate 8 east to the Japatul Road turnoff, then follow Highway 79 north for 15 miles to the lake.

There are many different species here to give your line a tug.
Photo by Howard Fisher.

Types of Fish
Rainbow trout, large and smallmouth bass, crappie, bluegill, catfish, and sturgeon.

Known Hatches & Baitfish
Midges, mayflies, dragonflies and damselflies, golden shiners, and bullfrog tadpoles.

Equipment to Use
Rods: 3–7 weight, 8–9 feet in length.
Reels: Standard click or disk.
Lines: WF or floating is usually all you need. Maybe pack a type-4 sink tip if the wind kicks up.
Leaders: For trout and panfish, 4X, 7–9 feet in length. For bass, 3X to 4X, 5–8 feet in length.
Wading: Chest-high waders and boots, or use a float tube on the entire lake.

Flies to Use
Dries: Light Cahill, Parachute Adams, Adams, Hendrickson, Callibaetis Emerger #14–20, Looping Callibaetis #16.
Nymphs: Hare's Ear, Prince Nymph, Scud #8–16, especially with beadhead.
Streamers & Poppers: Woolly Bugger and Olive Matuka #6–12, Gurgler #2.

When to Fish
For trout, February through July and September through November. For bass and panfish, May through October.

Seasons & Limits
Open year-round. Smallmouth bass fishing is strictly catch and release. Check current California regulations for other limits and restrictions.

Nearby Fly Fishing
Poke around. Some say you can find a couple of streams with some trout. Special regulations will apply, though, so check with local anglers or a fly shop.

Accommodations & Services
There are two campgrounds at the lake, each with RV sites with hookups, a launch ramp, tackle shop, boat rentals (including paddleboats), and a very good restaurant. You can also find restaurants and lodging in Julian, although weekends are likely to be crowded.

Rating
With lots of fish and lots of action in a pretty place, Cuyamaca reservoir rates a 9, assuming full recovery from the fire.

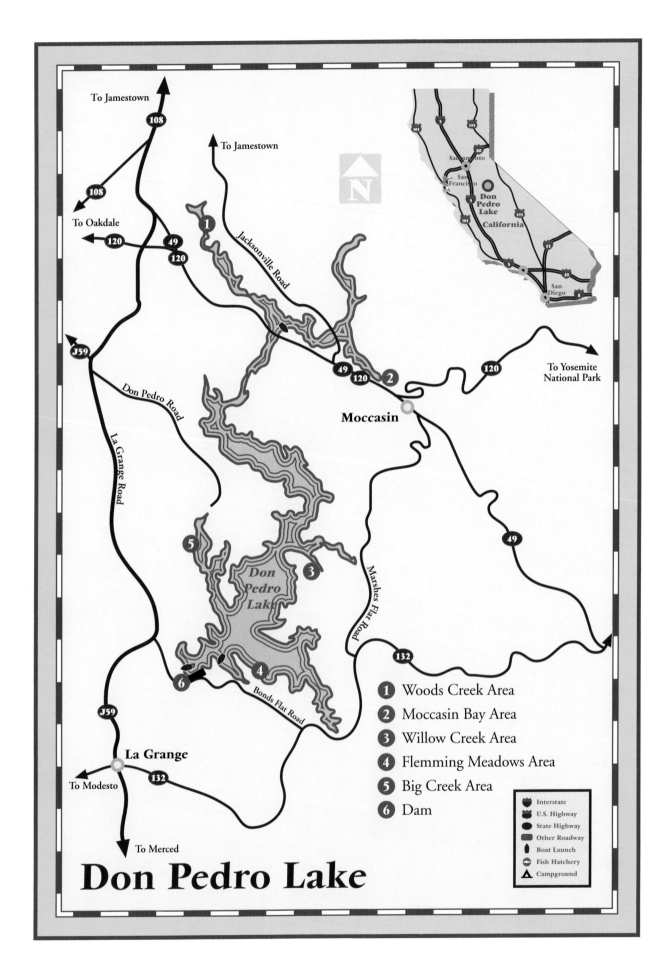

To Jamestown

108

108

To Oakdale

To Jamestown

Jacksonville Road

120

49

120

N

Don Pedro Road

J59

La Grange Road

49
120
2

120

To Yosemite National Park

Moccasin

49

Marshes Flat Road

5

Don Pedro Lake

3

4

6

132

Bonds Flat Road

J59

La Grange

132

To Modesto

To Merced

1 Woods Creek Area

2 Moccasin Bay Area

3 Willow Creek Area

4 Flemming Meadows Area

5 Big Creek Area

6 Dam

Interstate

U.S. Highway

State Highway

Other Roadway

Boat Launch

Fish Hatchery

Campground

Don Pedro Lake

Sacramento

San Francisco

Don Pedro Lake

California

San Diego

Don Pedro Lake

If you're afraid to lose some flies, don't go to this lake. If not, you'll work some of the best fish habitat in the foothills of northern California! The trout and bass you'll catch are worth a few missing flies.

Don Pedro, one of the best fly fishing destinations in the Sierra foothills gold country, is well stocked with trout, salmon, and bass. The Department of Fish & Game keeps virtually tens of thousands of fingerlings roaming this lake. The impoundment is huge, so plan on covering lots of water to maximize your fishing adventures. Be aware of boating patterns as you explore. As with most venues, the farther you travel from the parking lots and launch ramps, the less pressure the game fish receive.

The arms, coves, and inlets of Don Pedro are numerous, and all present you with fish cover to explore. Game fish have little problem finding and feasting on the healthy food chain in these areas. There are also plenty of places for them to retreat to when danger lurks.

Fly rodders should look for rocky habitat, timber, docks, and points for the most concentrated populations of game fish. The southern coves are teeming with bass. I recommend the Willow Creek and Big Creek areas. Dark-colored patterns are classics around these areas. The Woods Creek arm and the Moccasin Bay area are top choices for trout anglers, with the Flemming Meadows region being a solid second choice for trout.

Most folks drive to Don Pedro via Highway 120. Pass through the towns of Manteca and Oakdale, heading east. Exit onto J59, La Grange Road and go to Bonds Flat Road to reach the southern part of the reservoir. To access the north shore, just stay on 120 through Chinese Camp and continue to Moccasin Point.

Large trout and kokanee have given this reservoir a fine reputation. Photo by John Sherman.

Types of Fish
Rainbow trout, kokanee, largemouth, smallmouth, and spotted bass, crappie, bluegill, and some king salmon.

Known Hatches & Baitfish
Threadfin shad, bluegill, game fish fry, crayfish, leeches, frogs, callibaetis mayflies, caddisflies, damselflies, dragonflies, and hoppers.

Equipment to Use
Rods: 5–9 weight, 8½–10 feet in length.
Reels: Standard mechanical or palm drag.
Lines: WF floating for topwater and trout. Otherwise intermediate, sink tip type-4, modified sink tips of 130 to 200 grains, shooting heads type-4 or type-6.
Leaders: 2X to 6X, 6–12 feet in length.
Wading: Best fished from a motorboat. Bank angling is possible. It's a huge lake for float tubing.

Flies to Use
Dries & Topwater: Quigley Loopwing Callibaetis, Haystack Callibaetis #16, Parachute Madam X #8, Adams Irresistible #10, Griffith's Gnat #14, Adams #14–16, Madam X #8–12, Royal Stimulator #12, Whitlock's Red Head Hair Popper, Deer Hair Mouse, Swimming Frog, Loudmouth Shad #6, Gurgler #2, Gaines Bluegill Popper #12, Sponge Spider #10–12.
Nymphs: Putnam's Damsel #12, Kaufman's Dragonfly #8, Poxyback Callibaetis #16, Black Ant #10–14, Bug Eye Damsel #12, Gold Bead Bird's Nest #14, Poxyback Trico, Midge pupa #20.
Streamers: Burk's V-Worm #10, Black or Olive Woolly Bugger, Poxybou Crayfish, Whitlock Eelworm #4, Olive Matuka, Yellow Clouser Minnow #6, Blanton's Flash Tail series #6–8.

When to Fish
Trout: All year, prime in spring and fall.
Bass: February through October; prime times are March, April, and October.
Panfish: All year, prime time is early spring through summer.

Seasons & Limits
All-year access and, in general, year-round fishing, but contact local fly shops or the marina for assistance (Don Pedro Recreation Agency 209-852-2396, Don Pedro Marina 209-852-2369, Moccasin Point Marina 209-989-2206). Also refer to the current California Department of Fish & Game regulations booklet.

Accommodations & Services
This is a full-service facility with marinas, launches, boat rentals and supplies, and day-use fee. Campgrounds and boat-in camping abound.

Rating
Lots of trolling on this lake—at least a 7.

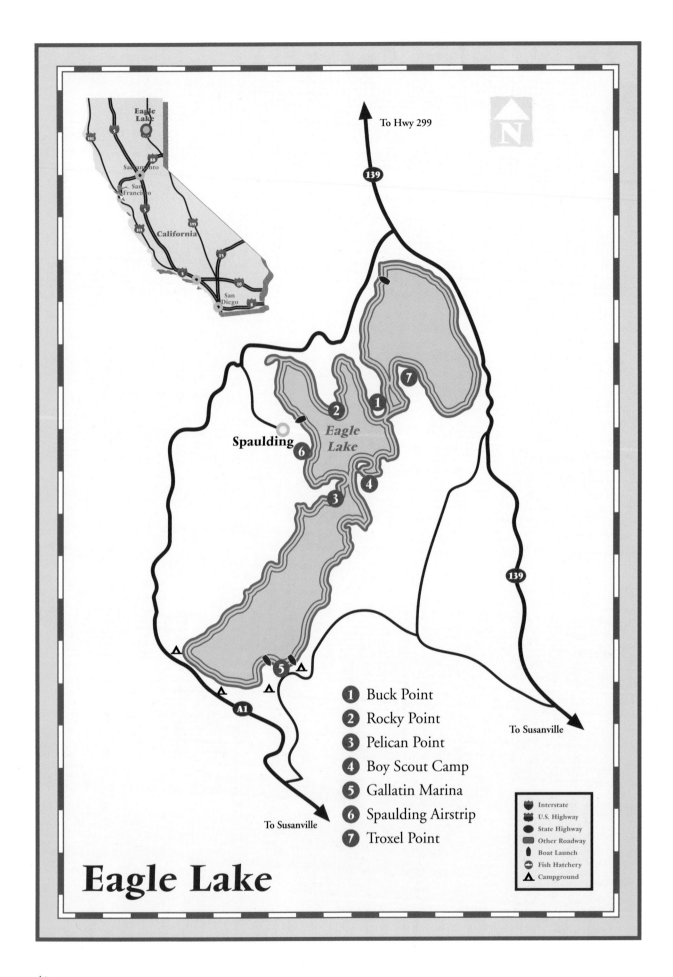

To Hwy 299

139

N

Eagle
Lake

Spaulding

2

1

7

6

4

3

5

A1

To Susanville

To Susanville

139

To Susanville

1 Buck Point
2 Rocky Point
3 Pelican Point
4 Boy Scout Camp
5 Gallatin Marina
6 Spaulding Airstrip
7 Troxel Point

Interstate
U.S. Highway
State Highway
Other Roadway
Boat Launch
Fish Hatchery
Campground

Eagle Lake

Eagle Lake
by Dave Stanley

I f you want to catch a giant rainbow trout in this part of the world, Eagle Lake is a good place to start. It is home to the Eagle Lake rainbow, a strain of the hardiest, fastest-growing trout in the West. More than 200,000 trout are planted in the lake annually. The authorities at the Reno Fly Shop say the key to fly fishing Eagle Lake is to hit it when it's "on," usually in spring and fall.

This large, alkaline body of water sits in the mountains just above Susanville. During the warm months of summer, fish tend to stay out in deep, cold water. When temperatures in the shallows remain cool—generally late May through early June or October through December—fly fishing excitement builds.

Large Eagle Lake rainbows make a habit of cruising near shore in search of food during these months and under these conditions. This is when fly fishers have the most success wading along rocky or tule-lined shores or casting from boats and float tubes. Scuds, leeches, minnows, and other aquatic insects populate these alkaline areas.

It's a good idea to target or pre-select the areas you want to fish and to get there early. The popular spots include the flats at the north end of the lake, around the marina at the south end, and along the shorelines near Spaulding, Pelican Point, and the old Boy Scout camp across from Pelican Point.

The weather at Eagle Lake sometimes ruins these fly fishing opportunities, making fishing conditions difficult if not downright nasty. If you're boating or float tubing when the wind comes up, head for shore. If you can put up with cold and wind, however, the trout are definitely worth the discomfort.

Early morning strike.
Photo by Ben Rualo, PDaCG.Com.

Gearing up for a great day of float tubing.
Photo by Ben Rualo, PDaCG.Com.

Type of Fish
A pure strain of Eagle Lake rainbow trout exists here.

Known Hatches & Baitfish
Not really a "hatch" lake, but there are some midges and damsels. Key in on scuds, leeches, and minnows.

Equipment to Use
Rods: 5–7 weight, 8–9 feet in length.
Reels: Palm or mechanical drag.
Lines: Floating or intermediate sink tip.
Leaders: Short and stout, 3X to 4X, 7½ feet in length.
Wading: Neoprene waders and felt-soled boots for the cold water. A float tube or boat is the best way to cover a lot of water.

Flies to Use
Dries: Of little importance, possibly suspended Midge Emergers.
Nymphs: Scud, Snail, Sheep Creek Special, Marabou and Mohair Leech, Small Olive Bird's Nest.
Streamers: Copper-Brown Krystal Bugger, Gray Zonker to imitate minnows, Staynor Ducktail.

When to Fish
Weeks after the lake opens in late May until warm water drives the fish deeper. Best fishing is from late September to the close of the season on December 31—if the water doesn't freeze.

Seasons & Limits
Open from the Saturday before Memorial Day until December 31. Always consult a fly shop or Department of Fish & Game regulations for current limits.

Accommodations & Services
There is plenty of motel and RV space in and around Susanville and several campgrounds around the lake. Limited motel and dining options exist in Spaulding and along the shore.

Rating
Dave Stanley and crew at Reno Fly Shop say that when it's on, Eagle Lake is an easy 10. Generally it's an 8.5.

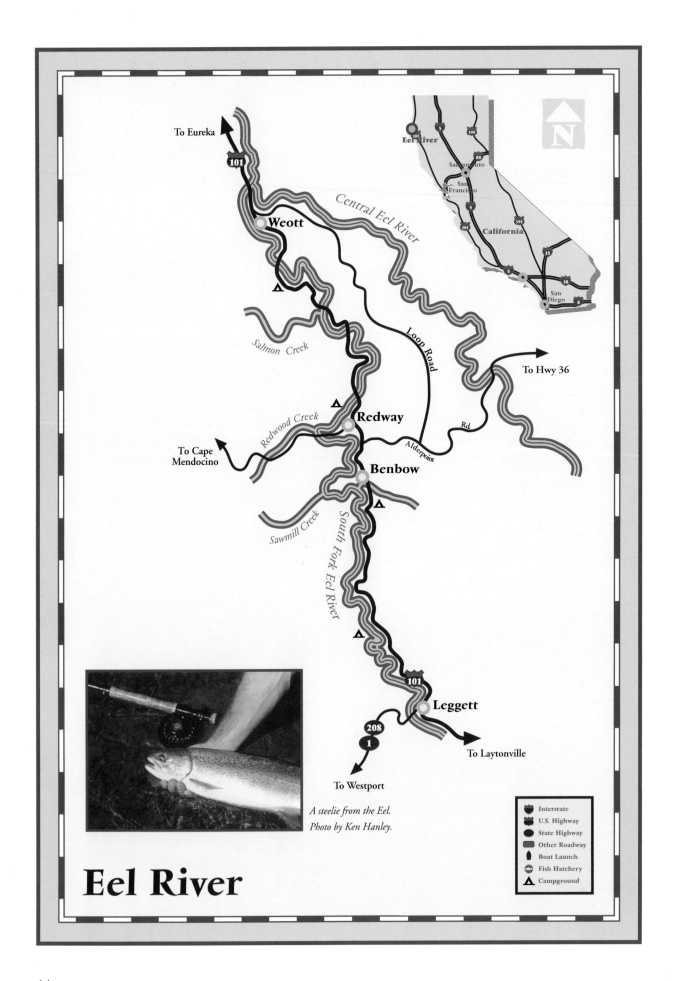

To Eureka

101

Central Eel River

Weott

Salmon Creek

Loop Road

To Hwy 36

Redwood Creek

Redway

Rd

Alderpoint

To Cape
Mendocino

Benbow

Sawmill Creek

South Fork Eel River

101

Leggett

To Laytonville

208

1

To Westport

A steelie from the Eel.
Photo by Ken Hanley.

Eel River

California

San Diego

San Francisco

Sacramento

Eel River

N

	Interstate
	U.S. Highway
	State Highway
	Other Roadway
	Boat Launch
	Fish Hatchery
	Campground

Eel River

Eel River

The Eel is a terrific river system for fly fishers who are afoot or afloat. It's also one of the prettiest and longest stream corridors in northern California, measuring 100 miles. It eventually hits the ocean near Ferndale. The beautiful fir, redwood, and other trees that line the river and the access along Highway 101 are remarkable. One can fly fish the river just about anywhere, from the tidewater environs to the upper waters at the town of Leggett.

As with any fishery connected to the coast, the river is susceptible to flooding during heavy rains. The Eel usually needs anywhere from a few days to a week to clear. When the river is in prime condition, your odds of tangling with a metallic steelhead or hefty Pacific salmon are first-rate. Check for steelhead behind rocks and in tailouts with moderate flows. Check the slow-moving sections of river and deep holes for salmon. Fishing from a drift boat for steelies usually provides the most success. The angler willing to travel the system is most likely to find active fish. You have to move, move, move, to get the best of this river's treasures. To check on stream flows and special closures, try the Department of Fish & Game recorded message line at (707) 442–4502.

The silver (coho) salmon runs on this river have become a major concern for the Department of Fish & Game. At the time of publication, California had implemented a no angling action for coho returning to any of our waters. At this point, you may not target the species. The silver populations just can't take any pressure and need time to recover.

To get to the Eel, just drive Highway 101. Access from the north is along approximately 90 miles of our dramatic coastline, through the towns of Crescent City, Arcata, and Eureka. Travelers from the south pass through San Francisco, Santa Rosa, Ukiah, Willits, and Leggett. The drive is roughly 200 miles from the San Francisco Bay Area.

The Eel is well known for its fall and winter runs of salmon and steelhead. Photo by John Sherman.

Types of Fish
King salmon (chinook), silver salmon (coho), steelhead, and shad.

Known Hatches & Baitfish
Concentrate on your fly selection, not bugs found in the field. In tidewater environs use shrimp and tiny baitfish patterns. In inland sections use traditional spawn patterns and attractor-style streamers and nymphs.

Equipment to Use
Rods: 7–9 weight, 8–10 feet in length. Spey rods are becoming more popular as well.
Reels: I prefer disk drag systems and large arbor designs with at least 75 yards of backing.
Lines: Sinking shooting head system or modified sink tips ranging from 150 to 300 grain weights.
Leaders: 1X to 3X, 6–10 feet in length.
Wading: Chest-high neoprene waders, or Gore-Tex clothes with proper insulating undergarments. Use felt-soled boots with cleats and a wading staff. Be prepared for cold and fast flows.

Flies to Use
Tidewater Area: Polar Shrimp #6, Joe's Prawn and General Practitioner #1/0 and #2, Krystal Bullet #4–6, Orange Comet, Fall Favorite #2.
Main Stream: Boss, Green-Butt Skunk #4–10, Brindle Bug, Silver Hilton #6–10, Pink Micro Egg #16, #4–10.

When to Fish
King Salmon: October through early January; prime time is late November into December.
Silver Salmon: Off-limits at present.
Steelhead: November through March; prime time is December through February.
Shad: Late spring through summer, in the lower river.

Seasons & Limits
This river is subject to low-flow closure. Restrictions on tackle, harvest, and access locations can change from season to season. Consult California Department of Fish & Game regulations or a local fly shop.

Nearby Fly Fishing
Give the Van Duzen River a try. It's well worth it.

Accommodations & Services
Find lodging, food, and supplies in Fortuna, Rio Dell, Garberville, and Leggett. Public and private campgrounds are located in Rio Dell, Weott, Myers Flat, Benbow, and the Leggett area.

Rating
If the river stays in shape throughout the winter, it can be a real winner. Overall, I find it to be a solid 6.5, and that's pretty darn good considering the volatile nature of our winter coastal rivers.

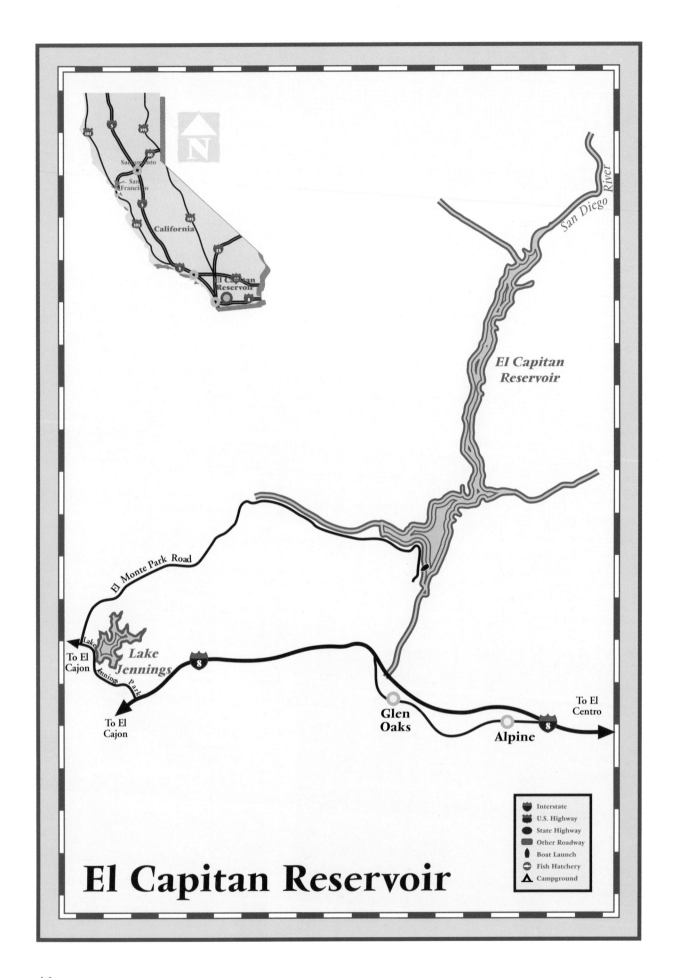

San Diego River

El Capitan
Reservoir

El Monte Park Road

Lake Jennings Park

To El Cajon

Lake
Jennings

To El
Cajon

To El
Cajon

Glen
Oaks

Alpine

To El
Centro

California

N

	Interstate
	U.S. Highway
	State Highway
	Other Roadway
	Boat Launch
	Fish Hatchery
	Campground

El Capitan Reservoir

El Capitan Reservoir

by Jeff Solis

A long with San Vicente and Lower Otay reservoirs and Lake Hodges, El Capitan is considered among the best warmwater fisheries in the southern reaches of California.

Distinguished by its long northern arm, El Capitan is a large reservoir that can produce big numbers of quality bass as well as the occasional 25-fish stringer of two-pound crappie, all caught on a fly.

At full capacity the reservoir is eight miles long with 20 miles of shore line. At time of publication it is operating at five miles in length.

Most of El Capitan's shoreline is relatively bare, but there is plenty of submerged structure such as trees and shrubs. Bottom fishing is slow, so work close to shore for bass. The upper reach of the reservoir's northern arm holds lots of crappie. Boat fishing is the ticket here–shore fishing with a fly rod is a waste of time.

The best days for fishing are during the week as water skiers and jet skiers find weekends popular.

You will want a boat to cover this large expanse of water.
Photo by Howard Fisher.

Photo by Howard Fisher.

Types of Fish
Largemouth bass, crappie, bluegill, blue and channel catfish, and sunfish.

Known Baitfish
Threadfin shad is the predominant baitfish.

Equipment to Use
Rods: 6–8 weight, 8–9 feet in length.
Reels: Standard click or disk.
Lines: WF, floating, and intermediate sink tip.
Leaders: 2X to 4X, 5–8 feet in length.
Wading: Not very productive for wade fishing. Use a boat; it's a long way to the best water.

Flies to Use
Streamers & Poppers: Hot Flash Minnow #6, Sponge Spider #12, Woolly Bugger, Clouser Minnow, Lefty's Deceiver (large) #1/0–2 for bass or (smaller) #2–6 for crappie.

When to Fish
Year-round.

Seasons & Limits
Year-round. A non-state fishing license is sold at the reservoir. Currently operated by the San Diego Water Department Lakes Recreation Program, days and hours of operation are limited, and subject to closure. Consult the City of San Diego Reservoirs and Recreation Program phone (619) 465-3474 for current schedule. At time of publication, open Fridays through Sundays, plus holidays.

Minimum size limit for bass is 15 inches and 10 inches for crappie.

Hike with care along the shoreline as rattlesnakes and poison oak are part of the natural environment.

Accommodations & Services
Boat rentals, bait, and tackle available at the reservoir. Use your own boat if possible; it's a long run to the best fishing. All services available in nearby El Cajon.

Rating
For bass, El Capitan Reservoir is a 7 to 8.

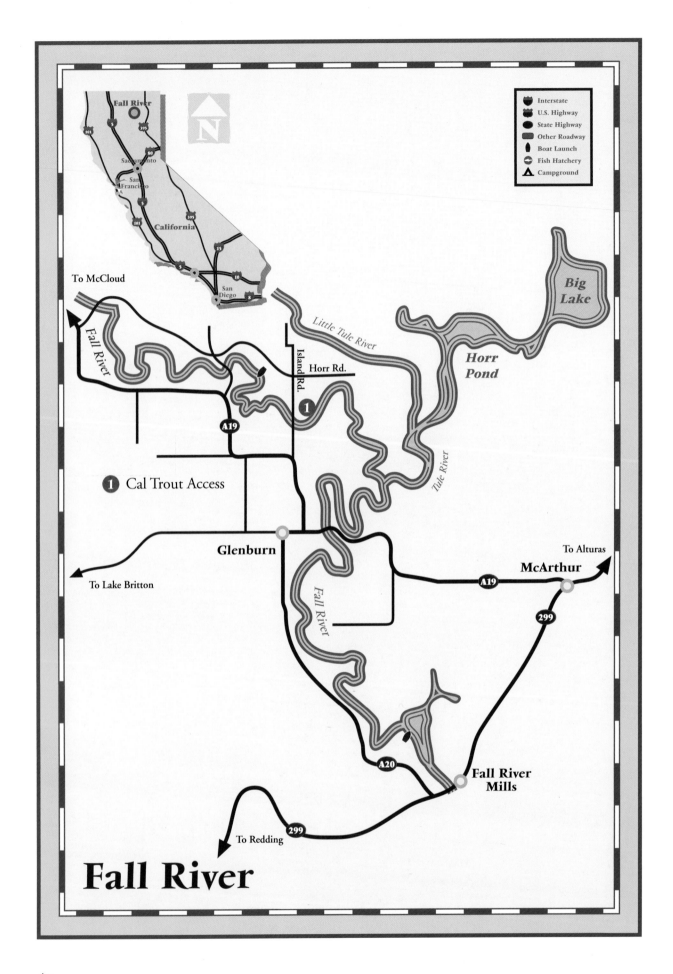

Fall River

Fall River

If you enjoy cool, clear, deep-running, classic spring-fed mountain rivers with thick and lush mats of vegetation, Fall River might just be your ticket to trout heaven. This is northern California trout water at its finest, but you'll need a boat or float tube to fly fish the best areas. The majority of the bank access is through private property. Prams and johnboats with electric motors are best for working this wide and spacious waterway—usually 100 to 250 yards across. A two-anchor system is a good way to position your boat. If you're a first-timer, a guide is the best way to learn this river.

Fall River was originally used to transport logs and was virtually a private watercourse. Anglers had limited access until the early 1970s. Today, fly fishers enjoy a bonus from the logging days. Many sunken logs provide cover and prime habitat for trout. These hefty, strong-fighting, wild trout run 16 to 20 inches. The average trout weighs two to three pounds. Every year enough 6- to 11-pound monsters are hooked to keep anglers on their toes!

Most fly fishers use a down-and-across presentation of short casts with line mends that extend the drift. This technique has earned the moniker "Fall River Twitch." Drag-free drifts and long leaders are critical for both nymph and dry fly presentations. Remember, this river is smooth, with little pocket water and few riffles.

Interstate 5 is the route to this wonderful fishery. Traveling from the north, as you pass the town of Mt. Shasta, keep an eye open for the McCloud exit, Highway 89. Follow 89 until it intersects with Highway 299. Travel east on 299 to Fall River Mills. Highway A20 then takes you directly to Glenburn and all the action. From the south, take Interstate 5 into the city of Redding. Exit onto 299 east and drive directly to Fall River Mills. The river is about a six-hour drive from the Bay Area.

Picturesque barns along the banks of the Fall River.
Photo by Ben Rualo, PDaCG.Com.

Types of Fish
Brown and rainbow trout.

Known Hatches
Spring & Fall: Baetis, pale morning dun (PMD), blue-winged olive.
June: Hexagenia mayfly, PMD.
July to August: Green drake, caddis, PMD.
All Year: Scuds, leeches.

Equipment to Use
Rods: 4–6 weight, 7–9½ feet in length.
Reels: Basic click and pawl or disk drag.
Lines: WF floating. For deepwater presentations, try a sink tip design type-2 or modified sink tip of 130 grain weight.
Leaders: 5X to 8X, 10–15 feet in length for surface work. 4X to 5X, 7–9 feet in length for subsurface presentations.
Wading: Take a boat for more fly fishing opportunities.

Flies to Use
Dries: Tan or Olive Paradun #16–20, Trico #18–20, Brown Elk Hair Caddis #14–16, Henryville Special #16, Hexagenia May #6, Olive or Brown Mayfly Emerger #16–20.
Nymphs: Olive Bird's Nest #12–14, Hunched Back Infrequens (HBI), Pheasant Tail #16–20, Green Sparkle Pupa #16–18, Damselfly Nymph #10–12, Scud #10–16, Poxyback Green Drake #12, Zug Bug #14–18, Hexagenia #6.
Streamers: Olive or Brown Woolly Bugger #8–10.

When to Fish
Rainbows: All season.
Browns: All season. Late summer/fall is best.

Seasons & Limits
Last Saturday in April through November 15. Barbless artificials only, two fish under 14 inches. Seasons and regulations change; check the California regulations or ask at a local fly shop before hitting the river.

Accommodations & Services
Lodging and supplies are available in Burney, Glenburn, and Fall River Mills.

Rating
Fall River is great for building visual skills, such as interpreting feeding behavior and holding lies and current seams. Without a doubt this fishery rates a 9.

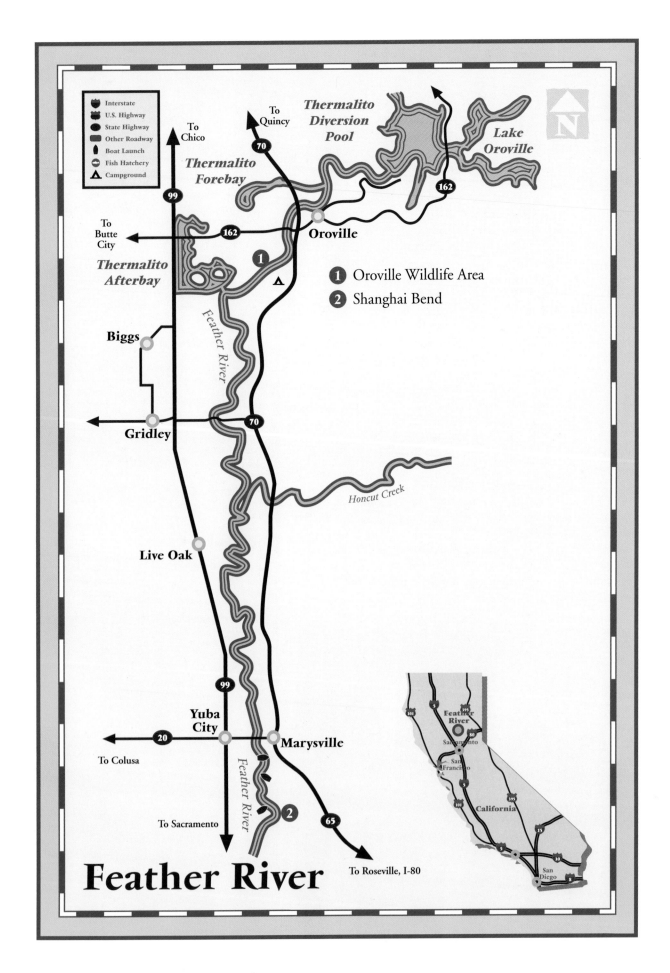

Feather River

Feather River
Lower Section

The lower Feather spills out of Lake Oroville and flows 50 miles south through the Central Valley. Before the Oroville Dam was built, the lower Feather was one of the state's top salmon rivers. Currently, this beautiful riverway contains about a dozen different game fish, including a number of anadromous species. Part of the fun here is picking the type of fish you wish to pursue. In nearly every month of the year fly fishing on the Feather can put a smile on your face.

As a general rule, the upper stretches run shallow and fast (over bedrock), while the lower river is wide, deep, and slow. Boaters have an advantage from Yuba City to Verona and the confluence with the Sacramento River. Bank angling access is best around Shanghai Bend and from Gridley Bridge to Thermolito Afterbay. The Oroville Wildlife Area offers more foot access, and farther downstream wading is possible in the Live Oak area. There are wadable areas below the town of Yuba City as well. The best access is during low-water periods.

The lower Feather holds a great year-round population of smallmouth bass. Look for them anywhere there is bass-type cover: logs, brush, stumps, undercut banks, etc. April to May is the best time for these one- to two-pounders.

Most anglers take Highway 99 from Sacramento (heading toward Marysville and Yuba City) to get to the Feather. To work the eastern shore, follow Highway 70 into Marysville and toward Oroville. To access the western shore, take the 99 split into Yuba City, through Live Oak, and on north. Local surface roads provide numerous access points to the water. From Sacramento to Yuba City/Marysville is about 45 miles. The drive into Oroville from the capital is close to 70 miles.

Fish on at the Feather.
Photo by John Sherman.

Types of Fish
American shad, smallmouth bass, striped bass, king salmon, steelhead, and rainbows.

Known Baitfish
Game fish fry, sculpins, crayfish, salmon roe.

Equipment to Use
Rods: 5–9 weight, 8–9 feet in length; Spey outfits are becoming more popular.
Reels: Basic click and pawl or disk drag systems. Smooth drags are key.
Lines: WF floating for low water or poppers; modified sink tip designs from 130 to 250 grain weights, or type-4 uniform full sinking line for streamers and nymphs.
Leaders: 3X to 5X, 6–10 feet in length.
Wading: Use chest-high waders, neoprene for winter months (or Gore-Tex with appropriate insulating undergarments), studded boots, and wading staff.

Flies to Use
Dries: Adams #12, Adams Irresistible #10, Yellow or Tan Humpy #14–16, Elk Hair Caddis #12.
Nymphs: Gold Ribbed Hare's Ear #12–16, Bird's Nest #12–16, Black AP Nymph #14, Tan and Olive Fox's Poopah #14.
Streamers: Hot Flash Minnow #6, Beaded Krystal Buggers #8, Muddler Minnow #2–8, Bullet Head #6, Poxybou Crayfish #4–8, Clouser Minnow #6, Sea Habit Bucktail (White Knight) #1/0, Flashtail Clouser #1/0–2, Single Egg #6.
Topwater & Subsurface: Gurgler #2, Whitlock's Deer Hair Popper #6–10.

When to Fish
American Shad: April through August; prime time is June and July.
Smallmouth Bass: All year; prime times are fall and spring.
Striped Bass: March through June; prime time is April and May.
Salmon: October and January.
Steelhead: September through February; October is prime time.
Trout: All year.

Seasons & Limits
Restrictions on access locations, tackle, harvest, and species vary throughout the year and throughout the river system. Always consult the California fishing regulations booklet. It's always a good idea to contact local fly shops in advance of your travels.

Accommodations & Services
Boat access is located at various spots along the river. Launch ramp and supplies are available at Verona Marina. Lake Oroville State Recreation Area has camping. Lodging and supplies are available in Oroville, Marysville, and Yuba City.

Rating
Crowds can build in the more popular runs during a hot bite period. Security can be an issue in outlying parking areas. Overall, the angling rates an 8.5.

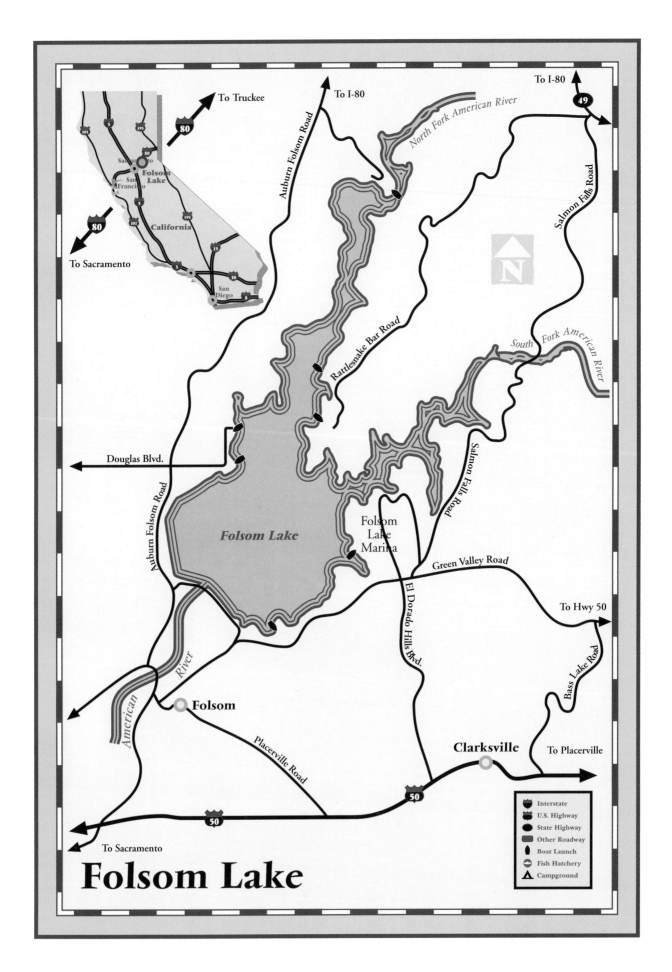

Folsom Lake

Folsom Lake

This reservoir, just 30 minutes from Sacramento, is a wonderful place for largemouth and smallmouth bass action. Folsom is also a pretty darn good trout fishery. The roaring American River provides high-quality water throughout the entire year, though droughts and seasonal conditions affect the lake's water levels. When the pond is full, you have about 12,000 acres to investigate. Trout plants begin around November and continue into April on most years. Bass are stocked year-round.

The reservoir has two forks, north and south. The trout love the cooler, oxygen-rich water of the North Fork habitat. Smallmouth also like to work this stretch, as there is no lack of rocky cover or structure. The South Fork arm also has trout, but the emphasis here is largemouth bass, found around submerged vegetation and timber. You can also target crappie near Browns Ravine (Folsom Lake Marina). In particular, look for these slabsides hanging around brush piles.

The topwater bass bite, usually during an early-morning or evening session, is worth pursuing. Chartreuse is a great color selection for this bite, especially in spring. Red and white poppers are excellent during summer and fall.

Folsom Lake is about 25 miles northeast of Sacramento. Take Interstate 80 to the Douglas Boulevard exit. Travel ten miles east to the Granite Bay entrance, or take Highway 50, El Dorado Hills Blvd. and Green Valley Road to the marina.

A nice smallmouth awaits you.
Photo by John Sherman.

Types of Fish
Rainbow trout, largemouth and smallmouth bass, crappie, and panfish.

Known Hatches & Baitfish
Bass: Pond smelt, threadfin shad, bluegill, game fish fry, crayfish, leeches, frogs.
Trout: Callibaetis mayfly, caddis, damselfly, dragonfly, hoppers, small baitfish.

Equipment to Use
Rods: 5–7 weight, 8–9½ feet in length.
Reels: Standard drag system.
Lines: WF floating, intermediate, sink tip type-4, modified sink tips of 130 to 200 grains, shooting heads type-4 or type-6.
Leaders: 1X to 6X, 6–12 feet in length for bass, 7–12 feet in length for trout.
Wading: Bank angling in hip boots is possible. The lake is terrific for float tubes, inflatables, prams, and boats.

Flies to Use
Dries: Quigley Loopwing Callibaetis #16, Parachute Madam X #8, Adams Irresistible #10, Griffith's Gnat #14.
Nymphs: Putnam's Damsel, Black AP #12, Kaufman's Dragonfly #8, Poxyback Callibaetis #16, Black Ant, Prince #14.
Streamers: Sea Habit Bucktail #1/0, Flashtail Clouser #1/0–2, Burk's V-Worm #10, Hot Flash Minnow, Purple Eelworm, Whitlock Near Nuff Sculpin, Zonker, Jansen's Threadfin Shad, Purple Eelworm, Black Hare Jig #6, Blanton's Flash Tail series #2–8, Whitlock Softshell Crayfish #8, Poxybou Crayfish #4–8, Black Woolly Bugger #4.
Topwater & Subsurface: Gurgler #2, Swimming Frog, Loudmouth Shad, Whitlock's Cocktail Hair Popper #6, Gaines Bluegill Popper #12, Sponge Spider 10–12, Deer Hair Mouse, Chartreuse Diver #4.

When to Fish
Trout: Concentrate your efforts from January through March.
Bass: March through November; prime times are April and May and October and November.
Crappie & Panfish: All year, summer is prime time.

Seasons & Limits
Fish for just about all species year-round. Harvest restrictions apply, so check local fly shops or the Department of Fish & Game regulations booklet for more exact information.

Accommodations & Services
There are four public launch ramps, a marina, boat rentals, concessions, and campgrounds at the lake. Lodging, gear, gas, and groceries are found in Sacramento.

Rating
Good opportunities year-round make this a fine 7.5 on most days, although summer crowds can make the fishing a bit crazy.

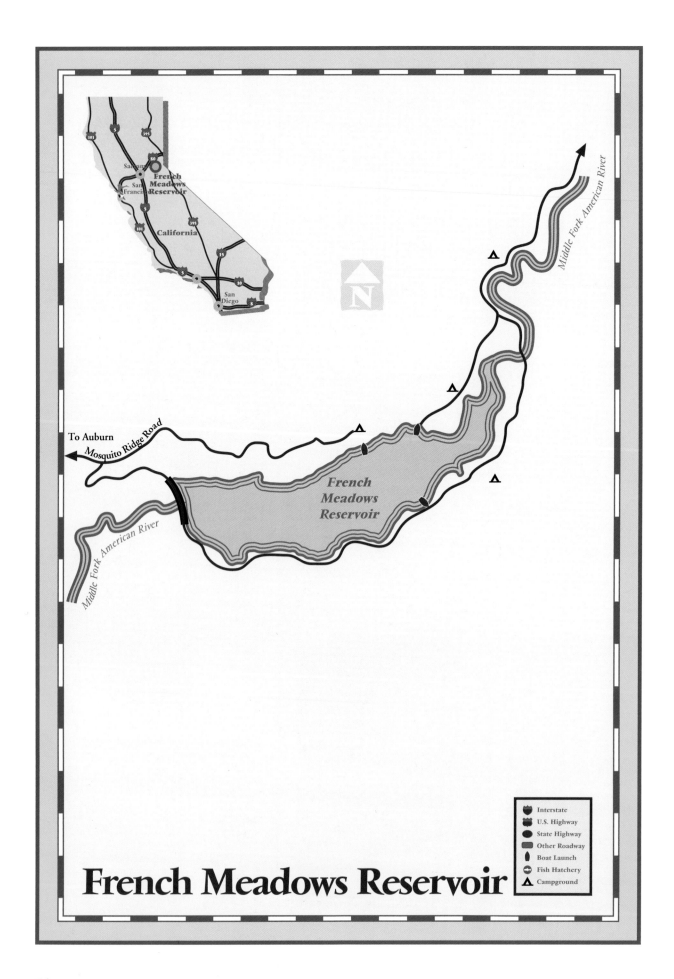

French Meadows Reservoir

French Meadows Reservoir

This Sierra Nevada gem is a classic mountain impoundment and heaven for trout, trout, and trout! They patrol submerged timber, stump fields, and stick-ups as their primary habitat, and the water is usually very clear. There are also some terrific boulders and shelves that add to the mix of structure and cover. This is the real deal for Sierra foothills trout.

French Meadows receives a good stocking of planted rainbows each year. There's also a sizable population of larger holdover trout. Most of the brown trout found in this reservoir are wild. They offer you some magical moments, to be sure. Adding to all this excitement is the ever-present chance of catching a hearty smallmouth bass. They aren't very numerous, but they are a terrific game fish on fly tackle.

The reservoir receives water from the Middle Fork of the American River. Flows are usually restricted in the fall, shrinking the lake considerably. At 5,300 feet in elevation, this place can get very cold, windy, and downright uncomfortable if you haven't prepared first. Don't forget your sunscreen either.

Getting to French Meadows can be tedious. Take your time and be patient, because it's well worth your effort, and the difficult access actually helps control the fishing pressure. From the foothills town of Auburn take the Forest Hill Road exit on the north side of town. In the town of Foresthill, after about 20 miles, turn right on Mosquito Ridge Road. It's about 37 miles to the reservoir.

A gem of a brown trout.
Photo by John Sherman.

Types of Fish
Rainbow and brown trout, smallmouth bass, panfish.

Known Hatches & Baitfish
Midges, callibaetis mayflies, caddis, damselflies, dragonflies, ants, game fish fry, and crayfish.

Equipment to Use
Rods: 5–7 weight, 8–10 feet in length.
Reels: Standard drag systems.
Lines: WF floating, intermediate, sink tip type-4; modified sink tips of 130 to 200 grains. Floating lines OK during calm periods.
Leaders: 3X to 6X, 9–12 feet in length.
Wading: Felt-soled boots and chest waders are OK, but bank angling and wading is limited. It's best to work from a skiff, canoe, pram, kayak, or inflatable if possible.

Flies to Use
Dries: Haystack Callibaetis, Quigley Loopwing Callibaetis #16, Adams #14–16, Parachute Madam X #8–12, Adams Irresistible #10, Griffith's Gnat #14, Royal Stimulator #12.
Nymphs: Midge Pupa, Poxyback Trico #20, Putnam's Damsel, Black AP #12, Kaufman's Dragonfly #8, Poxyback Callibaetis #16, Black Ant #10–14, Bug Eye Damsel #12, Gold Bead Bird's Nest #14.
Streamers: Flashtail Clouser #2–8, Bullet Head #10, Hot Flash Minnow, Whitlock Near Nuff Sculpin, Yellow Clouser Minnow, Olive Matuka #6, Black or Olive Woolly Bugger #4, Blanton's Flash Tail series #6–8.

When to Fish
Trout: Late May through September.
Bass: Prime time is June through September.
Panfish: Summer.

Seasons & Limits
Open all year. General state regulations with some limit restrictions. Consult a fly shop or the California fishing rules booklet.

Accommodations & Services
There are campgrounds and two launches at the lake. All supplies and lodging can be found in Auburn. Groceries and some supplies are available in Foresthill.

Rating
The access road is long and twisty but, hey, it keeps the place uncrowded and reduces fishing pressure. The still water fly fishing is awesome here. At least an 8.5!

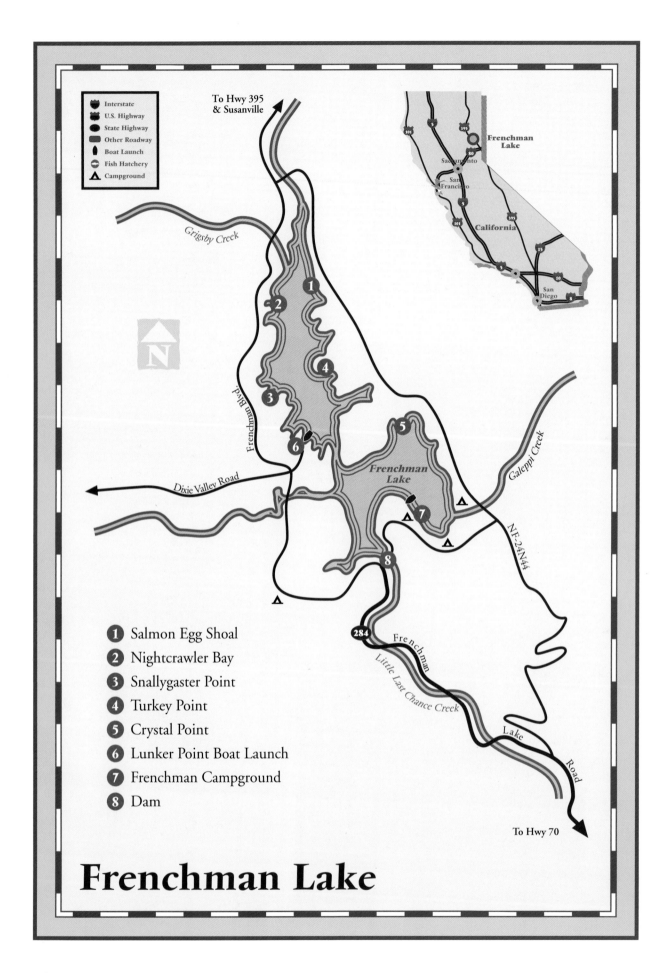

To Hwy 395
& Susanville

Grigsby Creek

Frenchman Lake

California

Sacramento

San Francisco

San Diego

Interstate
U.S. Highway
State Highway
Other Roadway
Boat Launch
Fish Hatchery
Campground

N

Frenchman Blvd.

Dixie Valley Road

Frenchman Lake

Galeppi Creek

NF-24N44

284

Frenchman

Little Last Chance Creek

Lake Road

To Hwy 70

1 Salmon Egg Shoal
2 Nightcrawler Bay
3 Snallygaster Point
4 Turkey Point
5 Crystal Point
6 Lunker Point Boat Launch
7 Frenchman Campground
8 Dam

Frenchman Lake

Frenchman Lake
by Dave Stanley

Photo by Richard Dickerson.

Frenchman Lake is a deep human-made impoundment about an hour's drive from Reno, 20 miles east of Lake Davis, and seven miles north of the town of Chilcoot, California. Dave Stanley at the Reno Fly Shop recommends this water if Lake Davis is off. Managed as a put-and-take fishery Frenchman receives hundreds of thousands of stockers each year. It is also subject to wind and cold weather, befitting an alpine setting of more than 5,000 feet in elevation.

It's best to fly fish in the large to pocket-sized, wind-protected bays that characterize most of the shoreline. At the northern end, where the main stream enters the lake, weed beds flourish, which support many aquatic life forms, including damsels, snails, mayflies, and midges.

Frenchman provides good evening surface activity during the summer, if the wind cooperates. Midges are the primary hatch, and a variety of surface and suspended patterns work well. Damsel and callibaetis mayfly hatches can be very productive from late May to July and are best fished while wading or from a floating craft in four feet or less of water. In the fall, snails and small leeches can create some spectacular fly action. Fish these patterns slowly on a floating or intermediate line.

Below the dam, Little Last Chance Creek offers plenty of trout in a tailwater-type fishery. These fish have been planted, but the easy access, pretty setting, and variety of fly fishing water make this creek worth checking out.

Frenchman Lake was poisoned in 1994 to rid it of illegally stocked northern pike and a large trash fish population. The fishery now flourishes, the trout are much healthier, and the fly fishers are happier.

Types of Fish
Rainbow and brown trout.

Known Hatches
Primary hatches include blood midges, damsels, and callibaetis. There are some evening caddis hatches during the summer months.

Equipment to Use
Rods: 4–6 weight, 8–9½ feet in length.
Reels: Standard trout reels are fine.
Lines: Floating, 4–6 weight. Intermediate or sinking, 2–4 weight.
Leaders: Wet lines for deep water, short and stout, 3X to 4X, 7½ feet in length. Intermediate and dry, 4X to 6X, 9–12 feet in length.
Wading: Use neoprene waders and felt-soled boots in cold weather. Wet-wade in warm weather. Easily fished from shore or a small boat.

Flies to Use
Dries: Suspended Midge Emerger, Callibaetis Emerger, Adams Parachute, Damsel.
Nymphs: Snail, Sheep Creek Special, Dragonfly, Timberline Emerger, Marabou Damsel, Pheasant Tail, Small Olive and Black Bird's Nest.
Streamers: Black, Gray, and Olive Leeches; Brown Woolly or Krystal Buggers.

When to Fish
The lake fishes well from ice-out until mid- to late July. The best time to fish Frenchman is from mid-September until the lake ices over.

Seasons & Limits
Frenchman is open year-round. Check California Department of Fish & Game regulations for current limits.

Accommodations & Services
Motel and RV spaces, restaurant, laundry, and auto services are best in and around Portola or forty miles away in Reno. There is a general store with gas in Chilcoot and several good, convenient campgrounds around the lake.

Rating
Generally, Frenchman rates a 7 or 7.5. During the best hatch times, this rating increases to the 8.5 to 9 range.

Anglers brave the cold in pursuit of Frenchman's trout.
Photo by Richard Dickerson.

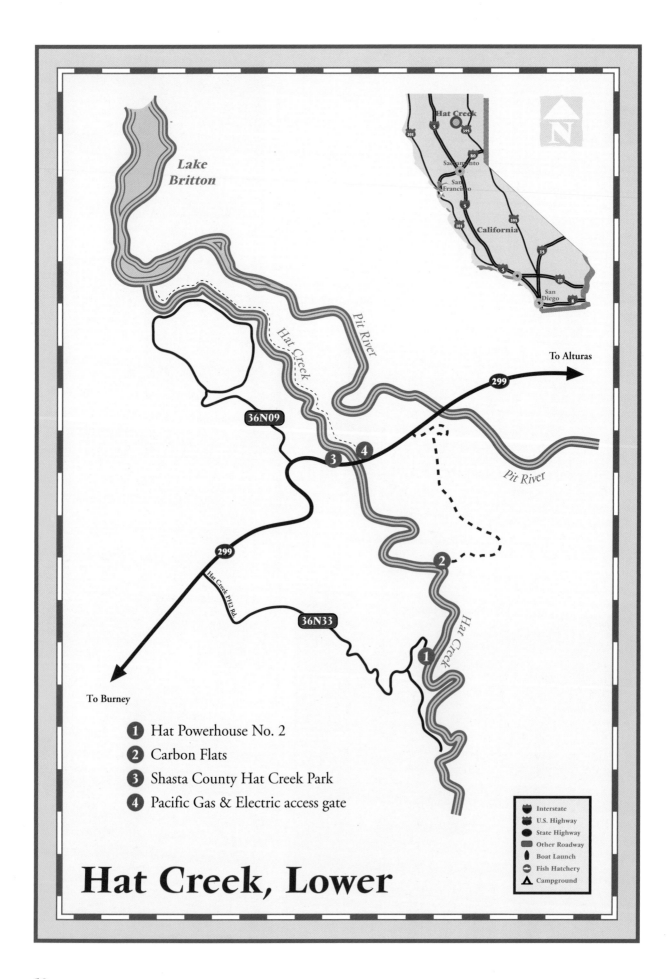

Lake Britton

Pit River

Hat Creek

To Alturas

299

Pit River

36N09

3

4

299

Hat Creek Ph2 Rd.

36N33

Hat Creek

2

To Burney

1

Hat Creek

1 Hat Powerhouse No. 2

2 Carbon Flats

3 Shasta County Hat Creek Park

4 Pacific Gas & Electric access gate

Hat Creek

Hat Creek, Lower

Interstate
U.S. Highway
State Highway
Other Roadway
Boat Launch
Fish Hatchery
Campground

California

Hat Creek

Sacramento

San Francisco

San Diego

Hat Creek, Lower

With headwaters in Lassen Volcanic National Park, Upper Hat Creek is a rumbling mountain stream. People fish here with all forms of flies, lures, and bait. Anglers can camp streamside and haul in all sorts of hatchery trout.

In the valley, highly regarded Lower Hat Creek is a blue-ribbon meadow-meandering wild trout stream. These 3.5 miles of river have all the ingredients many fly rodders dream about: gin-clear water, tricky currents, wild fish, and a complex food chain. Add this up and you've got quite a fly fishing test on a world-class trout stream.

In 1968 all non-game fish were purged from the lower river, which was then replanted with native and wild trout. Regulation changes, a halt to fish stocking, and natural propagation have resulted in an outstanding population of wild trout. Hat Creek and Fall River are perhaps California's (if not the West's) best classic fly fishing streams.

The Lower Hat features extraordinarily long, glassy, deep pools and a series of shallow riffles. The streambed has lots of cover, concealing wary trout that average 10 to 16 inches. The banks are verdant, with hardwoods, shrubs, and a mixture of grasses. Hatches are many and often nearly simultaneous. Don't limit yourself to dry fly action, as sight nymphing can be dynamite on this river!

Hat Creek "central" is the town of Burney on Highway 299, 51 miles east of Redding (which is on Interstate 5). From Burney take 299 northeast about eight miles to the stream.

Fish on at Hat Creek!
Photo by Ken Hanley.

Types of Fish
Rainbow and brown trout.

Known Hatches
April & May: Salmonflies, golden stones, and PMDs.
May & June: Green drakes, PMDs, pale evening duns, caddis.
July & August: Baetis (blue-winged olives), tricos, little yellow stones, caddis.
September & October: Large October caddis.
All Year: Small caddis.

Equipment to Use
Rods: 3–5 weight, 7½–9 feet in length.
Reels: Mechanical or palm drag.
Lines: Floating. For deep water and caddis pupa, use Hi-speed, Hi-D sink-tip.
Leaders: 4X to 7X, 10–12 feet in length.
Wading: Chest-high neoprene waders and felt-soled boots.

Flies to Use
Dries: Mahogany Dun #18, Harrop Haystack Callibaetis #14–16, Loopwing Paradun Olive #20, Trico #20, Burk's CDC Stone #14, Brown Elk Hair Caddis #14, Orange or Gold Stimulator #8, Dave's Hopper #8, Yellow Humpy #4, Black Ant #12–14, Green Drake Paradrake #8–10, various Mayfly Cripples and Spinners.
Nymphs: Bird's Nest #14, Hare's Ear Beadhead #10–14, Hunched Back Infrequens (HBI) #16–18, Pheasant Tail Nymph #16–18, Poxyback Golden Stone & PMD #6–8, Black Rubber Legs #6, Bead October Poopah #8, Green Sparkle Pupa #14.
Streamers: Muddler Minnow #4–8, Olive Matuka Sculpin #2–6.

When to Fish
May and October are prime times. Mornings and evenings and hatch periods are usually the best times of day to fly fish, especially in the summer.

Seasons & Limits
Usually open the last Saturday in April through November 15. Upper Hat, limit five fish. Lower Hat from Lake Britton to Powerhouse #2, barbless flies and lures only, two fish, 18 inches minimum. Special restrictions on harvest and tackle can change, so always check with a fly shop or in the California fishing regulations booklet.

Accommodations & Services
Lodging, fly shops, and supplies are in Burney, Cassel, and Fall River Mills. Camping is best at McArthur–Burney Falls Memorial State Park or the PG&E Camp in Cassel. A fine option is the Clearwater Lodge on the Pit River, www.clearwaterlodge.com.

Rating
On the upper section a 7, on the lower reaches an 8.5.

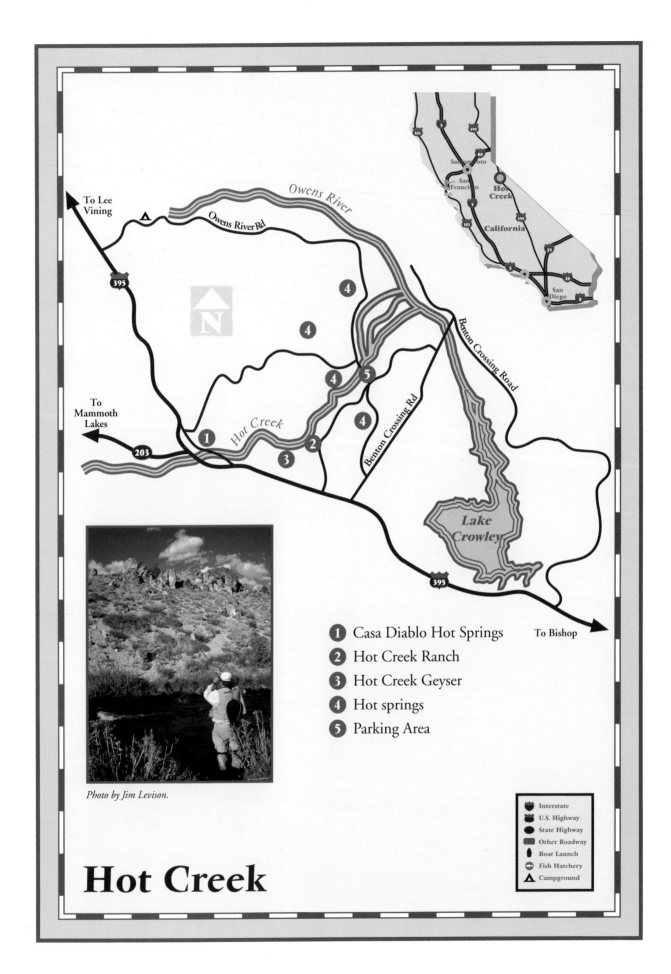

To Lee Vining

Owens River

Owens River Rd

To Mammoth Lakes

Hot Creek

Benton Crossing Road

Benton Crossing Rd

Lake Crowley

To Bishop

Sacramento
San Francisco
Hot Creek
California
San Diego

1 Casa Diablo Hot Springs
2 Hot Creek Ranch
3 Hot Creek Geyser
4 Hot springs
5 Parking Area

Photo by Jim Levison.

Interstate
U.S. Highway
State Highway
Other Roadway
Boat Launch
Fish Hatchery
Campground

Hot Creek

Hot Creek

by Cheryl Hoey

Amazing and magical are two words that spring to mind when I think of Hot Creek. Amazing is the statistic that Hot Creek is the most productive stream in the western United States. A California Department of Fish & Game electroshock survey once counted 11,000 fish per mile—a remarkable number for such a narrow creek 7,000 feet above sea level and managed entirely as wild trout water. Such an abundance of fish draws anglers from everywhere to Hot Creek.

Magical is the astounding natural beauty of the area. The stream carves a deep canyon through an active geothermal area just east of the Sierra Nevada. Puffs of steam rise from the water's edge, and hot springs bubble from the ground along the trail. In addition to giving the creek its name, these springs also keep the water between 55 and 60 degrees F, nurturing abundant plant and insect life, and creating an ideal habitat for trout.

While I was the manager of the Orvis store in San Francisco, I had the opportunity to fish in some very special places. Hot Creek, however, remains my favorite. In addition to the fishing experience and unbelievable beauty, it holds many of my favorite personal memories. When I learned I was pregnant with my daughter, although overjoyed, I realized that my idle fishing days were numbered. The only sensible thing to do that summer was fish a lot. I spent most of my fishing days that summer at Hot Creek. I didn't need waders at my favorite spot, an ideal place for a woman who couldn't bend from the waist. Five years later, my husband, Jack, and I had the pleasure of watching our Leslie select the perfect fly, cast, catch, and release her first fish.

Effectively fishing Hot Creek rarely requires casts of more than 20 feet. Standing on the bank, you can see fish working close by. I emphasize standing on the bank because wading is discouraged and unnecessary, except to release a fish. Moreover, the creek's fish are not easily spooked and seem unfazed by the presence of anglers. These conditions generally make Hot Creek excellent for beginners, although there are times when extremely selective fish, weeds, and high desert winds combine to challenge even the most skilled angler.

The public section of water between Hot Creek Ranch and the parking area at Owens River Road is approximately two miles long. The Owens River Road end has public restrooms and a paved trail down to the creek. Bathing and swimming areas are located at the foot of the trail. Many tired anglers discover that a warm soak offers the perfect ending to a day of fishing this beautiful, small stream.

From Bishop take Interstate 395 north to Owens River Road.

Photo by John Sherman.

Types of Fish
Brown and rainbow trout.

Known Hatches
Baetis, caddis, scuds, ants, and hoppers.

Equipment to Use
Rods: 9 feet in length, 4–6 weight.
Reels: Standard spring and pawl or disk drag.
Lines: WF, floating.
Leaders: 9–12 feet in length, 5X to 7X.
Wading: Wading discouraged and not required.

Flies to Use
Dries: Blue-Winged Olive, CDC Caddis, Madam X, Hopper, Ant, and Beetle.
Nymphs: Beadhead Pheasant Tail, Scud, and Brassie.
Streamers: Black or Olive Leech patterns.

When to Fish
Because of consistent water temperatures, Hot Creek fishes well all day throughout the season.

Seasons & Limits
From the last Saturday in April through November 15. Barbless hooks only. No kill, zero limit.

Nearby Fly Fishing
Owens River, Lake Crowley, and June Lake Loop (Highway 158).

Accommodations & Services
The Mammoth Lakes area has hotels, restaurants, gas, and fly shops.

Rating
Hot Creek provides opportunities for beginners and a challenge for seasoned anglers—a solid 8.

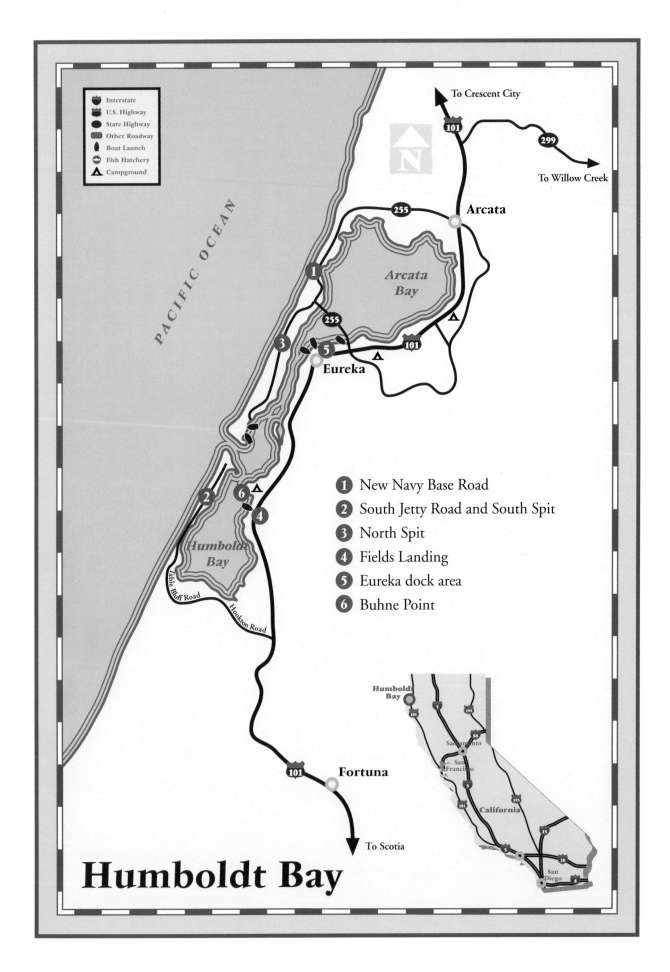

Humboldt Bay

Legend:
- Interstate
- U.S. Highway
- State Highway
- Other Roadway
- Boat Launch
- Fish Hatchery
- Campground

To Crescent City

101

299

To Willow Creek

255

Arcata

PACIFIC OCEAN

Arcata Bay

255

101

Eureka

① New Navy Base Road
② South Jetty Road and South Spit
③ North Spit
④ Fields Landing
⑤ Eureka dock area
⑥ Buhne Point

Humboldt Bay

Table Bluff Road

Hookton Road

101

Fortuna

To Scotia

Humboldt Bay

Sacramento

San Francisco

California

San Diego

Humboldt Bay

I've said it before, and I'll say it again: This place rocks! It's a diverse saltwater fishery that's still untapped. Why? I don't know. Perhaps because it's so far north nobody makes the effort to explore it. But I do know that it produces some great action for rockfish, flatfish, smelt, and much more. Let me push a button for you—fish it or miss the fun! See you on the water.

Humboldt Bay is California's second largest enclosed bay system. Two huge spits protect the long inner bay from the pounding Pacific surf. Shore angler and skiff pilot alike can reap the benefits around this location. It's a perfect place for kayaks and canoes as well. Wading and shorebound fly fishers will enjoy Buhne Point, South Spit, Fields Landing, and the Eureka dock areas. Access is limited along the North Spit.

The rugged shoreline protects perfect habitat for many bottom fish. Just inside the southern part of the bay is an artificial reef that attracts greenling and rockfish galore. Perch are found throughout the entire system. The central and northern regions are home to healthy flatfish populations. The South Jetty offers opportunities for bottom fish and salmon. Night fish along this jetty and you'll probably catch trophy-sized rockfish and even lingcod at times. By the way, this is no place to work with wimpy tackle. Come equipped to handle heavy hydraulics and tough game fish.

If you're looking for a saltwater fly rod outing without much pressure, explore Humboldt Bay. The entire north coast provides magnificent views of coastal wilderness. Put in the miles and make this drive. Take Highway 101 to Eureka. The bay and access are west off the town of Fields Landing or Road 255.

Fishing the shallows at Humboldt Bay.
Photo by Ken Hanley.

Types of Fish

King salmon (chinook), silver salmon (off-limits for now), bottomfish (including rockfish, cabezon, lingcod, greenling, and starry flounder), leopard shark, jack smelt, surfperch.

Known Baitfish

Smelt, anchovy, game fish fry, shrimp, crab, marine worms.

Equipment to Use

Rods: 7–10 weight, 8½–10 feet in length.
Reels: I prefer a large arbor and disk drag design. Lots of backing helps.
Lines: Intermediate, type-4 sinking, modified sink tips of 200 to 400 grains, shooting heads type-6 or LC-13. Floating line for poppers or sliders.
Leaders: 0X to 2X, 3–6 feet in length (sometimes longer and lighter in extremely calm, clear conditions).
Wading: Chest-high neoprene waders (or Gore-Tex with appropriate insulating undergarments), felt-soled boots over mudflats (studs help on rocks slippery with seaweed). Boats provide unlimited access.

Flies to Use

Streamers: Sea Habit Bucktail (White Knight) #1/0, Tan Flashtail Clouser #2, Sar Mul Mac Anchovy #3/0, Lefty's Deceiver #1/0, Popovic's Deep Candy Bendback and Popovic's Jiggy #2–4, ALF Baitfish #2, Rusty Squirrel Clouser #4–6.
Topwater & Subsurface: Gurgler #1/0, Crease Fly #1/0, Milt's Minnow #1/0, Crystal Popper #2/0–1.

When to Fish

Salmon: July through December; prime time is July to September.
Bottom Fish: All year.
Leopard Shark: All year, prime times are spring and fall.
Flounder: All year, prime times are fall and early spring.
Smelt & Perch: All year.

Seasons & Limits

Restrictions on tackle, access, and harvest do apply. Refer to the California Fish & Game regulations booklet and call local fly shops for timely updates. Currently, silver salmon may not be harvested.

Accommodations & Services

There are campgrounds at North Spit, KOA Campground, King Salmon Resort, and Ebb Tide RV Park. Lodging and supplies are available in Arcata and Eureka. Find public launch ramps and marina at Fields Landing (south) and north of Eureka.

Rating

Humboldt Bay is wild and it's worth the trip—a big 9! Just don't expect a stocked pond atmosphere and catch ratio.

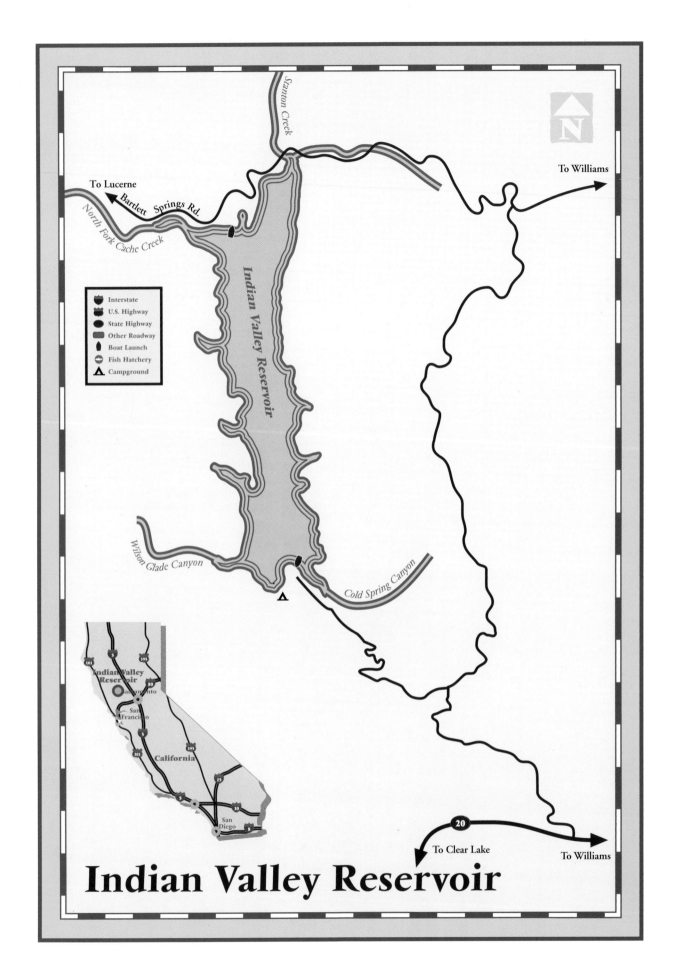

To Williams

To Lucerne

Santon Creek

Bartlett Springs Rd.

North Fork Cache Creek

Indian Valley Reservoir

Interstate
U.S. Highway
State Highway
Other Roadway
Boat Launch
Fish Hatchery
Campground

Wilson Glade Canyon

Cold Spring Canyon

Indian Valley Reservoir
Sacramento
San Francisco
California
San Diego

20

To Clear Lake

To Williams

Indian Valley Reservoir

Indian Valley Reservoir

This place is hands down one of my favorite still-water locations. I like the challenge of working amongst timber, stumps, and stick-ups. Boy, oh boy, does this place answer that calling! Bass, crappie, and wood make a terrific combination, though this habitat is not for the faint of heart. Expect to lose some flies, but expect to catch some wonderful fish in return! The water is usually clear and warm. Canoes and kayaks can give you an edge maneuvering around this tight cover.

All this wood can demand some precision presentations on your part. A moderate sink tip or floating line coupled with long leaders is a super setup for working this cover. Think "vertical presentations" before you cast. Use whatever combination of terminal tackle you're comfortable with to achieve a near-vertical retrieve path (or drop zone if necessary). Make your presentations tight to the cover. Poppers escaping the timber zone can produce some serious fun for you as well. With all this rough wood, be sure to constantly check your leader and tippet for nicks or abrasion damage.

Generally, the best fly fishing is inside the small coves scattered around the lake. Don't forget to work the points of these coves. They represent transition zones that bass use all year. You can fish this lake 24 hours a day to extend your angling pleasure.

The only drawback to Indian Valley Reservoir is the access roads. They're long, twisty, and slow to travel on. This does, however, help limit the pressure on the lake. A good way to get there is from Interstate 5 and the town of Williams. Take Highway 20 west 10 miles, where you'll take a right turn on Leesville Road. Just past Leesville, turn left on Bear Valley Road, for a couple of miles, then take Brim Road which runs into Bartlett Springs Road to the lake.

A boat allows anglers to fully expore all areas of Indian Valley Reservoir. Photo by Don Vachini.

Types of Fish
Largemouth smallmouth, and spotted bass; crappie; panfish; rainbow trout.

Known Hatches & Baitfish
Threadfin shad, bluegill, game fish fry, crayfish, leeches, frogs, damselflies. dragonflies, midges.

Equipment to Use
Rods: 5–8 weight, 8½–10 feet in length (heavy rods help around the timber).
Reels: Standard drag systems.
Lines: WF floating, intermediate, sink tip type-2 or -3, modified sink tips of 130 to 200 grains.
Leaders: 0X to 4X, 6–9 feet in length.
Wading: It's best to work from a boat. Bank angling is possible but limited.

Flies to Use
Dries: Parachute Madam X #8, Adams Irresistible #10, Griffith's Gnat #14.
Nymphs: Putnam's Damsel #12, Kaufman's Dragonfly #8, Black Ant #14, Black AP #12, Prince #14.
Streamers: Olive Matuka #6, Flashtail Clouser #1/0–2, Purple Eelworm #6, Burk's V-Worm #10, Hot Flash Minnow #6, Whitlock Near Nuff Sculpin #6.
Topwater & Subsurface: Gurgler #2, Swimming Frog #6, Loudmouth Shad #6, Gaines Bluegill Poppers #12, Sponge Spiders #10–12.

When to Fish
Bass: All year, prime times are March, April, and October.
Panfish: All year, prime is early spring through summer.
Trout: Winter months are best (work near the inlets and dam).

Seasons & Limits
All-year access. Harvest restrictions apply, so check with local fly shops or in the Department of Fish & Game booklet for current information.

Accommodations & Services
Two launch ramps, a supply store, rental boats, and some campsites are available at the lake. Lodging and supplies in Williams.

Rating
The roads to the area are not the best, but the solitude is a real plus—a nice 8.

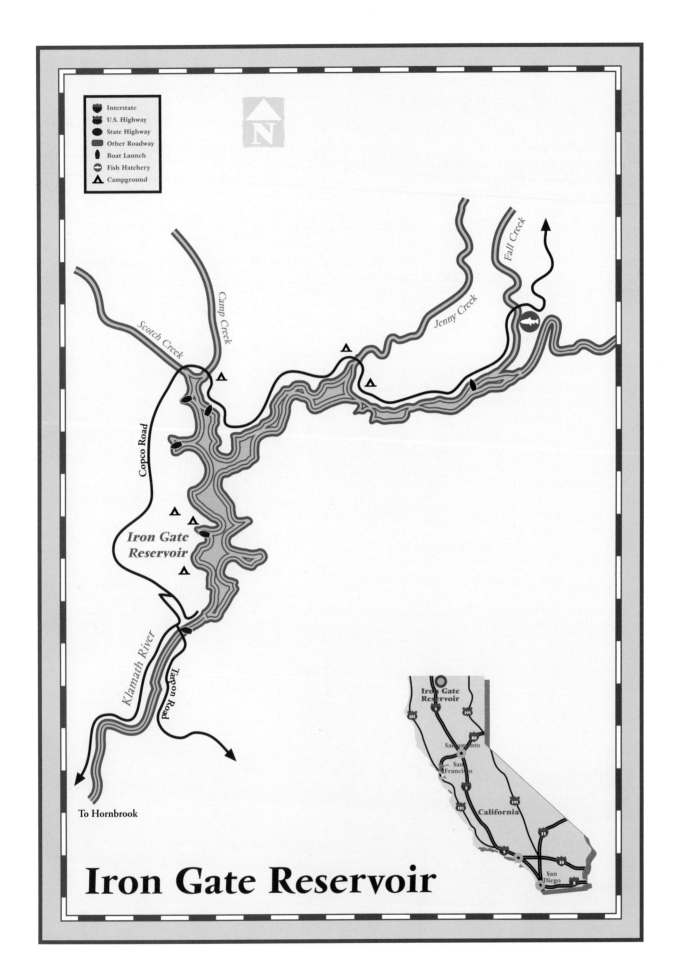

Iron Gate Reservoir

Iron Gate Reservoir

Iron Gate is in extreme northern California and relatively remote but very accessible. The yellow perch in Iron Gate are worth any effort you have to make to reach this water. They're a virtual bonanza for fly rodders! Red patterns are the ticket to reaching perch nirvana around here. A sunken Royal Red Humpy or San Juan Worm is like candy to these game fish. It's a perfect game for four-weight outfits.

The cover around the reservoir contains cattails and a variety of weed carpets. Concentrate on the green cover edges and you'll find success with trout and bass. Cast into the 'tails and you're likely to find perch, bass, and crappie. Using a small boat or inflatable will undoubtedly expand your opportunities. For another game, you can target the beautiful steelhead strain of wild trout in deeper waters. These fish are landlocked and not planted. Streamers are the best approach to entice these fish to the fly. When the powerhouse turbines are releasing water, the food chain gets a mega boost, and the trout become very active feeders.

Iron Gate is actually the lower of two reservoirs in the area. Copco Lake is about two miles, on a gravel road, from Iron Gate. Both waters fish about the same and both have launch ramps and no limits on perch. To get to the reservoirs, drive almost to Oregon on Interstate 5. Just north of Yreka take the Henley-Hornbrook Road exit and drive eight miles east on Copco Road.

Iron Gate Reservoir offers opportunities for trout, bass and yellow perch just south of the Oregon border. Photo by Tom Chadwell.

Types of Fish
Rainbow and brown trout; largemouth, smallmouth, and spotted bass; crappie; yellow perch.

Known Hatches & Baitfish
Threadfin shad, pond smelt, sculpin, game fish fry, crayfish, leeches, frogs, callibaetis mayflies, caddis, damselflies, dragonflies, and hoppers.

Equipment to Use
Rods: 4–7 weight, 8½–10 feet in length.
Reels: Standard drag systems.
Lines: WF floating, intermediate, sink tip type-4, modified sink tips of 130 to 200 grains, shooting heads type-4 or type-6.
Leaders: 1X to 5X, 6–12 feet in length.
Wading: It's best to work from a boat. Bank angling is possible but limited.

Flies to Use
Dries: Royal Red Humpy #12, Quigley Loopwing Callibaetis #16, Parachute Madam X #8, Adams Irresistible #10, Griffith's Gnat #14.
Nymphs: Fire Red San Juan Worm #8–14, Putnam's Damsel #12, Kaufman's Dragonfly #8, Poxyback Callibaetis #16, Black Ant #14, Black AP #12.
Streamers: Flashtail Clouser #2, Purple Eelworm #6, Burk's V-Worm #10, Hot Flash Minnow #6, Whitlock Near Nuff Sculpin #6.
Topwater & Subsurface: Dave's Hopper #8, Gurgler #2, Swimming Frog #6, Loudmouth Shad #6, Gaines Bluegill Popper #12, Sponge Spiders #10–12.

When to Fish
Trout: Late fall, winter, and early spring.
Bass: March to November; prime times are April, May, October, and November.
Perch & Crappie: March to November.

Seasons & Limits
All-year access. Harvest restrictions apply, so check with local fly shops or in the Department of Fish & Game regulations for current information.

Nearby Fly Fishing
Copco Lake.

Accommodations & Services
Free camping is available around the lake. Try Long Gulch Park, Mirror Cove Camp, and Jenny Creek Park. Supplies are available at the convenience store in Iron Gate.

Rating
If you want to catch a mess of feisty fish, go to Iron Gate. It's at least a 7 for trout and bass. Yellow perch deserve a 9 rating.

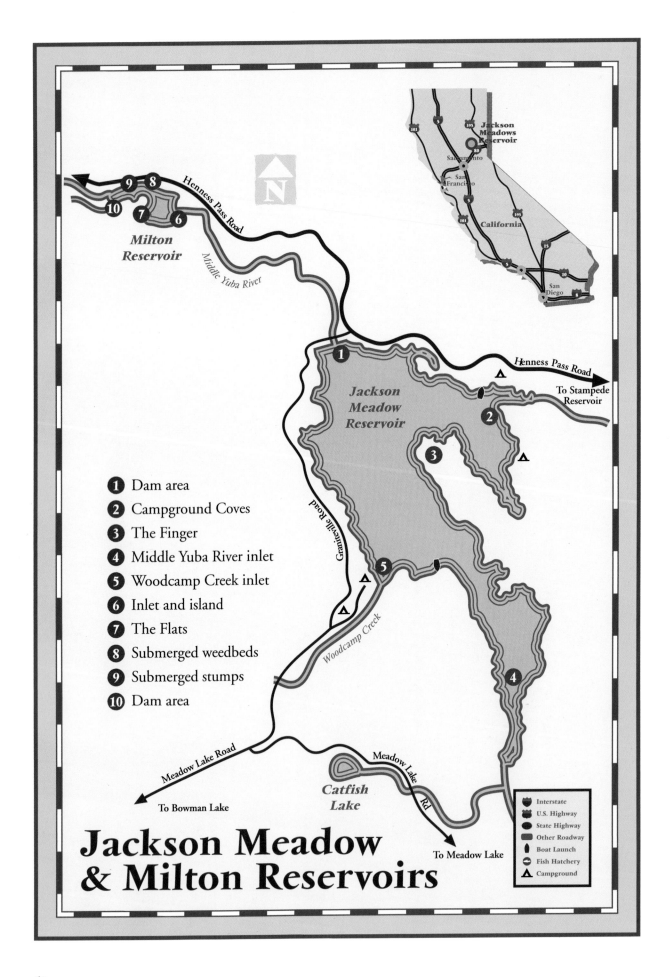

1 Dam area

2 Campground Coves

3 The Finger

4 Middle Yuba River inlet

5 Woodcamp Creek inlet

6 Inlet and island

7 The Flats

8 Submerged weedbeds

9 Submerged stumps

10 Dam area

Milton Reservoir

Jackson Meadow Reservoir

Henness Pass Road

Middle Yuba River

Graniteville Road

Woodcamp Creek

Henness Pass Road

To Stampede Reservoir

Meadow Lake Road

Meadow Lake Rd

To Bowman Lake

Catfish Lake

To Meadow Lake

California

Jackson Meadows Reservoir

Sacramento

San Francisco

San Diego

Interstate

U.S. Highway

State Highway

Other Roadway

Boat Launch

Fish Hatchery

Campground

Jackson Meadow & Milton Reservoirs

Jackson Meadow & Milton Reservoirs

by Dave Stanley

Jackson Meadow, at more than 6,000 feet in elevation, provides a typical picturesque and forested Sierra Nevada lake. An additional benefit is that it's easy to get to. Located 25 miles north of Truckee (most anglers take Highway 89 north), the reservoir is a convenient staging area for backpackers and others heading into the forest. Don't let this deter you. This drive-up convenience and easy access are plusses for the fly fisher.

A boat or float tube is necessary on most of the water due to the steepness of the banks. But you won't have to pack it very far. The reservoir has a boat ramp and several access areas for tubers. The best fly fishing area is the upper end where the Middle Yuba River enters the reservoir. Fishing the evening midge hatch is most productive for fly casters.

Milton is a small, 70-acre reservoir located 1.5 miles below the Jackson Meadow dam. Milton is even prettier than Jackson—one of the most scenic still waters in the eastern Sierra. It can also be very productive for fly fishing.

The water at Milton is very clear and cold most of the season. Presentation and fly selection here are critical, because cruising trout, particularly in the shallows, can be very selective. Dry fly activity is excellent early and late in the season.

The Middle Fork of the Yuba River, which connects the two reservoirs, is also a fun and challenging fishery during the summer months. Both reservoirs are planted with rainbow trout each year.

Tiny Milton Reservoir sits just below Jackson Meadow Reservoir. Photo by Don Vachini.

Types of Fish
Both lakes hold healthy populations of rainbow and brown trout, with the occasional cutthroat.

Known Hatches
Midges: All year.
Callibaetis: May and September.
Damsel Migrations: June and July.
Siphlonurus (Grey Drakes): Early June.
Flying Ants: June.
Evening Caddis: All summer.

Equipment to Use
Rods: 3–6 weight, 8½–9 feet in length.
Reels: Click or disk drag balanced to rod.
Lines: Floating, intermediate sink, or type-2 full sink lines to match the rod.
Leaders: on floating lines, 9–12 feet, 5X to 7X, on sinking lines: 6–7½ feet, 3X to 4X.
Wading: Chest-high neoprene waders and felt-soled boots. Wading is limited at Jackson Meadow due to steep banks. Wade The Flats at Milton. A float tube or boat works well on both waters.

Flies to Use
Dries: Suspended Midge, Callibaetis Paranymph, Parachute Adams. on summer evenings try Small Caddis.
Nymphs: Damsel, Pheasant Tail, Hare's Ear, midge larva imitations like Brassie or Small Bird's Nest.
Streamers: Olive, Brown, and Black Woolly Buggers and Leeches; baitfish imitations, Matukas, and Zonkers.

When to Fish
Late May to early August and from mid-September to October.

Seasons & Limits
Open the last Saturday in April to November 15. Jackson Meadow has general limits and regulations. Milton has a two-fish-under-12-inches limit and single barbless hook regulations. Check the California Department of Fish & Game Regulations.

Accommodations & Services
The closest services are 25 miles away in Truckee. There are improved Forest Service campgrounds at Jackson Meadow and free, first-come, first-served camping spots at Milton.

Rating
Jackson Meadow is a 5, but Milton rates an 8 or 9.

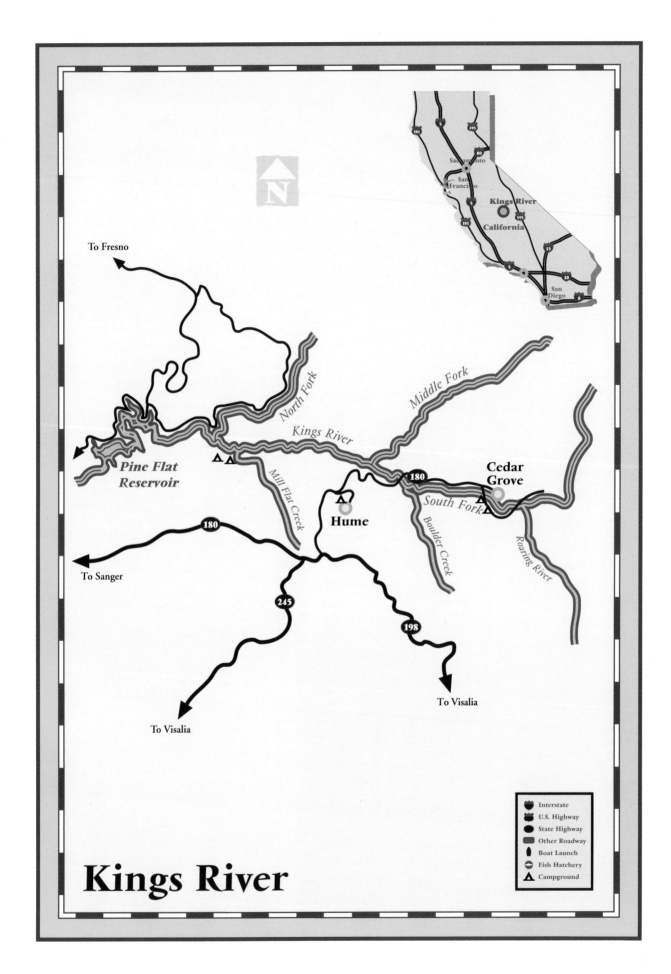

To Fresno

North Fork

Middle Fork

Kings River

Pine Flat
Reservoir

Mill Flat Creek

Hume

180

Cedar
Grove

South Fork

Boulder Creek

Roaring River

180

To Sanger

245

198

To Visalia

To Visalia

Kings River

Interstate
U.S. Highway
State Highway
Other Roadway
Boat Launch
Fish Hatchery
Campground

Kings River
California

Kings River

The Kings is a wild place. Really. It's a designated Wild and Scenic River that's home to wild trout and planters as well. You'll find rainbows, browns, brookies, and even a few goldens in this waterway. The river is well worth your time and effort: The scenery is truly magnificent, and the angling is of high caliber.

This is a classic freestone habitat. It does experience fluctuations in flow and depth dependent on runoff or drought conditions. Don't be dismayed, however, as the river is loaded with insects, crustaceans, and minnow life throughout the drainage. Trout in these environs generally have no problem feasting under any conditions. Accordingly, stock your fly boxes with a good variety of imitations, from tiny bugs to chunky crayfish.

If you wade the river from late fall through midwinter, especially above Pine Flat Reservoir, be alert for spawning trout. It's wise to keep your wading at a minimum so as not to disturb their spawning grounds.

Those of you looking to change the pace can find smallmouth bass located on the stretch between Avocado and Sanger. I really enjoy the bass action in these parts. I work from a canoe to maximize my success. The river produces best during low flow periods when the water is crystal clear. I especially pay attention to areas of rocky cover and deep pools. Crawdads, tiny minnows, and hopper imitations are tops for feeding these terrific game fish.

Access to the river is via the city of Fresno. To reach the Lower/Middle Kings section, take Highway 180 east to Centerville. Go left onto Trimmer Springs Road and continue past Pine Flat Reservoir. Those wishing to access the Upper Kings, in Kings Canyon National Park, take Highway 180 east into Big Stump Grove. Turn north on 180 and continue past Boyden Cavern.

Flows on the upper stretches of the wild Kings River can remain fairly high during the summer. Photo by Brian Milne.

Types of Fish
Rainbow and brown trout, smallmouth bass.

Known Hatches & Baitfish
In October, find caddis, spotted sedge, American grannon, sulphur mayfly, blue-winged olive, PMD, mahogany dun, salmon fly, black stone, little yellow stone, game fish fry, sculpin, crayfish, hoppers, and ants.

Equipment to Use
Rods: 3–6 weight, 8½–9 feet in length.
Reels: Basic click and pawl or disk drag systems.
Lines: WF floating, modified sink tip design with 130 grain weight, or type-4 uniform full sinking line.
Leaders: 3X to 5X, 6–10 feet in length.
Wading: Use chest-high waders, neoprene for winter months (or Gore-Tex with appropriate insulating undergarments), studded boots, and wading staff.

Flies to Use
Dries: Madam X #6, Stimulator #6–8, Sparkle Dun or Thorax Dun #12–16, Adams #12, Adams Irresistible #10, Yellow or Tan Humpy #14–16, Brown or Tan Elk Hair Caddis #12, Light Cahill #12–16, Little Yellow Stone #16, Dave's Hopper #6.
Nymphs: Hunched Back Infrequens #16, Mercer's Z-Wing Caddis #10–14, Gold Ribbed Hare's Ear #12–16, Bird's Nest #12–16, Black AP #14, Tan and Olive Fox's Poopah #14.
Streamers: Beaded Krystal Bugger #8, Muddler Minnow #2–8, Bullet Head #6, Poxybou Crayfish #4–8.

When to Fish
Smallmouth Bass: All year, prime months are August through October.
Trout: All year.

Seasons & Limits
Restrictions on access locations, tackle, harvest, and species vary throughout the system. Always consult the California fishing regulations booklet. It's also a good idea to contact local fly shops in advance of your travels.

Accommodations & Services
Lodging is plentiful around Fresno, Visalia, and Sanger. Campgrounds in the Lower Kings area exist around Pine Flat Reservoir and along the river, including at Garnet Dike Camp. Supplies are available in Piedra. For campgrounds, lodging, and supplies in the Upper Kings region, go to Kings Canyon National Park.

Rating
Overall, the angling rates an 8.5 to 9. It's hard to find a better freestone experience, particularly in the winter.

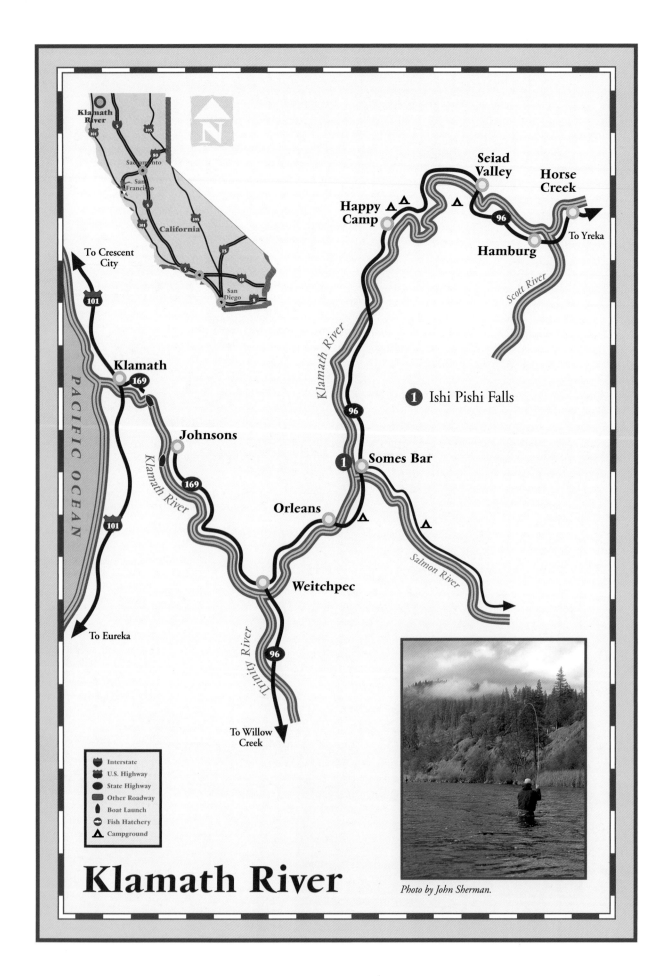

Klamath River

Klamath River

To Crescent City

PACIFIC OCEAN

101

Klamath

169

Johnsons

169

Klamath River

To Eureka

Orleans

Weitchpec

Trinity River

96

To Willow Creek

Seiad Valley

Horse Creek

Happy Camp

96

Hamburg

To Yreka

Scott River

Klamath River

96

1 Ishi Pishi Falls

1 Somes Bar

Salmon River

California

To Crescent City

San Diego

Legend:
- Interstate
- U.S. Highway
- State Highway
- Other Roadway
- Boat Launch
- Fish Hatchery
- Campground

Klamath River

Photo by John Sherman.

Klamath River

The Klamath is one of the great and historic blue ribbon rivers of the United States. Thick timber, rough canyons, wildlife, and a fishing-friendly local economy create a beautiful and comprehensive setting for the fly fisher.

There are 200 miles of big river: big pools, big currents, big structure, big schools and, thankfully, big fish. There can also be big crowds, but there's big space. Some of the best fly fishing is on the lower river, from the village of Weitchpec to the ocean. This region is vast (100 to 200 feet across), so you'll need a boat to access the prime waters.

Upriver, from Johnsons Bar to Hamburg, there's plenty of bank angling. Drive Highway 96 and look for likely spots. Fall and spring are peak periods for steelhead. Use floating line, sink tip, greased line, and streamer presentations. The middle river is a popular one- to three-day float trip section. The 40 miles of upper river (from Iron Gate Dam to Hamburg) has lengthy riffles and extensive pools with plenty of shore access. Steelhead run here from about September to March.

For salmon, use deep nymph and attractor techniques and heavy sinking lines. Come May and June, the shad runs offer terrific action for fly rodders. Look for schools moving in the tidewater and lower river systems. In late summer, large concentrations of fish usually show up around the Ishi Pishi Falls area near Somes Bar.

The Klamath starts below the dam at Iron Gate Reservoir, just east of Interstate 5 and north of the town of Yreka. Highway 96 runs along most of the river. The mouth of the Klamath is located off Highway 101, 20 miles south of Crescent City.

The lower Klamath is a major river that runs both deep and wide. Photo by Brian O'Keefe.

Types of Fish
King salmon (chinook), steelhead, shad, and trout.

Known Baitfish
Various baitfish, isopods, and shrimp in the tidewaters. Upstream, imitate minnows and various nymphs for salmon and steelhead.

Equipment to Use
Steelhead and Salmon:
Rods: 5–9 weight, 8½–10 feet in length, Spey outfits as well.
Reels: Excellent drag with lots of backing.
Lines: WF Floating, type-2 or type-4 shooting heads, sink tip of 130 to 250 grains.
Leaders: 0X to 3X, 7–9 feet in length.
Wading: Chest-high waders, neoprene in winter (or Gore-Tex with appropriate insulating undergarments), felt-soled or studded boots, and wading staff.
Trout:
Rods: 4–7 weight, 8½–9½ feet in length.
Reels: Standard click and pawl or disk drag.
Lines: WF Floating, type-2 sink tip to match rod weight.
Leaders: 4X to 5X, 7–9 feet in length.
Wading: Chest-high waders, neoprene in winter (or Gore-Tex with appropriate insulating undergarments), felt-soled or studded boots, and wading staff.

Flies to Use
Dries: Madam X #6–8, Steelhead Caddis #8, Steelhead Skating Muddler #2, Waller Waker #4.
Nymphs: Dark Scud #12–14, Red Fox Squirrel #10–14, Gold Bead Bird's Nest #12, Golden Stone Nymph #6–10, Rubber Legs #4–6, Black Woolly Bugger #6, Gold Ribbed Hare's Ear #8–12.
Streamers: Bucktail Coachman #6; Burlap, Brindle Bug, Silver Hilton, or Green-Butt Skunk #6–10; Purple Peril #6; Boss #4–10; Freight Train #6; Woolhead Sculpin #4; various Shad patterns #6–12.

When to Fish
Salmon: Summer and fall.
Steelhead: Fall and spring, prime time is September to late November.
Shad: May to September, prime time is June and July.

Seasons & Limits
The Klamath is subject to low-flow closures and restrictions on tackle, access, and harvest. Special regulations for the Klamath River below Iron Gate Dam are reviewed annually in the spring and published in a special DFG supplement in May. Consult the California Department of Fish & Game regulations or inquire at a local fly shop.

Accommodations & Services
Lodging and supplies are available in Happy Camp, Orleans, and Klamath Glen. Camping is best near Hamburg, Seiad Valley, Happy Camp, Dillon Creek, Bluff Creek, and the Orleans region.

Rating
In fall the river could get crowded for bank anglers, but overall the Klamath is a great river worthy of an 8. The "half pounder" run of steelheads is an awesome show to behold.

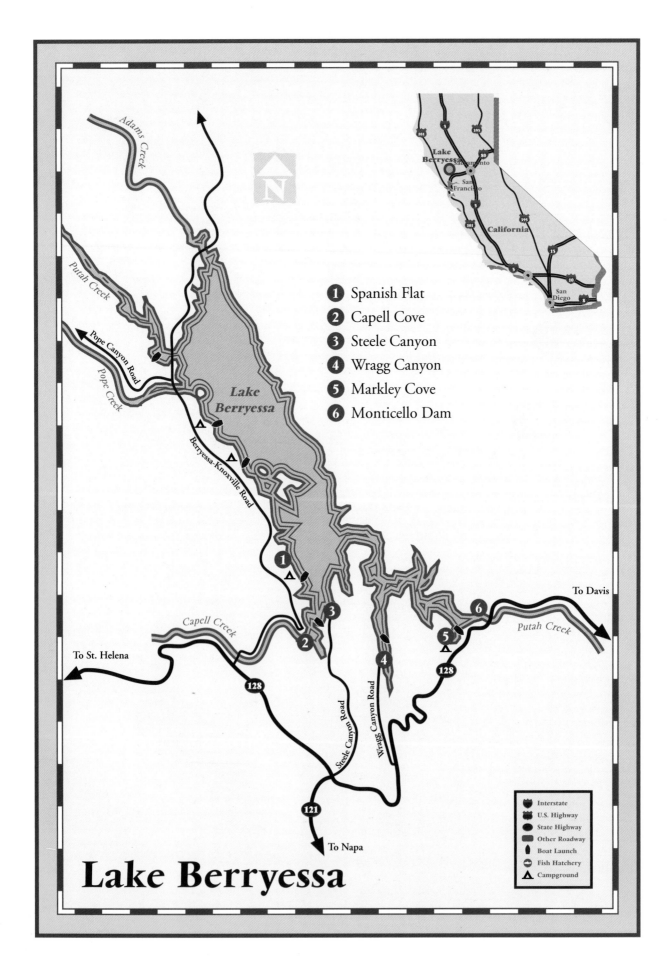

1 Spanish Flat
2 Capell Cove
3 Steele Canyon
4 Wragg Canyon
5 Markley Cove
6 Monticello Dam

Lake Berryessa

Interstate
U.S. Highway
State Highway
Other Roadway
Boat Launch
Fish Hatchery
Campground

Lake Berryessa

I have a conflict with this place. I love it and I hate it! This 25-mile lake is probably one of the most heavily used water resources in the state. Therein lies the problem. The fishing, however, always pays off for me. Here's why: The lake is loaded with fish! It's a bass angler's dream, as well as home to an outstanding trophy trout fishery. The lake is easy to get to, is scenic, offers plenty of camping and services, and can be a fun picnic or party spot—hence, the potential for overpopulation on some weekends. Stay sharp amidst all the boat traffic. Better yet, try to be on the water at midweek. You'll appreciate the difference.

Bass in Lake Berryessa follow the classic calendar. They're active in the shallows during the spring spawning cycle and the autumn minnow bite, cruising brush and rocky points. Work from an inflatable in the lake's southern arms, especially Steele and Wragg canyons. Smallmouth often congregate at the north end of Berryessa near Pope and Putah creeks.

Berryessa is stocked with a large number of trout each year, ranging from 10 to 20 inches in length. Expect to find them down deep in the summer months. In fact, they're downright tough to catch unless you use a heavy modified sink tip line for deepwater presentations. Figure on trout hanging in the 20- to 30-foot depth range during this time. In autumn when the lake "turns over," you'll find trout closer to the surface and within easy range of most line designs.

Throughout the year Berryessa plays host to many fishing tournaments. To avoid the competition, contact one of the lake's resorts or the Lake Berryessa Visitor Information line (707) 966–2111. The lake is 50 miles west of Sacramento and 65 miles north of San Francisco.

An early morning boater works Lake Berryessa.
Photo by Don Vachini.

Types of Fish
Rainbow and brown trout; largemouth, smallmouth, and spotted bass; panfish; and catfish.

Known Hatches & Baitfish
Shad, game fish fry, crayfish, frogs, worms, grubs, damselflies and dragonflies. For trout, imitate small baitfish and callibaetis mayflies and midges.

Equipment to Use
Rods: 5–9 weight, 8½–10 feet in length.
Reels: Standard drag systems.
Lines: Intermediate full sinking, type-4 or type-6 sinking shooting heads, or modified sink tips of 130 to 200 grains. WF floating on occasion.
Leaders: 1X to 4X, 7–12 feet in length.
Wading: A terrific lake for float tubes and prams. Bank angling is somewhat limited.

Flies to Use
Dries: Quigley Loopwing Callibaetis #16, Parachute Madam X #8, Adams Irresistible #10, Griffith's Gnat #14.
Nymphs: Burk's Damsel, Putnam's Damsel #12, Kaufman's Dragonfly, Prince or Hare's Ear Aggravator #6.
Streamers: Tan and White Flashtail Clouser #2, Sea Habit Bucktail (White Knight) #2–1/0, Blanton's Flash Tail series #2–8, Whitlock Near Nuff Sculpin, Zonker, Jansen's Threadfin Shad, Hot Flash Minnow, Purple Eelworm, Black Hare Jig #6, Burk's V-Worm #10, Whitlock Softshell Crayfish #8, Poxybou Crayfish #4–8, Crystal Rubber Bugger, Black Woolly Bugger #4.
Topwater: Gurgler #2–1/0, Swimming Frog, Whitlock's Red Head Hair Popper #6, Deer Hair Mouse, Chartreuse Diver #4.

When to Fish
Bass: March through November; prime time is April, May, October and November.
Trout: Fall and winter; prime time is October and early November.
Crappie: Spring and summer.
Catfish: Summer.

Seasons & Limits
You can fish for something just about any time of the year. Check current California fishing regulations or ask at one of the fly shops or marinas for specific information.

Accommodations & Services
This place has it all: seven full-service resorts and marinas with ramps and campsites galore. Berryessa is also a great lake for a houseboat expedition.

Rating
Crowded weekends not withstanding, there are quality fish to be had on this lake. Overall, I'm confident with a solid 8 rating, though it's closer to a 9 on most outings.

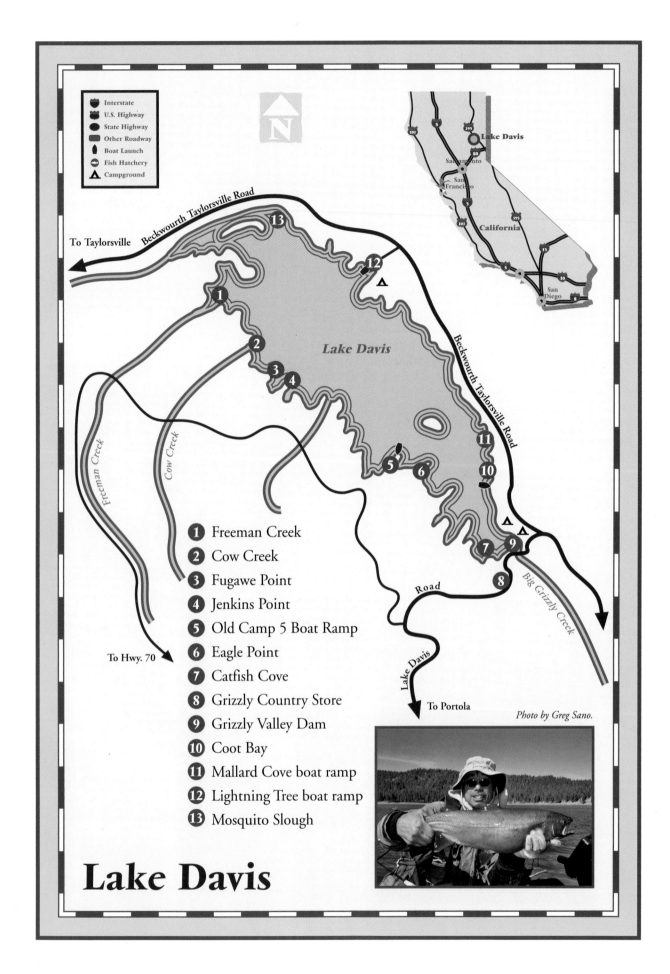

Interstate
U.S. Highway
State Highway
Other Roadway
Boat Launch
Fish Hatchery
Campground

N

Beckwourth Taylorsville Road

To Taylorsville

California

Lake Davis

13

12

1

2

3

4

Freeman Creek

Cow Creek

Beckwourth Taylorsville Road

11

5

6

10

7   9

8

Road

Big Grizzly Creek

Lake Davis

To Hwy. 70

To Portola

1 Freeman Creek
2 Cow Creek
3 Fugawe Point
4 Jenkins Point
5 Old Camp 5 Boat Ramp
6 Eagle Point
7 Catfish Cove
8 Grizzly Country Store
9 Grizzly Valley Dam
10 Coot Bay
11 Mallard Cove boat ramp
12 Lightning Tree boat ramp
13 Mosquito Slough

Photo by Greg Sano.

Lake Davis

Lake Davis

by Dave Stanley

There's nothing quite like fly fishing Lake Davis from mid-June through July, when the damsels are out and about. This one-of-a-kind experience scores a perfect 10 rating. During other months of the season, the fishing still rates quite high by anyone's standards.

Lake Davis is about 50 miles north of Reno, Nevada, and 7 miles north of Portola, California, in the forests at about 5,700 feet in elevation. The lake (reservoir) was built as a water supply for the small town of Portola; hence, there's no swimming, water skiing, jet skiing, or other forms of motorized mayhem.

Lake Davis is not particularly deep, except near the dam. The majority of this water can be fly fished effectively, especially around the huge, lush weed beds. These sprout up along the western shore during the summer months. Try fishing from Eagle Point up to Mosquito Slough and where Freeman and Big Grizzly Creeks enter the lake. Summer is also a good time to fish for bass.

The Davis weed beds support healthy populations of snails, scuds, damsels, dragons, midges, mayflies, caddisflies, leeches, and baitfish. There are even stoneflies near the creek mouths and a fairly predictable carpenter ant hatch in late May and June.

Large midge and caddis hatches are common at Davis. When the fish are "on" these bugs, fishing can be exceptional. In the fall Davis becomes much less crowded, and casting to hungry, cruising trout in the shallows is very productive.

Despite the bountiful bugs, the most exciting time to fish Davis is during the damsel migration. This generally begins in mid-June and often lasts until the end of July. At this time large rainbows, up to seven pounds, come to the surface and into the shallows to slash greedily among hundreds of thousands of damsel nymphs as the insects are making their way to shore. It's not uncommon to hook the trout of the summer, or even of a lifetime, in less than two feet of water!

Lake Davis is great for float tubing or wading the western shore. Photo by Ben Rualo, PDaCG.Com.

Types of Fish
Primarily rainbow trout, also some browns and a large population of illegally stocked largemouth bass and northern pike. The illegal introduction of northern pike (a voracious non-native species) into Lake Davis threatens the entire aquatic ecosystem and the fisheries of much of Northern California's rivers, delta and San Francisco Bay. The Department of Fish and Game currently plans a pike eradication program in late 2007 at Lake Davis and a replanting of the reservoir with trout. Consult their website www.dfg.ca.gov for current information. Following the eradication the trout fishing can be expected to return to be as strong as ever.

Known Hatches
Because of the extensive and varied biomass of Davis, there is not room to list all known hatches. The lake is best fished with surface flies during the summer blood midge emergence, callibaetis hatch, and world-class damsel migration.

Equipment to Use
Rods: 4–6 weight, 8½–9 feet in length.
Reels: Palm or mechanical drag.
Lines: Floating, 4–6 weight; intermediate, sinking 2–4 weight.
Leaders: Intermediate and dry lines, 4X to 6X, 9–12 feet in length. For deep wet lines, 3X to 4X, 7½ feet in length.
Wading: Use neoprene waders or felt-soled boots for cold water. Otherwise, wet-wade or use a boat or float tube.

Flies to Use
Dries: Suspended Midge and Callibaetis Emergers, Parachute Adams, dry Damsel patterns, small Caddis.
Nymphs: Snail patterns, Sheep Creek Special, Dragonfly Nymph, Marabou Damsel, Pheasant Tail, small Olive and Black Bird's Nest, Blood Midge pupa.
Streamers: Leech patterns such as Black, Olive, or Brown Woolly or Krystal Buggers.

When to Fish
If accessible, ice-out is an excellent time to fish Davis, as is mid-June through July and again from mid-September until the lake ices over.

Seasons & Limits
Open year-round. Limits can change, so check the California Game & Fish Regulations booklet or ask at a local fly shop.

Accommodations & Services
Motel and RV spaces, as well as restaurants, laundry, and auto services are in and around Portola. There are several very good campgrounds and a general store at the lake. Grizzly Store and Resort (530) 832-0270.

Rating
Year in and year out, this is one of the eastern Sierra's best fisheries. During the damsel migration, Lake Davis is a solid 10. The rest of the year, it's an 8.5, or maybe even a 9.

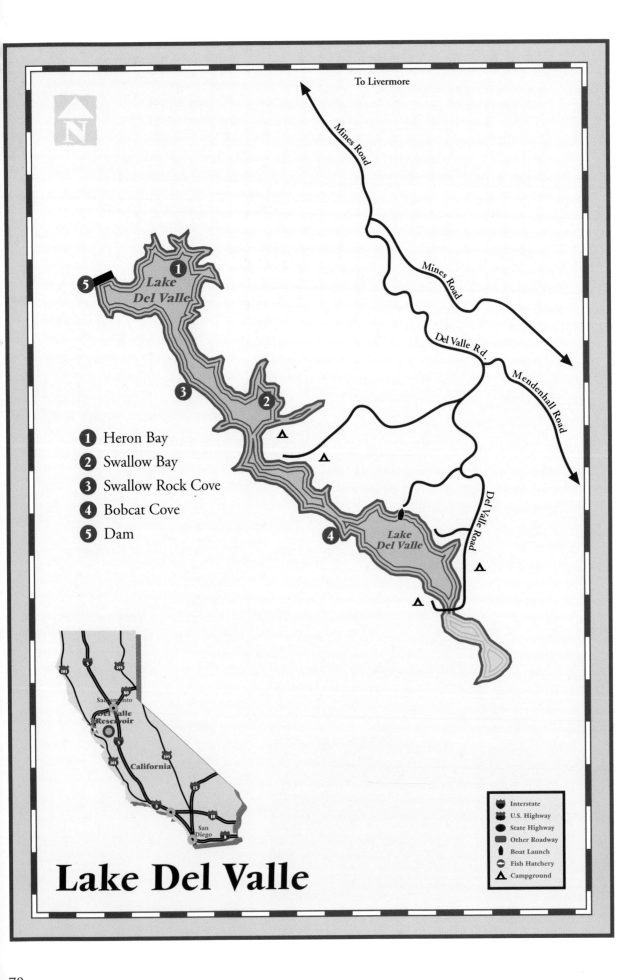

To Livermore

Mines Road

Mines Road

Del Valle Rd.

Mendenhall Road

Del Valle Road

Lake
Del Valle

Lake
Del Valle

1 Heron Bay
2 Swallow Bay
3 Swallow Rock Cove
4 Bobcat Cove
5 Dam

Del Valle Reservoir
Sacramento
California
San Diego

	Interstate
	U.S. Highway
	State Highway
	Other Roadway
	Boat Launch
	Fish Hatchery
	Campground

Lake Del Valle

Lake Del Valle

Here's a cool canyon reservoir with a lot to offer the Bay Area angler. Lake Del Valle, also referred to as "DV," is located just ten miles southeast of Livermore, past some wine country and rural life. The water is situated in a wonderful setting of rolling hills, grasslands, and oak woodlands. Turkey, deer, fox, and bobcat are just a few of the creatures residing around the impoundment. Though minutes away from the hectic inner-city scene, Del Valle is a quality outing, inviting a slower pace and tugs on your line. There are plenty of hiking, boating, and year-round camping opportunities for your enjoyment as well.

DV is a long, narrow, canyon-like fishery. You'll fish deep waters, sheer rock walls, tapering points, small coves, and just a few shallow grassy flats. The steep, rocky structure and cover provide high-quality habitat for smallmouth bass. Bronzebacks and autumn go hand in hand on this reservoir.

Trout aficionados have their best opportunities during the winter months. The East Bay Regional Park District and the California Department of Fish & Game plant thousands of half-pounders weekly during the cooler months. DV's cold waters keep the trout frisky and near the surface, within easy reach of most fly rodders. Watch out, though—a huge striped bass might just inhale the trout you've hooked. I've seen it happen—pretty wild! By the way, in 1994, Del Valle yielded a rainbow trout of more than 17 pounds.

Stripers are more likely to be found cruising around the deeper waters near the dam. It's a long run to the northwest end, but that's where the striper addicts can play the game with confidence. Largemouth bass, on the other hand, covet the southern territory, where there are timber, stumps, and warmer waters. Their spawning cycle is very short in DV, so be on the water during May or miss the action. The minnow bite occurs in fall, and both stripers and largemouth are on the attack. The shoreside coves and shallow flats are home to large populations of panfish. They're a great place for ultralight outfits.

To get to Del Valle, head east on Interstate 580 to Livermore. Take Livermore Avenue south to Tesla Road to Mines Road. After about three miles turn right on Del Valle Road, which takes you to the recreation area entrance.

You'll find a wide variety of fish and plenty of accessible shoreline at Del Valle. Photo by Brian Sak.

Types of Fish
Largemouth, smallmouth, and striped bass; bluegill; rainbow trout, and catfish.

Known Hatches & Baitfish
Threadfin shad, bluegill, game fish fry, crayfish, leeches, frogs, callibaetis mayflies, caddisflies, damselflies, dragonflies, and hoppers.

Equipment to Use
Rods: 5–9 weight, 8½–10 feet in length.
Reels: Mechanical or disk drag.
Lines: Intermediate, sink tip type-4, modified sink tips of 130 to 200 grains, shooting heads type-4 or type-6 (LC-13 is best for working near the dam for stripers).
Leaders: 1X to 6X, 6–12 feet in length.
Wading: Felt-soled boots, hippers, or chest waders okay. It's best to work from a boat or inflatable if possible.

Flies to Use
Dries: Quigley Loopwing Callibaetis #16, Parachute Madam X #8, Adams Irresistible #10, Griffith's Gnat #14.
Nymphs: Putnam's Damsel, Black AP #12, Kaufman's Dragonfly #8, Poxyback Callibaetis, Pheasant Tail #16, Black Ant, Prince, Jansen Callibaetis, Zug Bug #14.
Streamers: Sea Habit Bucktail #1/0, Flashtail Clouser #1/0–2, Purple Eelworm, Hot Flash Minnow, Whitlock Near Nuff Sculpin #6, Burk's V-Worm #10.
Topwater & Subsurface: Gurgler #2, Swimming Frog, Loudmouth Shad, Dave's Hopper #6, Gaines Bluegill Popper #12, Sponge Spider #10–12, Gaines Micro Popper #8–10.

When to Fish
Bass: March through November; prime times are April, May, October and November.
Panfish: All year, but summer is prime.
Trout: Prime time is November through April. With high winds in the winter, casting is best in the early mornings and evenings.

Seasons & Limits
All-year access. Changing limit restrictions apply to various species. Check local fly shops or the Department of Fish & Game booklet for up-to-date information.

Accommodations & Services
Public launch ramp, marina, boat rentals, concessions, and campgrounds are at the lake. Lodging, gear, groceries, and gas are available in nearby Livermore.

Rating
A good setting for beginner and pro alike, and a fun place to boat—a 7.

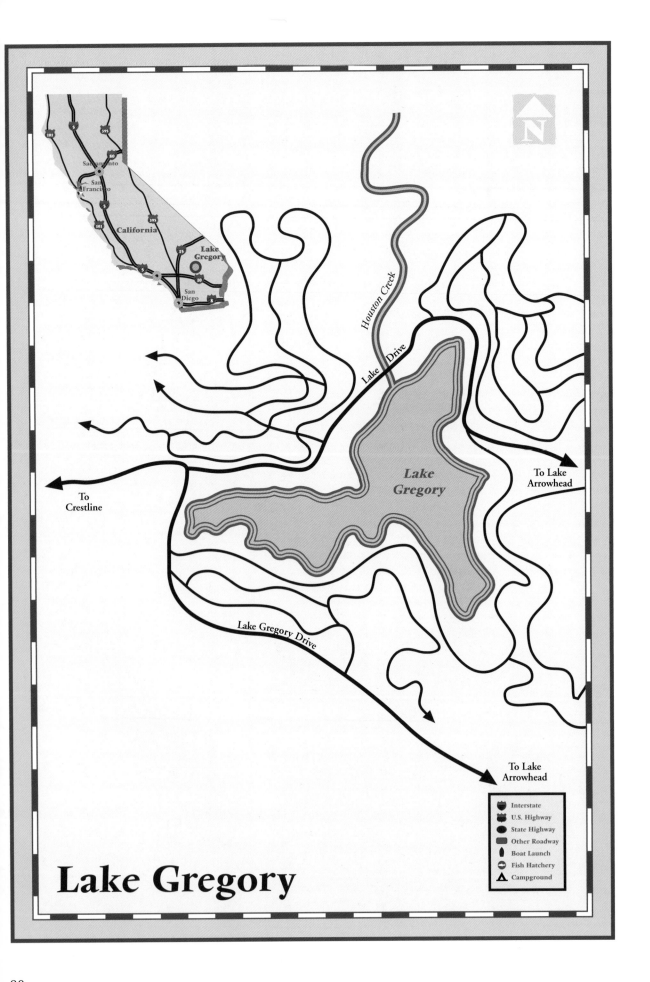

Lake Gregory

Lake Gregory

by Jeff Solis

Only 14 miles north of San Bernardino, Lake Gregory offers fly anglers the opportunity to fish for high-quality planted trout, largemouth bass, and panfish. As of this writing the lake record trout is 11 pounds.

Lake Gregory sits at 4,500 feet in elevation in the San Bernardino Mountains and boasts approximately 3 miles of shoreline. Shore fishing is open and productive year-round, especially during some great summer hatches. A float tube, though, is really the best way to cover the most water and explore the lake. The preferred float tube technique is to slowly retrieve a sink tip line with an attractor-style fly.

In addition to quality fly fishing, Lake Gregory has many nearby amenities, including a swimming beach and water slide. This is one of those places where you can fish before or after work, which just happens to be when the fishing is best. Better yet, take a day off and bring the whole family.

Lake Gregory is approximately 70 miles east of Los Angeles. From Los Angeles, take Interstate 10 east to Waterman Avenue (Highway 18), then proceed north through Waterman Canyon. Take 138 to Crestline and Lake Gregory.

A winter's day at Lake Gregory.
Photo by Howard Fisher.

Types of Fish
Trout, largemouth bass, crappie, and channel catfish.

Known Hatches & Baitfish
Midges, callibaetis mayflies, and minnows.

Equipment to Use
Rods: 5–7 weight, 8–9 feet in length.
Reels: Standard click or disk.
Lines: WF or floating for dries, full sink or types 4–6 sink tip for nymphs and streamers.
Leaders: 2X to 7X, 7–10 feet in length.
Wading: Wading is not permitted, but float tubes are.

Flies to Use
Dries: Light Cahill #12–16, Parachute Adams, Adams #12–18, Loopwing Callibaetis #14–16, and Black and Cream Midge Patterns #18–22.
Nymphs: Poxyback Callibaetis #14–16, Pheasant Tail, Hare's Ear #10–16, Prince Nymph #8–16, Zug Bug #12–16, Brassie #16–22.
Streamers & Poppers: Woolly Bugger, Matuka, Black Nosed Dace #4–10, Woolly Worm #8–10, Wiggle Bug #2–6, and Foam or Deer Hair Popper #4–8.

When to Fish
For trout, fish year-round. For bass, fish April through November. For crappie, spring, summer, and fall.

Seasons & Limits
Open year-round for shore fishing. Check current California Department of Fish & Game regulations or contact a local fly shop for other seasons, limits, and restrictions.

Nearby Fly Fishing
Lake Arrowhead, Big Bear Lake, Silverwood Lake, Deep Creek, and Bear Creek.

Accommodations & Services
There is no camping at the lake, but lodging and other accommodations are nearby. Boat rentals are available April through November.

Rating
For convenience and proximity, Lake Gregory rates a 7.

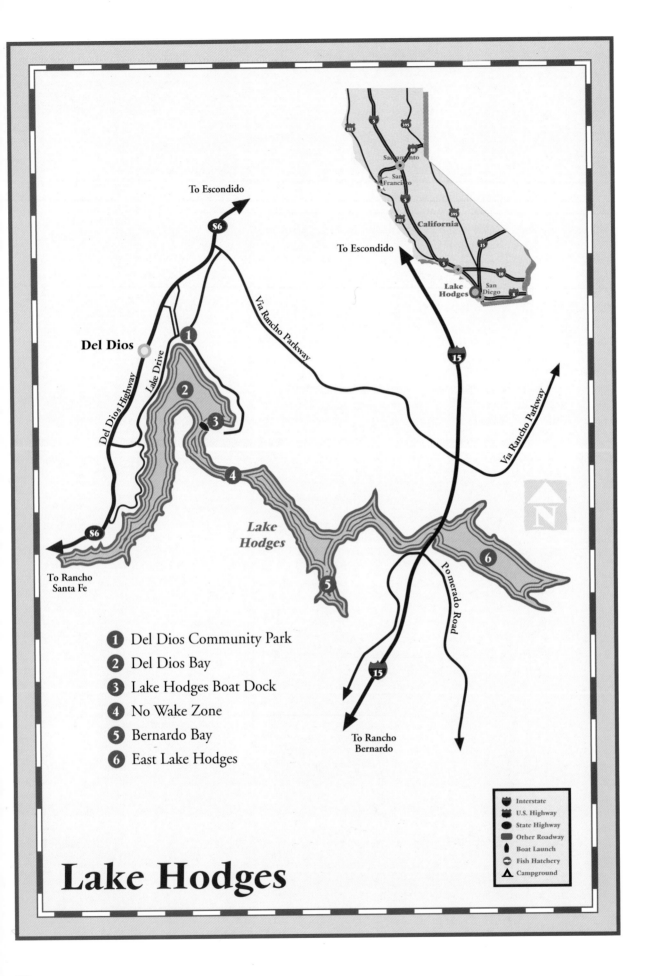

Lake Hodges

1 Del Dios Community Park
2 Del Dios Bay
3 Lake Hodges Boat Dock
4 No Wake Zone
5 Bernardo Bay
6 East Lake Hodges

Lake Hodges

by Jeff Solis

The bass and crappie in Lake Hodges are the largest in San Diego County. The lake record for bass, when this book went to press, was more than 20 pounds, and crappie run to four pounds. This is a popular, urban, often crowded spot, but there aren't many fly anglers. If you need a great, convenient warmwater fishery, here's a place where you can easily hook a "toad"—but landing it is another matter.

The east side of Lake Hodges is relatively shallow with lots of fishable areas near brush piles and submerged stumps. The western two-thirds of the lake has good shoreline that is best worked from a boat. Float tubes also work well for both bass and crappie, but beware of boating traffic. Target tules (bulrushes) and other structures. A short walk from a parking area south of the Bernardo arm leads to a good spot to launch a float tube.

Floating lines; heavy leaders; and big, flashy flies cast close to and into submerged structure are the ticket for connecting with Lake Hodges' monster bass. Work small streamers around bridge supports to take crappie.

To reach Lake Hodges from the San Diego area, go north about 30 miles on Interstate 15 almost to Escondido, and exit on Via Rancho Parkway, go west to Lake Drive, then left to the lake entrance.

With 27 miles of shoreline and 1,234 surface acres at capacity, a boat can be very helpful. Photo by Howard Fisher.

Types of Fish
Largemouth bass, crappie, bluegill and channel catfish.

Known Baitfish
Crayfish and shad.

Equipment to Use
Rods: 9 feet in length; 8–10 weight for bass, 6 weight for crappie.
Reels: Standard click or disk.
Lines: WF, floating, and sink or sink tip types-4–6.
Leaders: 4–6 feet in length, 1X to 3X for bass; 6 feet in length, 3X to 4X for crappie.
Wading: This is not a good lake to wade; it's best fly fished from shore or a float tube.

Flies to Use
Streamers & Poppers: Deer Hair Frog, Dahlberg Diver #6, or Flashy Clouser #2 for bass. Small Clouser or Mickey Finn #6 for crappie.

When to Fish
Morning or late afternoon.

Seasons & Limits
At time of publication the lake is open Wednesdays and weekends. All state boating and fishing regulations apply. The following fish limits apply to Lake Hodges: 5 bass, 5 catfish, 25 crappie. Days and hours of operation are limited and subject to closure. Consult the City of San Diego Reservoirs and Recreation Program phone (619) 465-3474 for current schedule. At time of publication, open on Wendesdays, Saturdays, Sundays, plus holidays during the season.

Nearby Fly Fishing
Miramar Reservoir and the San Diego coastline.

Accommodations & Services
Like other city-run lakes, there are boat rentals, a boat launch, and a concession stand. The city of Escondido is very close and has all other services. The San Diego Wild Animal Park is also nearby.

Rating
Lake Hodges rates a 7.

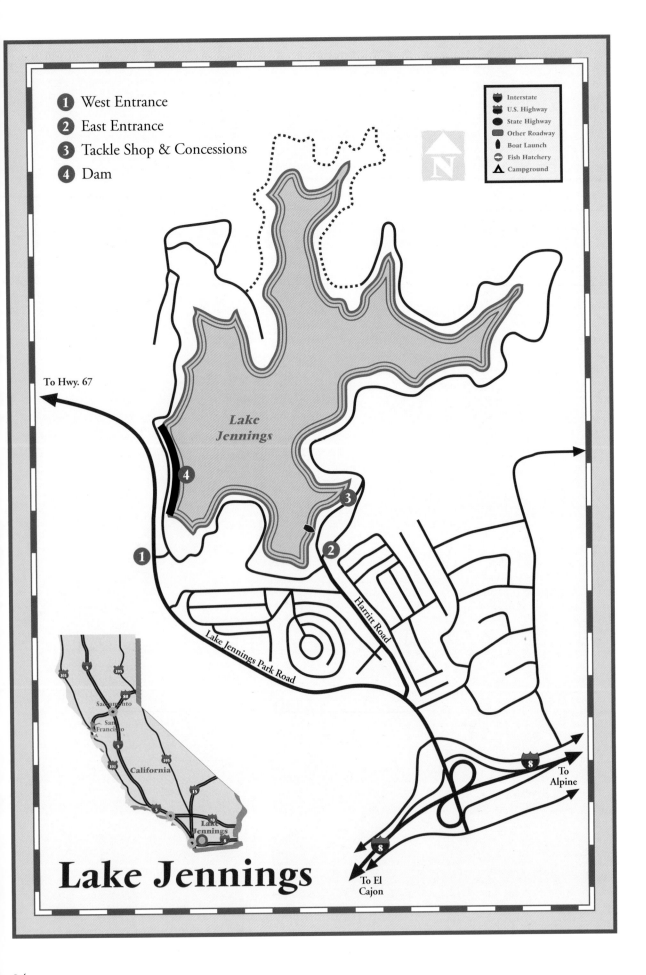

1 West Entrance
2 East Entrance
3 Tackle Shop & Concessions
4 Dam

Interstate
U.S. Highway
State Highway
Other Roadway
Boat Launch
Fish Hatchery
Campground

N

To Hwy. 67

Lake Jennings

4

1

3

2

Harritt Road

Lake Jennings Park Road

8

To Alpine

8

To El Cajon

California

Sacramento

San Francisco

Lake Jennings

Lake Jennings

Lake Jennings

by Jeff Solis

Lake Jennings County Park offers the city-bound angler the opportunity to fly fish for stocked trout, bass, and bluegill in a country setting. Though popularly regarded as a place to soak PowerBait, for fly anglers, especially those short on time, Lake Jennings is possibly San Diego's best-kept bass secret. Abundant bird life, including ospreys, call this reservoir home, and if you pay attention, you'll even spot the occasional deer as it comes down to the water's edge. At times like this, it's hard to believe that you're just 15 minutes from downtown San Diego.

Surrounded by a steep, tree-lined shoreline, Lake Jennings runs as deep as 120 feet. Its surprisingly clear water wraps around numerous small points and long coves where you can walk and cast to pods of cruising trout. If you visit this reservoir, however, you'll want to go after its warmwater denizens.

At times, especially in the spring when the fish are on their spawning beds, the bass action on Jennings can be a truly exhilarating—or, more accurately, humbling—experience. The best way to chase these aggressive fish is from a boat. Cast tight to shoreline cover, let your Clouser Minnow or Crayfish Pattern sink, then slowly retrieve it along the bottom. Winter brings some shad action; casting a Clouser or Deceiver to the edge of a school is likely to produce strikes.

To get to the lake from San Diego, take Interstate 8 east to Lake Jennings Park Road. Turn north and continue for a half-mile to the water.

A small oasis in a desert region, Lake Jennings is best covered by boat. Photo by Howard Fisher.

Types of Fish

Stocked rainbow trout, stocked catfish, largemouth bass, crappie, and bluegill.

Known Hatches & Baitfish

Midges, mayflies, damselflies, and shad.

Equipment to Use

Rods: 9 feet in length, 4–6 weight.
Reels: Standard click or disk.
Lines: WF, floating or sink tip, type-4, intermediate.
Leaders: For trout, 9–10 feet in length, 5X; for bass, 6 feet in length, 3X; for bluegill, 6–7 feet in length, 5X.
Wading: Wading and tubing are not permitted. Walk and cast or, preferably, fish from a boat.

Flies to Use

Dries: For trout, use Light Cahill #12, Callibaetis Emerger #16. For bluegill, use Stimulator #8, Humpy #6.
Nymphs: Hare's Ear #12, Olive Damsel #6, Soft Hackle #14.
Streamers & Poppers: White or Chartreuse Woolly Bugger #2–8, Olive Hornberg #10, Clouser Minnow #2–6, Deceiver #2, Crayfish #4.

When to Fish

For trout, December through May. For bass, late February through August. For bluegill, April through September.

Seasons & Limits

Operated by Helix Water District. Schedule at time of publication is Friday, Saturday and Sunday. Check for current information. Trout are stocked October through May, catfish stocked June, July and August. Limits: 5 trout, 5 bass, 5 catfish and 25 bluegill.

Nearby Fly Fishing

Lake Murray.

Accommodations & Services

County campground, concession stands, rowboat and motorboat rental, concrete launch ramp are at the lake. Nearby El Cajon has all services.

Rating

Other, more productive lakes are nearby, so Lake Jennings rates a 5. But there are days when it can be in the 7 range, and it is easily accessed from the San Diego metro area, so don't rule it out.

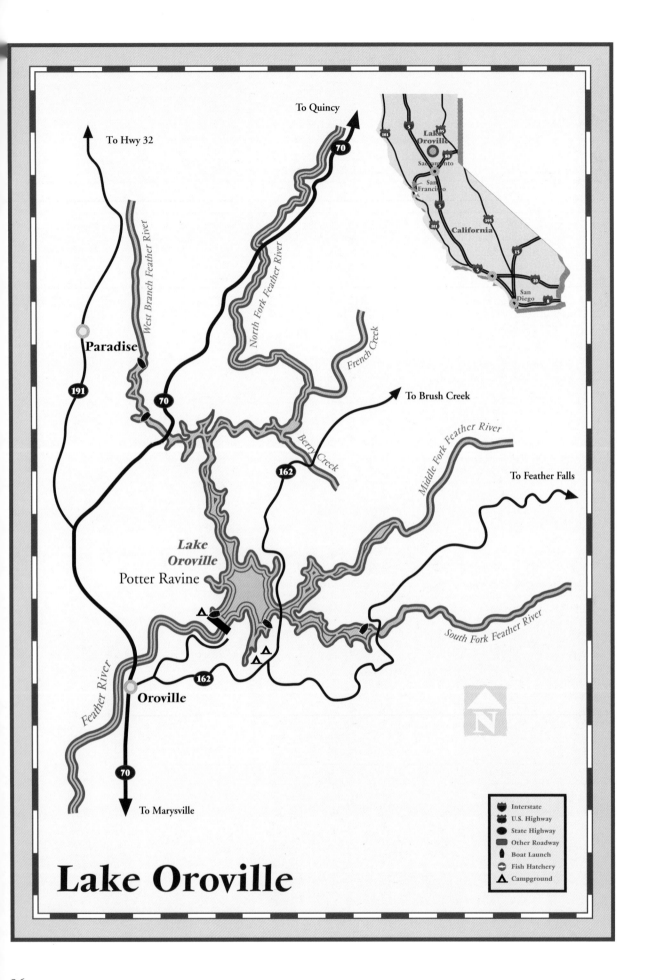

To Hwy 32

To Quincy

Paradise

West Branch Feather River

North Fork Feather River

French Creek

To Brush Creek

Middle Fork Feather River

To Feather Falls

191

70

70

Berry Creek

162

Lake
Oroville

Potter Ravine

South Fork Feather River

Feather River

162

Oroville

70

To Marysville

California

Lake
Oroville

Sacramento

San
Francisco

San
Diego

	Interstate
	U.S. Highway
	State Highway
	Other Roadway
	Boat Launch
	Fish Hatchery
	Campground

N

Lake Oroville

Lake Oroville

Lake Oroville, a young lake, has much to offer in the way of fishing and outdoor recreation. This impoundment is all about bass: smallmouth, largemouth, and spotted. Oroville is similar to Lake Shasta: big, with steep, rocky banks and points that taper down deep. The lake's three long, narrow arms can provide plenty of structure and secluded waters to explore. When these shallow spawning areas aren't left high and dry (due to fluctuations from dam releases), you can experience a fly fishing bonanza. Spotted bass in particular do well in this environment.

A good way to cast to monster bass is to work this lake at night. Under cover of darkness, bass are in the topwater and very aggressive. Fly fish around any structure at Berry Creek, Potter Ravine, and the Middle or South forks of the Feather River.

Trout fishing around this lake can be frustrating due not only to fluctuations in water levels but also the water temperature. In the summer months, the warm surface waters drive the trout to deeper haunts out of reach of most lines. You'll need to adapt your tackle to super fast-sinking designs such as an LC-13 head to get any shot at these fish. On the other hand, the trout are on top during the winter and spring "turnover" cycle. Try the arms of the West Branch and North Fork Feather River.

The lake is about 12 miles east of Oroville, which is 70 miles north of Sacramento or about 60 miles south of Red Bluff. Take Interstate 5 or Highway 70.

As the second largest reservoir in California, Oroville is best known for its spotted bass. Photo by Brian Sak.

Types of Fish
Largemouth, smallmouth, and spotted bass, rainbow trout, chinook salmon, crappie, and panfish.

Known Hatches & Baitfish
Threadfin shad, bluegill, game fish fry, crayfish, leeches, frogs, callibaetis mayflies, caddis, damselflies, and dragonflies.

Equipment to Use
Rods: 5–8 weight, 8½–10 feet in length.
Reels: Standard drag systems.
Lines: Intermediate, sink tip type-4, modified sink tips of 130 to 200 grains, shooting heads type-4 or type-6, LC-13.
Leaders: 1X to 4X, 6–12 feet in length.
Wading: It's best to work from a boat or inflatable if possible as wading is limited.

Flies to Use
Nymphs: Putnam's Damsel #12, Kaufman's Dragonfly #8, Poxyback Callibaetis #16, Black Ant #14, Black AP #12, Prince #14.
Streamers: Sea Habit Bucktail #1/0, Flashtail Clouser #1/0–2, Purple Eelworm #6, Burk's V-Worm #10, Hot Flash Minnow #6, Whitlock Near Nuff Sculpin #6.
Topwater & Subsurface: Gurgler #2, Swimming Frog #6, Loudmouth Shad #6, Gaines Bluegill Popper #12, Sponge Spider #10–12.

When to Fish
Bass: March through November, prime times are April, May, October, and November.
Trout: Late fall and winter into early spring
Crappie & Panfish: All year, prime times are spring and fall

Seasons & Limits
All-year access. Harvest restrictions apply so check with local fly shops or consult the Department of Fish & Game booklet for current information.

Accommodations & Services
Supplies and lodging are available in the town of Oroville. There are marinas, public launch ramps and moorings, boat rentals, and campgrounds at the north and south ends of the lake.

Rating
If you like bass, you'll find the lake rates a 7. Check water levels before you go.

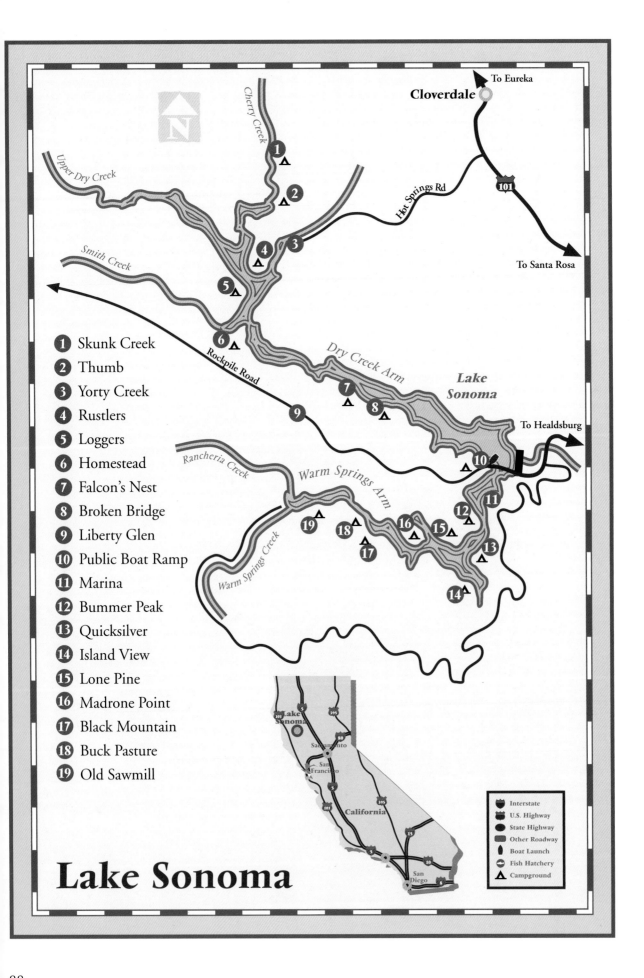

1 Skunk Creek
2 Thumb
3 Yorty Creek
4 Rustlers
5 Loggers
6 Homestead
7 Falcon's Nest
8 Broken Bridge
9 Liberty Glen
10 Public Boat Ramp
11 Marina
12 Bummer Peak
13 Quicksilver
14 Island View
15 Lone Pine
16 Madrone Point
17 Black Mountain
18 Buck Pasture
19 Old Sawmill

Lake Sonoma

Lake Sonoma

Located in the lovely coastal foothills north of Santa Rosa, this gem is known for sizzling bass fly fishing. There's plenty of structure and cover such as timber stick-ups and submerged vegetation—classic bass habitat where the fish breed and feed. This is all by design.

Lake Sonoma, behind Warm Springs Dam, finished filling a two-creek drainage in 1985. Much of the brush and vegetation was left, creating an excellent warm-water environment for fish and fly fishers. Some of the holdover steelhead trout can be caught. They're a minor concern, however, and generally limited to the very deep water at the dam. Concentrate on the bass and sunfish. Water skiing is restricted to the central body of water, so skiers do not disrupt the fishing environments.

Most of the shoreline at Lake Sonoma is good bass water. Most of the coves are great bass water. And there are hundreds of coves. Threadfin shad is the main forage for the largemouth bass and the landlocked steelhead. The aggressive smallmouth prefer crayfish and meaty nymphs. If you want to concentrate on the topwater bite, try Skunk Creek Cove and Upper Dry Creek. Other good bass locations include the areas near Quicksilver and Black Mountain camps.

As with most bass fisheries, you'll find much of the action below the surface. Sinking shooting heads can help you probe the deeper water. When boating or tubing, be cautious around all the sunken wood.

Lake Sonoma is off Highway 101 at Canyon Road in the town of Geyserville. Canyon Road turns into Dry Creek Road and takes you right to the lake. From the coast, the lake makes a good day trip from Sea Ranch or Bodega Bay.

With two extensive arms, Lake Sonoma offers both cold and warmwater fisheries. Photo by Don Vachini.

Types of Fish
Smallmouth and largemouth bass, landlocked steelhead, and panfish.

Known Hatches & Baitfish
Threadfin shad, game fish fry, crayfish, callibaetis mayflies, various caddis, damselflies, and dragonflies.

Equipment to Use
Rods: 5–8 weight, 8½–10 feet in length.
Reels: Standard drag systems.
Lines: WF Floating, intermediate, sink tip type-4, modified sink tips of 130 to 200 grains, shooting heads type-4 or type-6, LC-13.
Leaders: 0X to 4X, 6–9 feet in length.
Wading: It's best to use a boat or inflatable as shoreline access is limited.

Flies to Use
Nymphs: Putnam's Damsel #12, Kaufman's Dragonfly #8, Poxyback Callibaetis #16, Black Ant #14, Black AP #12, Gold Bead Prince #14.
Streamers: Flashtail Clouser #1/0–2, Purple Eelworm #6, Burk's V-Worm #10, Hot Flash Minnow #6, Whitlock Near Nuff Sculpin #6, Black Woolly Bugger #4.
Topwater & Subsurface: Gurgler #2, Loudmouth Shad #6, Gaines Bluegill Popper #12, Sponge Spider #10–12, Callibaetis Spinner #16, Elk Hair Caddis #10.

When to Fish
Bass: March through October, prime times are April and May and September and October.
Steelhead: Early spring and early fall (though always deep and tough to catch).
Panfish: April through October, prime in summer.

Accommodations & Services
Campsites are all around the lake; lodging and supplies are available in Cloverdale, Healdsburg, and Geyserville. Find launch ramps at Warm Springs Bridge and Yorty Creek Recreation Area. Rent boats at the Lake Sonoma Marina. There's a small store just south of the lake.

Seasons & Limits
All-year access. Harvest restrictions apply, so check with local fly shops or in the Department of Fish & Game regulations booklet for current information.

Rating
Overall, an 8.

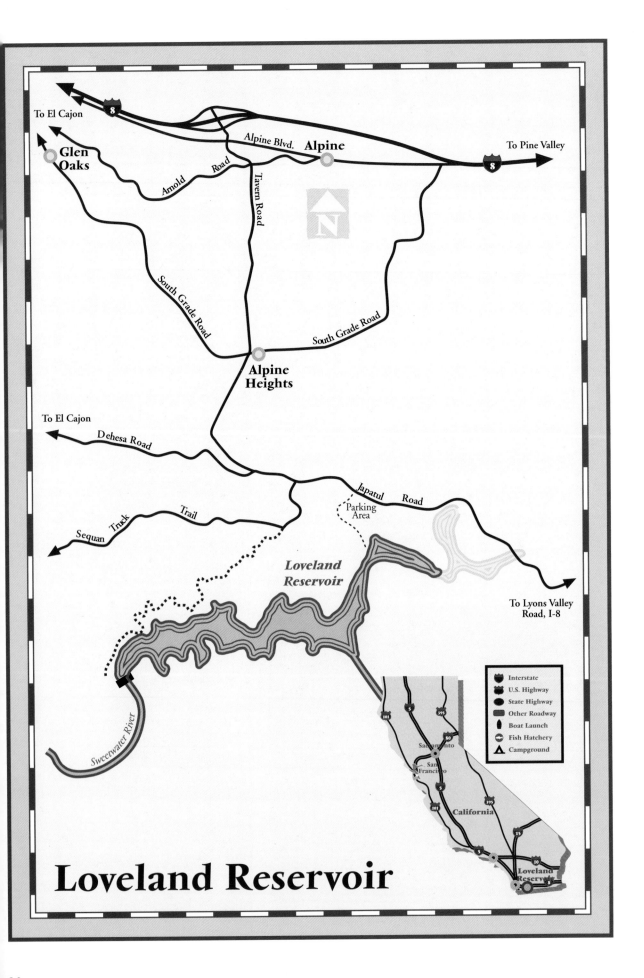

Loveland Reservoir

Loveland Reservoir

by Jeff Solis

Photo by Howard Fisher.

I f chugging big shad patterns or Dahlberg Divers along the edge of a fishy-looking stick-up sounds like a good time, try this lake. Mr. Bucketmouth will be waiting.

A deep impoundment surrounded by very steep, chaparral-covered hills, Loveland Reservoir is San Diego County's only no fee fishery. Here you'll find lots of bassy-looking water, particularly at the east end of the reservoir, where the Sweetwater River enters. During high water periods, this tree-covered meadow often becomes flooded, creating almost ideal warmwater habitat where you'll find hot fly rod action for bass over five pounds, as well as trophy panfish.

A proven technique at Loveland is to fish surface poppers when and where shad school. Also try slowly working a crayfish pattern around areas of submerged structure. Keep a few mini poppers and large dry flies handy for the lake's monster bluegill and red-ear sunfish.

Bank access only. No boats, kickboats or float tubes. Leave your waders and wading boots as no water contact is allowed. Plus you'll need your hiking boots. Watch your footing on the steep half-mile path down to and up from the water.

To get to Loveland Reservoir, take Interstate 8 east to Tavern (Alpine) Road. Turn south, and the road will take you right to the lake's parking lot.

Types of Fish
Largemouth bass, bluegill, catfish, and red-ear sunfish.

Known Hatches & Baitfish
Dragonflies, damselflies, and shad.

Equipment to Use
Rods: For bass 9 feet in length, 7–9 weight; for panfish 9 feet in length, 5–7 weight.
Reels: Standard click or disk.
Lines: WF or floating is all you'll need.
Leaders: For bass, 4–6 feet in length, 1X to 3X. For panfish, 4–8 feet in length, 3X to 4X.
Wading: No wading and no body contact with the water allowed!

Flies to Use
Dries: Stimulator and Humpy #10–12.
Nymphs: Carey Special #12, Damselfly Nymph #8, and Soft Hackle #14 (for panfish).
Streamers & Poppers: Big Woolly Bugger #4, Shad-colored Dahlberg Diver #2, Clouser Minnow #2–6, natural Deer Hair Popper #6, Mini Poppers #12.

When to Fish
Bass fishing is best in February and March and again in September and October. Panfish fishing stays consistent from April through September.

Seasons & Limits
Open year-round. See California Fish & Game regulations for limits. Currently 5 bass (12" minimum), 5 catfish, no limit on bluegill and sunfish.

Accommodations & Services
None. Limited services in Alpine.

Rating
Loveland Reservoir deserves a rating of 7.5.

Some areas can offer room to backcast. At others you'll need a good roll cast. Photo by Howard Fisher.

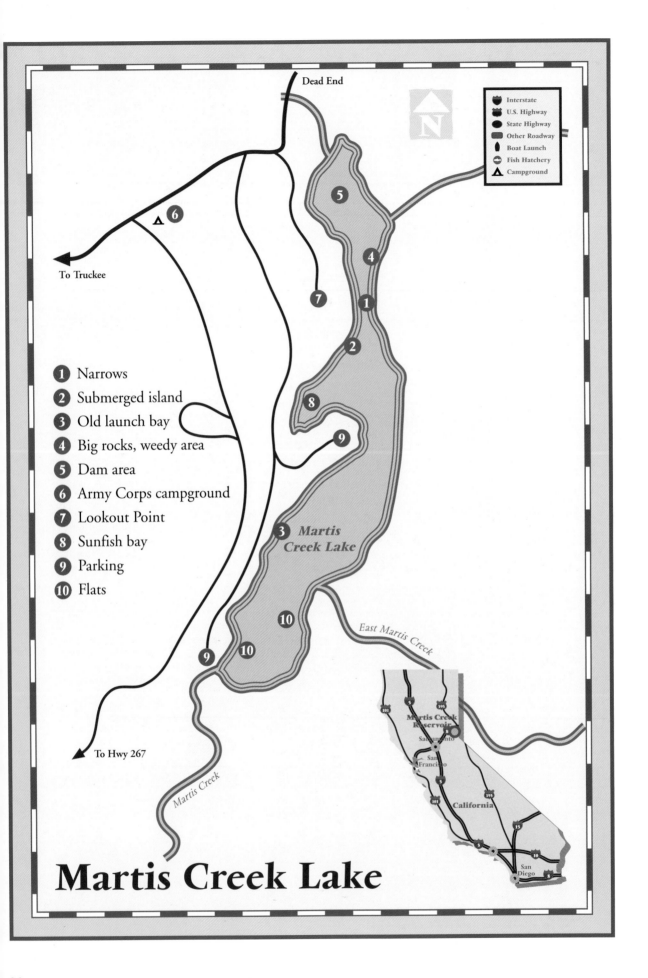

N

Legend:
- Interstate
- U.S. Highway
- State Highway
- Other Roadway
- Boat Launch
- Fish Hatchery
- Campground

Dead End

To Truckee

5

6 △

4

7

1

2

8

9

1 Narrows
2 Submerged island
3 Old launch bay
4 Big rocks, weedy area
5 Dam area
6 Army Corps campground
7 Lookout Point
8 Sunfish bay
9 Parking
10 Flats

3 *Martis Creek Lake*

10

10

9

10

East Martis Creek

To Hwy 267

Martis Creek

California — Martis Creek Reservoir, Sacramento, San Francisco, San Diego

Martis Creek Lake

Martis Creek Lake

by Dave Stanley

It began as a basic 70-acre lake built by the Army Corps of Engineers for flood control. Then it was selected as the first still water for California's Wild Trout Program. Since 1979 no boat motors (either gas or electric) and strict catch and release rules have helped grow fine trout in this lake. Regulations also include the use of single barbless hooks. Cutthroat trout, which flourished in the 1980s, are now all but gone, replaced by good populations of rainbows and browns. At the Reno Fly Shop we have observed over the years that fluctuating water levels and other unknown factors have affected trout growth and survival here. Ongoing efforts by the California Department of Fish & Game will, we hope, reverse this trend in the near future.

Located only about four miles southeast of Truckee, Martis Creek Lake is an extremely easy lake to get to and enjoy. It is a convenient "after work" fly fishing outing for many Reno-, Truckee-, and Lake Tahoe-area locals.

Martis Creek Lake is barely 25 feet deep at minimum pool. It has large numbers of green sunfish and other minnows, as well as a good crayfish population. Using a fast sinking line or shooting head with these imitations can produce surprising results. During non-hatch periods, fishing a blood midge pupa three to six feet under an indicator will often produce strikes.

Martis Creek, which flows into the reservoir, is a rainbow and brown trout spawning stream and is closed to all fishing. The outflow stream is a spawning tributary of the Truckee River and can produce some big trout early in the season. Please practice catch and release and tread lightly if you fish this stream.

The inlet channel is a prime starting point at Martis Creek Lake. Photo by Don Vachini.

Types of Fish

Primarily rainbow and brown trout. There may still be some cutthroats left from the reservoir's initial population. Also, illegally introduced green sunfish.

Known Hatches

Callibaetis, small mayflies, damselflies, and midges. The most important midge is the giant blood midge. Caddis during the summer evenings. Some little yellow stoneflies near the mouths of the two creeks that feed the reservoir.

Equipment to Use

Rods: 3–6 weight, 8½–9 feet in length.
Reels: Click or disk drag balanced to rod.
Lines: Floating, intermediate sink, and type-2 full sink lines to match rod.
Leaders: Sinking, 6–7 feet in length, 3X to 4X. Floating, 9–12 feet in length, 5X to 7X.
Wading: Neoprene waders and felt-soled boots during cold weather. Wet-wade during warm weather. Generally, wading is limited in the lake. A float tube or pram is very handy here.

Flies to Use

Dries: Suspended midge patterns, especially the Giant Blood Midge, Callibaetis Paranymphs, Elk Hair Caddis, Parachute Adams, and Parachute Hare's Ears. Adult Damsels, Spent Rusty Spinners, and small Caddis.
Nymphs: Damsel, Pheasant Tail, Hare's Ear, Blood Midge pupa. Brassies and imitations of small midge larva and pupas. Soft Hackle flies also work well.
Streamers: Olive and Black Woolly Buggers and Leeches. In fall, use large Brown Woolly Buggers to imitate the abundant crayfish population. Use Olive Matukas and Zonkers to imitate baitfish.

When to Fish

Spring and fall are the best times to fish Martis, especially during the predictable evening hatches of blood midges. Early spring runoff can cause the water level to rise, affecting the fly fishing. The dog days of mid-July to mid-September are less productive and are best fished with a fast-sinking line in deeper water.

Seasons & Limits

Open the last Saturday in April until November 15. Barbless, artificial lures only, catch and release. All tributaries are closed all year. Check current California Department of Fish & Game regulations for any changes.

Accommodations & Services

Closest services are four miles away, either at the Northstar Resort or in Truckee, or sixteen miles over the pass in Kings Beach, at the edge of Lake Tahoe. There is an excellent improved campground one-half mile above Martis. Run by the Corps of Engineers, it takes campers on a first-come, first-served basis.

Rating

The fly fishing deserves a 7.5 to 8 rating due to the predictable blood midge hatch and the dry fly action it provides. First-time visitors should know that Martis receives heavy pressure in May and June, especially in the evenings.

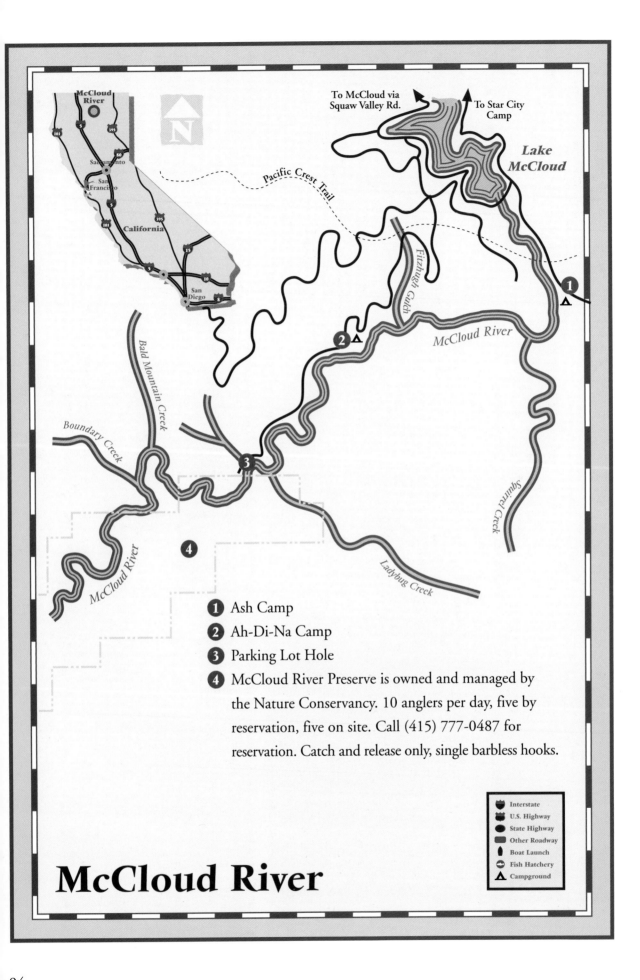

To McCloud via
Squaw Valley Rd.

To Star City
Camp

Lake
McCloud

Pacific Crest Trail

Fitzhugh Gulch

McCloud River

1

2

Bald Mountain Creek

Boundary Creek

3

Squirrel Creek

4

McCloud River

Ladybug Creek

McCloud
River

California

Sacramento

San
Francisco

San
Diego

1 Ash Camp

2 Ah-Di-Na Camp

3 Parking Lot Hole

4 McCloud River Preserve is owned and managed by
the Nature Conservancy. 10 anglers per day, five by
reservation, five on site. Call (415) 777-0487 for
reservation. Catch and release only, single barbless hooks.

	Interstate
	U.S. Highway
	State Highway
	Other Roadway
	Boat Launch
	Fish Hatchery
	Campground

McCloud River

McCloud River

This river runs cold and clear with water born from the glaciers of Mt. Shasta and Lake McCloud. At times the glacial silt imbues the water column with a handsome green tint (much like you'd find in a classic steelhead stream). If you hear that the McCloud's "running a bit green," grab your fly rod, because the fishing may be magical! A note for the fly fishing newcomer to the McCloud: The river's quirks can be tough to learn, but once you pay your dues you'll be hooked forever!

The stream is full of stone structure. Boulders of all sizes create a playing field of pocket water, riffles, and big pools. The upper river offers more habitat variety, especially small pocket water, riffles, and narrow meadow meanders. Long deep pools, tail outs, and larger pockets are more characteristic of the lower river. Stream banks are typically overgrown with vegetation, making wading techniques key to your success. A bonus to angling on the McCloud is the wildlife in the nearby forest. It's not uncommon to find signs of black bear or wild turkey as you patrol the banks.

McCloud rainbows average 10 to 13 inches throughout the system. Occasionally fly fishers catch larger fish in the 17- to 20-inch range. If you want big trout, target the browns. Spawning browns will average 17 to 22 inches. Larger, 26- to 30-inch whoppers show up every year as well.

To reach the McCloud River, take Interstate 5 toward the town of Mt. Shasta. Exit onto Highway 89 and travel into the town of McCloud. In McCloud, look for Squaw Valley Road (heads due south). Be patient as you follow this long, winding route around Lake McCloud and eventually down to the river.

The McCloud is known the world over as a great trout stream. Photo by Brian O'Keefe.

Types of Fish
Rainbow and brown trout.

Known Hatches & Baitfish
Spring: Golden stones, March browns.
June: Green drakes.
July, August: Little yellow stones, pale evening duns.
Fall: October caddis, sculpins, and trout fry.
All Season: Miscellaneous caddis, blue-winged olives, hoppers, and terrestrials.

Equipment to Use
Rods: 5–7 weight, 8–9 feet in length.
Reels: Mechanical or palm drag with 50 yards of backing.
Lines: Use floating for main stream; Hi-speed or Hi-D sink tip for fast flows or deep presentations. For deepwater streamers, use a #4 uniform sink line or 130- to 200-grain shooting head.
Leaders: 1X to 6X, 7–12 feet in length.
Wading: Chest-high neoprene or breathable waders, boots, cleats, and a wading staff.

Flies to Use
Dries: Light Cahill; Parachute Adams; Parachute Hare's Ear #14–18; Elk Hair Caddis #12–16; Orange, Yellow, or Gold Stimulator #8; Dave's Hopper #8–10; Yellow or Red Humpy #12–16; Black Ant #12–14.
Nymphs: Bird's Nest, Hare's Ear #10–16; Hunched Back Infrequens (HBI) #14–16; Poxyback Golden Stone #6–8; Poxyback PMD & Green Drake #16; Black or Olive Poxyquill #14–18; Black AP #12–14; October Caddis Emerger #6–8; Caddis, Pheasant Tail, or Prince #12–16; Dark Stonefly, Black Rubber Legs; Kaufman's Stone #4–8.
Streamers: Chartreuse & White Thunder Creek Marabou #2-6, Olive Matuka Sculpin, Zonker #2–6, Woolly Bugger #2–10 in assorted colors, Muddler Minnow #2–8, Matuka or Leech #2–4.

When to Fish
May through July and October through November 15 are prime times. November is best for big brown trout fishing. Afternoon and evening are generally the best times of day to fish.

Season & Limits
Open the last Saturday in April through November 15. Restrictions on tackle and harvest vary by stream location; refer to the Department of Fish & Game booklet for current information. Generally, regulations are as follows:
McCloud Dam Downstream to Ladybug Creek: artificial lures with barbless hooks, two-trout limit.
Ladybug Creek Downstream to Lower Boundary of U.S. Forest Service Loop: artificial lures and barbless hooks, no trout.
U.S. Forest Service loop downstream to the McCloud River Club: closed all year.

Accommodations & Services
Lodging and supplies in are available in McCloud or Mt. Shasta. Camping is best at Fowler's Camp and Ah-Di-Na Campground.

Rating
One of my favorites—certainly a blue ribbon experience. Hands down a solid 9.

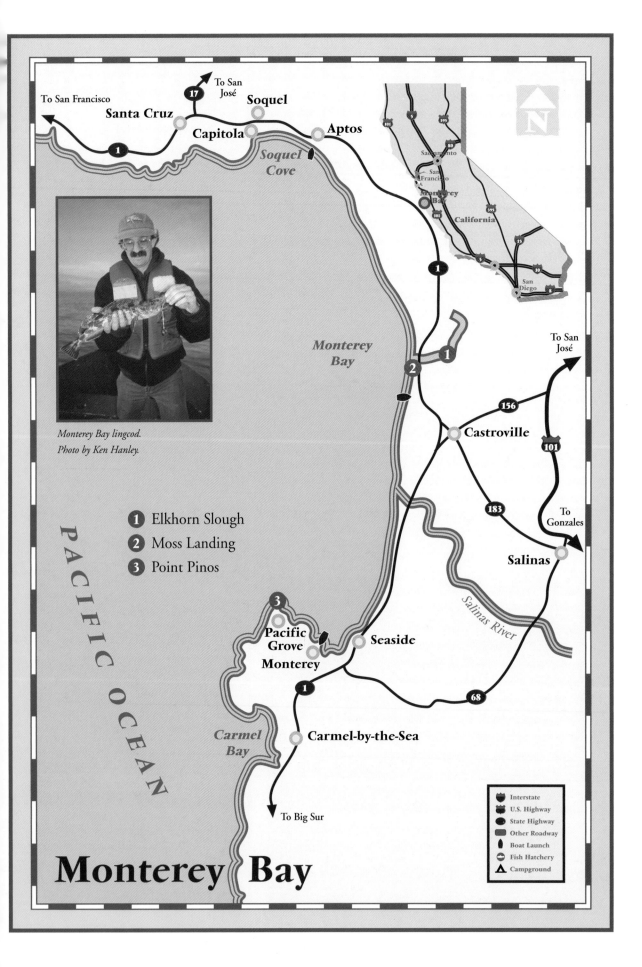

To San Francisco

To San José

Santa Cruz

Soquel

Capitola

Aptos

Soquel Cove

17

1

Monterey Bay lingcod.
Photo by Ken Hanley.

Monterey Bay

California

To San José

156

Castroville

101

183

To Gonzales

Salinas

1

2

1 Elkhorn Slough
2 Moss Landing
3 Point Pinos

Salinas River

PACIFIC OCEAN

3

Pacific Grove

Monterey

Seaside

68

1

Carmel Bay

Carmel-by-the-Sea

To Big Sur

Monterey Bay

Interstate	
U.S. Highway	
State Highway	
Other Roadway	
Boat Launch	
Fish Hatchery	
Campground	

Monterey Bay

This bay features some of central California's most beautiful coastline. Combine excellent saltwater fly fishing, abundant sea life, famous golf links, resorts, shopping, and fun attractions, and you can easily find an excuse to fly fish in this area.

Monterey Bay is a 90-mile crescent curving from the city of Santa Cruz on the north to Point Pinos and Monterey's Cannery Row at the south. The bay features more than two dozen beaches and 40 miles of beachhead. For the fly rodder there are three wharves, two harbors with jetty access, acres of floating kelp beds, and plenty of reef structure to explore.

From April through November fly fish from shore, as most of the inshore species are available in fairly shallow water. Catch game fish in the churning surf or in waters from 3 to 30-plus feet deep. A small seaworthy skiff is also a good way to fish near shore. Either way, you can cast to all kinds of fish.

Striped bass and halibut range from 3 to 15 pounds. Rockfish weigh from 1 to 5 pounds. Perch and smelt are typically less than one pound, though plenty of chunky two-pounders are available. To tag a shark you'll need a boat to go farther offshore, where the pelagic species roam. Blues weigh from 65 to 100 pounds!

Access the region from Highway 1 if you're coming from the north, from Highway 17 over the Santa Cruz Mountains from the inland, northeast, or from Highway 101 when traveling from the south. Take Highway 156, which intersects Highway 1 near Castroville or Highway 68 from Salinas. Coastal Highway 1 from Big Sur offers stunning views but is a slower way to get to the region. Once there, travel around the bay is easy on scenic Highway 1.

The shoreline can be very rocky in places while offering some fishy spots. Photo by Captain Albert E. Thebridge, NOAA Corps (ret.)

Types of Fish
Striped bass, rockfish, blue shark, halibut, jack smelt, surfperch.

Known Baitfish
Anchovy, herring, mackerel, smelt, squid, shrimp, and crabs.

Equipment to Use
Rods: 8–10 weight, 9–10 feet in length.
Reels: I prefer a large arbor and disk drag design with large backing capacity.
Lines: Type-4 sinking line or heavy sinking shooting heads of 300 to 500 grains; floating line for poppers.
Leaders: 0X to 2X, 4–7 feet in length. Lengths will vary with choice of fly.
Wading: Use chest-high neoprene waders with booties for the sandy surf. For hopping around rocks or jetties, wear warm, loose-fitting clothes and heavy hiking boots.

Flies to Use
Streamers: ALF Baitfish, Flashtail Clouser #2/0–2, Sea Habit Bucktail (White Knight) #2/0, Sar Mul Mac Anchovy #3/0, Popovic's Surf Candy or Popovic's Jiggy #2, Squid Fly #1/0–3/0, Rusty Squirrel Clouser, 10–40 Sandworm, Surf Grub #4.
Topwater & Subsurface: Gurgler #2/0, Llamahair Baitfish #1/0.

When to Fish
Striped Bass: June through September, August is prime.
Rockfish: All year, prime time is late July through September.
White Sea Bass: Summer.
Halibut: June through September.
Surfperch: All year, prime time is May through September.
Blue Shark: June through December, prime time is August through October.
Jack Smelt: All year.

Season & Limits
There are some restrictions on tackle and harvest, which vary from time to time. It's best to check at local bait and fly shops or consult the California Department of Fish & Game regulations.

Accommodations & Services
Supplies and lodging are available in Santa Cruz, Soquel, Capitola, Moss Landing, and Monterey. Camping is available at New Brighton State Beach and Sunset State Beach. Public launches and marinas are located throughout the bay system. Boat rentals are available in Santa Cruz and Capitola.

Rating
For variety, beauty, and accessibility, a 9.

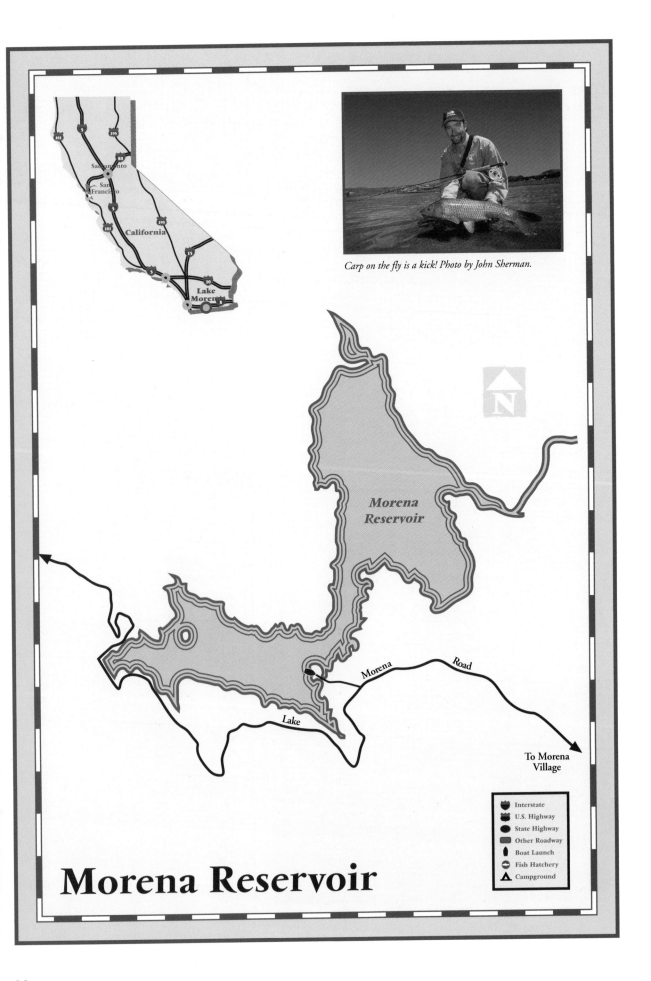

Carp on the fly is a kick! Photo by John Sherman.

California

Lake Morena

Morena Reservoir

Morena Road

Lake

To Morena Village

	Interstate
	U.S. Highway
	State Highway
	Other Roadway
	Boat Launch
	Fish Hatchery
	Campground

Morena Reservoir

Morena Reservoir
by Jeff Solis

Although it is one of the most remote lakes in San Diego County, Lake Morena is a very popular fishing destination for Southern California fly anglers. Granite boulders and oak trees shade most of the shoreline, making Lake Morena an ideal spot for campers, picnickers, or anyone on a family fishing outing. It's best to plan on a full weekend to visit this beautiful still water.

At approximately 1,500 surface acres, Lake Morena provides opportunities to catch trout, largemouth bass, crappie, and bluegill. The reservoir is open year-round and is an incredible winter trout fishery. In early spring, trophy bass begin to get aggressive, and panfish action shifts into high gear by summer.

It's possible to fish Lake Morena effectively from the shore with floating lines or sink tips, but most anglers use float tubes and sink tip or full sink fly lines. Small, slowly retrieved streamer and nymph patterns produce the most consistent results. In early spring, big bass stay in deeper water, making a full sink line or shooting head a must. Panfish can be taken on small nymphs and dry flies throughout the year.

Morena is approximately 60 miles east of San Diego. To get there, take Interstate 8 east to Buckman Springs Road (Highway S1). Turn south (right) on Buckman Springs Road to Oak Drive. Turn right on Oak Drive and make another right on Lake Morena Road to get to the lake.

There are many species at Morena to test your skill.
Photo by John Sherman.

Types of Fish
Trout, bass, catfish, crappie, bluegill, and carp.

Known Hatches & Baitfish
Midges, callibaetis mayflies, dragonflies and damselflies, leeches, crayfish, and game fish fry.

Equipment to Use
Rods: 8–10 feet in length, 4–8 weight.
Reels: Standard click or disk.
Lines: WF, floating, full sink, type-4–6 sink tip and shooting head.
Leaders: For trout 7–12 feet in length, 4X to 7X. For bass 6–10 feet in length, 1X to 4X. For panfish 7–10 feet in length, 5X to 7X.
Wading: Lots of wadable water on the north and south ends of the lake. Float tubes and boats are okay, too.

Flies to Use
Dries: Adams & Parachute Adams #12–18, Looping Callibaetis Dry & Emerger #14–16, Special Emerger, Black and Cream Adult Midge, Griffith's Gnat #18–22.
Nymphs: Flashback Beadhead Hare's Ear #10–16, Beadhead PT #10–18, Prince #8–14, Brassie #18–22.
Streamers & Poppers: Woolly Bugger #4–10, Leech #4–8, Small Alf #2/0–2, Clouser Minnow #1/0–8, Wiggle Bug, Foam and Deer Hair Poppers, Crayfish #4.

When to Fish
Prime time for trout is October through February. The best time for bass is February through October. Crappie and bluegill fishing is prime in the spring and summer.

Seasons & Limits
Open year-round, a half-hour before sunrise until a half-hour after sunset. Limits: 5 trout, 5 bass (12-inch minimum), 10 catfish, 25 crappie, and as many bluegill as you can catch.

Nearby Fly Fishing
Cuyamaca Reservoir and the Sweetwater River.

Accommodations & Services
Morena Reservoir has boat rentals and a launch ramp. Currently there are 58 campsites with water and electricity for rent. There are also 28 campsites with no hook-ups, for rent. RVs can also park at the private Lake Morena RV Park, which offers complete hook-ups. For more information contact Stroud Tackle or the San Diego Fly Shop.

Rating
Lake Morena rates an 8.5.

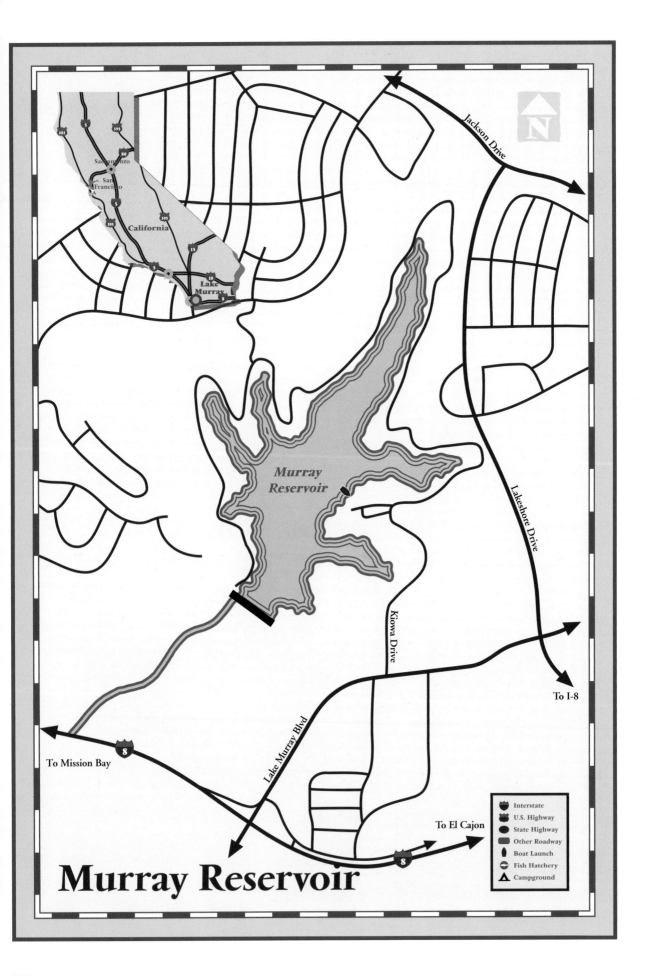

Murray Reservoir

Murray Reservoir

by Jeff Solis

Murray Reservoir offers year-round, world-class bass and wonderful winter trout fly fishing for anglers short on time. Located just ten miles from downtown San Diego, Murray Reservoir is the most centrally located reservoir in the county, yet its proximity to a large population center doesn't seem to adversely affect the quality of the angling experience. This fishery consistently produces largemouth bass in the 15- to 20-pound class. It offers steady action in the winter for stocked rainbows up to five pounds, and provides the panfish enthusiast a year-round chance to hook dinner-plate-sized crappie or bluegill.

The access road that runs completely around Lake Murray enables walk-and-wade anglers to fish the entire reservoir, especially the more remote, reed-lined banks where bass are likely to hold. Watch your back cast, however; you might hook one of the many walkers or joggers who also enjoy using the lake.

While shore fishing can produce good results, a boat or float tube is still the best way to fish Murray Reservoir. Bass usually hold tight to reeds and other subsurface structure, and a full sink or sink tip fly line will allow you to get your fly down to them. You'll want to keep a floating line handy, however. The surface action on the reservoir occasionally heats up, and well-presented dry flies can produce jolting strikes.

To get to this great bass fishery, take Interstate 8 to Lake Murray Blvd., go north to Kiowa Drive, then take a left to the lake. You won't be disappointed.

When full the reservoir covers 171 surface acres. The shoreline is accessible though you'll probably want to be on the water. Photo by Howard Fisher.

Types of Fish
Stocked rainbow trout, Florida largemouth bass, and panfish.

Known Hatches & Baitfish
Midges, mayflies, dragonflies and damselflies, shad, shad, and more shad!

Equipment to Use
Rods: For trout, 8–9 feet in length, 3–5 weight. For bass, 9 feet in length, 5–8 weight.
Reels: Standard click or disk.
Lines: WF or floating and a sink tip (type-4) for some situations.
Leaders: 7–9 feet in length, 4X to 6X for trout. 6–9 feet in length, 3X to 4X for bass.
Wading: Most of this lake is better for float-tubing than wading. Either way, have watertight waders.

Flies to Use
Dries: Poxyback Callibaetis Emerger #14–16, Adams #12–18, Parachute Baetis #14–18.
Nymphs: Hare's Ear #10–18, Prince #8–16, Beadhead PT #10–14, Dragon & Damsel, Poxyback Callibaetis #16.
Streamers & Poppers: Woolly Bugger #4–8, Clouser Minnow #2–6, Shad-Colored Deceiver, Foam Popper #2.

When to Fish
Trout: November through May.
Bass: Year-round, best surface action July through September.
Panfish: November through May.

Seasons & Limits
Days and hours of operation may be limited and subject to closure. Consult the City of San Diego Reservoirs and Recreation Program phone (619) 465-3474 for current schedule, or check their web site. Limit 5 trout, 5 bass with a 12-inch minimum, 25 panfish.

Accommodations & Services
Many shoreline picnic sites, concession stands, boat rental, and launch ramp. The San Diego Fly Fishers offer free casting lessons every Sunday at 9 a.m.

Rating
Lake Murray is at least a 7 for largemouth bass opportunities and convenience.

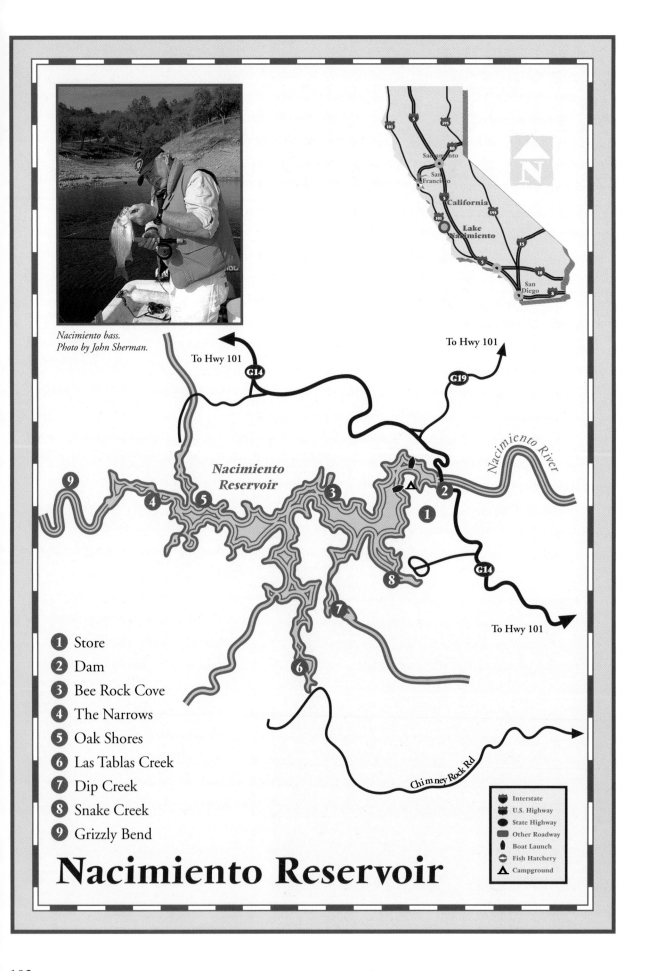

Nacimiento bass.
Photo by John Sherman.

To Hwy 101

G14

To Hwy 101

G19

Nacimiento River

Nacimiento Reservoir

9

4

5

3

2

1

8

7

6

To Hwy 101

Chimney Rock Rd

1 Store
2 Dam
3 Bee Rock Cove
4 The Narrows
5 Oak Shores
6 Las Tablas Creek
7 Dip Creek
8 Snake Creek
9 Grizzly Bend

Nacimiento Reservoir

Interstate
U.S. Highway
State Highway
Other Roadway
Boat Launch
Fish Hatchery
Campground

California

Sacramento
San Francisco

Lake
Nacimiento

San Diego

Nacimiento Reservoir

This water is best known for its white bass population. The game fish are indeed doing just fine in this reservoir. It is, in fact, the only water left in California with such a fishery. During the spring these bass head toward the narrows and the river mouth to spawn. It's a popular time to work the deep pools in this water (though the boat ride to these environs does take a while). Throughout the summer season, when the white bass return to the open lake, you can spot them as they crash on baitfish at the surface. Look for topwater boils, diving birds, or a ring of boats targeting the bass. These fish can really put on a show for you! Boats are a real necessity to maximize your white bass action.

Rocky habitat is a premier element in the bronzeback territory around the reservoir. Smallmouth bass love this type of structure, and there's seemingly no end to it, as it snakes around the 160 miles of shoreline! Work the tapering points around each cove and arm. In the Las Tablas arm you'll find plenty of timber habitat and scads of smallies to challenge your skills. I suggest you take some time to work around the Oak Shores area as well. A successful brushpile restoration program has enhanced this stretch of water.

Most of the bass in "Naci" are in the one- to four-pound range. The reservoir's lunkers generally stay in the deepest waters, hugging any cover or structure. Deepwater tactics and tackle are necessary to catch any of these trophy-sized bass.

Nacimiento is open 24 hours a day for angling access. That's a lot of casting! The smallmouth topwater bite is terrific during the summer evening cycle. To avoid heavy-pressure days, think about planning a midweek adventure.

To reach this 5,000-acre impound, take Highway 101 toward Paso Robles. Coming from the north, access Nacimiento from the town of Bradley by taking County Road G18 west to G19 (Nacimiento Lake Road). From the south, take Highway 101, pass through Paso Robles and head to the water on County Road G14.

White bass on the fly.
Photo by John Sherman.

Types of Fish
Largemouth, smallmouth, and white bass; crappie; panfish.

Known Hatches & Baitfish
Threadfin shad, bluegill, game fish fry, crayfish, leeches, damselflies, dragonflies, and hoppers.

Equipment to Use
Rods: 5–7 weight, 8–10 feet in length.
Reels: Standard drag systems.
Lines: WF, floating, intermediate, sink tip type-4, modified sink tips of 130 to 200 grains, shooting heads type-3 or type-6.
Leaders: 2X to 6X, 6–12 feet in length.
Wading: It's best to work from a boat. Bank angling is marginal due to private land.

Flies to Use
Nymphs: Putnam's Damsel #12, Kaufman's Dragonfly #8.
Streamers: Flashtail Clouser #1/0–2, Poxybou Crayfish #4, Burk's V-Worm #10, Hot Flash Minnow, Milt's Pond Smelt, Whitlock Near Nuff Sculpin #6.
Topwater & Subsurface: Crease Fly #1/0, Gurgler #2–1/0, Loudmouth Shad #6, Gaines Bluegill Popper #12, Sponge Spider #10–12.

When to Fish
Smallmouth Bass: All year, prime time is January through March.
Largemouth Bass: All year, prime time is March to April, and October.
White Bass: Spring spawn, schooling activity during the summer.
Crappie & Panfish: All year, prime time is early spring through summer.

Seasons & Limits
All-year access. Harvest restrictions apply, so check with local fly shops or consult the Department of Fish & Game regulations.

Accommodations & Services
This is a full-service facility, with marina, launch ramps (at both ends of the lake), and boat rentals, plus camping nearby. Supplies are available in Paso Robles and Bradley.

Rating
An excellent resource located in central California. A solid 8 on most days.

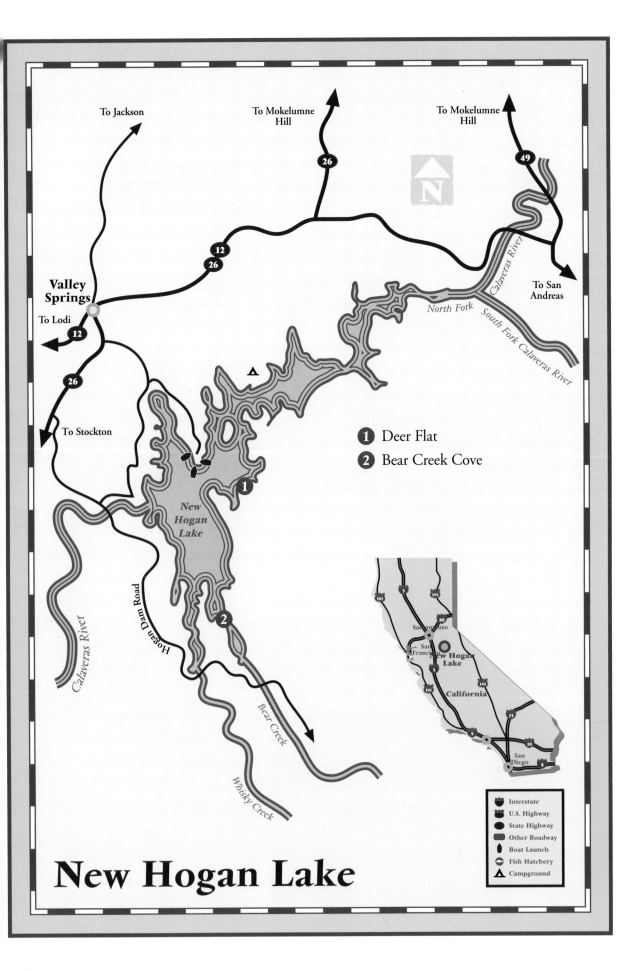

To Jackson

To Mokelumne Hill

To Mokelumne Hill

26

49

Valley Springs

12
26

Calaveras River

North Fork

South Fork Calaveras River

To San Andreas

To Lodi

12

To Stockton

26

1 Deer Flat
2 Bear Creek Cove

New Hogan Lake

1

2

Calaveras River

Hogan Dam Road

Bear Creek

Whisky Creek

California

Sacramento
San Francisco
New Hogan Lake
San Diego

	Interstate
	U.S. Highway
	State Highway
	Other Roadway
	Boat Launch
	Fish Hatchery
	Campground

New Hogan Lake

New Hogan Lake

Located in the lower Sierra foothills region, New Hogan is just east about 4 miles from Camanche Reservoir. It's not the hottest ticket for fly fishing, but it is a good add-on to any foothills adventure. The main sport fish here is striped bass, but you do have four other species of game fish to pursue with a fly.

Stripers go on a short topwater spree starting in September and ending in late October. Watch for birds diving, swirls on the surface, or busting bait, and get over to the action pronto! These are strong predatory fish, and the feeding frenzies are sporadic throughout the lake. If you prefer trout, you'll find the most consistent-producing region is in the Calaveras arm. Largemouth bass are typically concentrated in Bear Creek Cove, located in the southern reaches of the lake.

A bonus for this reservoir is the boat-in campgrounds, especially around Deer Flat. These camps give you great access to a wide variety of cover and structure around the lake.

New Hogan Lake is in the Sierra foothills, about 40 miles east of Stockton on Highway 26. Travel east on 26 to Valley Springs. From here many local surface roads take you toward the Calaveras River arm. To work the reservoir's north end, take Highway 12 east from Valley Springs toward San Andreas.

New Hogan can be very popular at times but there's plenty of water to spread out. Photo by U.S. Army Corps of Engineers.

Types of Fish
Rainbow and brown trout, largemouth and striped bass, panfish.

Known Hatches & Baitfish
Threadfin shad, bluegill, game fish fry, crayfish, leeches, frogs, callibaetis mayflies, caddis, midges, damselflies, and dragonflies.

Equipment to Use
Rods: 5–9 weight, 8½–10 feet in length.
Reels: Standard drag systems.
Lines: Intermediate, sink tip type-4, modified sink tips of 130 to 200 grains, shooting heads type-4 or type-6, and LC-13.
Leaders: 0X to 6X, 6–12 feet in length.
Wading: Bank access is possible but a boat or inflatable is best. Felt-soled boots, hippers, or chest waders are okay.

Flies to Use
Dries: Madam X #8–12, Loopwing Callibaetis #16, Royal Stimulator #12.
Nymphs: Poxyback Trico #20, Midge Pupa #20, Putnam's Damsel #12, Kaufman's Dragonfly #8, Poxyback Callibaetis #16, Black Ant #14, Black AP #12, Prince #14.
Streamers: Sea Habit Bucktail #1/0, Flashtail Clouser #1/0–2, Purple Eelworm #6, Burk's V-Worm #10, Hot Flash Minnow #6, Whitlock Near Nuff Sculpin #6.
Topwater & Subsurface: Gurgler #2, Crease Fly #2, Loudmouth Shad #6, Gaines Bluegill Popper #12, Sponge Spider #10–12.

When to Fish
Trout: All year, prime January to April.
Striped Bass: All year, fall months are best for shallow water opportunities.
Largemouth Bass: February through September, prime time is March through May.
Panfish: All year, summer is prime time.

Seasons & Limits
Access is year-round but harvest restrictions apply. Check with local fly shops, the Camanche Store, or the Department of Fish & Game regulations booklet.

Accommodations & Services
Two boat-in and two drive-in camping areas, public launch ramp, supplies and groceries, boat rentals, and marina are at the lake.

Rating
New Hogan makes a nice two-day camping and fishing outing. Overall a 5.5.

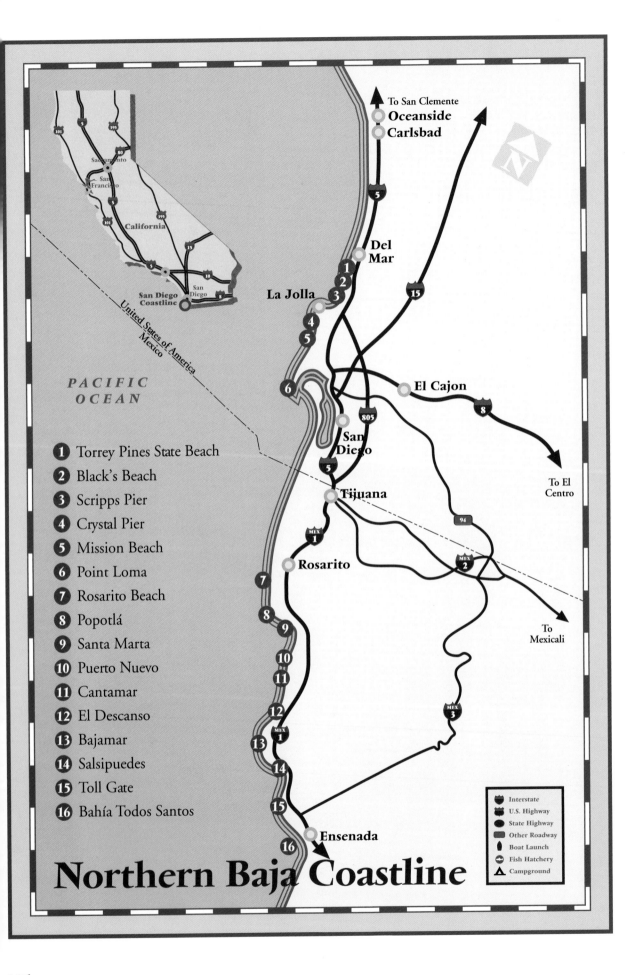

Northern Baja Coastline

1 Torrey Pines State Beach

2 Black's Beach

3 Scripps Pier

4 Crystal Pier

5 Mission Beach

6 Point Loma

7 Rosarito Beach

8 Popotlá

9 Santa Marta

10 Puerto Nuevo

11 Cantamar

12 El Descanso

13 Bajamar

14 Salsipuedes

15 Toll Gate

16 Bahía Todos Santos

PACIFIC
OCEAN

United States of America
Mexico

California

San Diego
Coastline

San
Diego

To San Clemente

Oceanside

Carlsbad

Del
Mar

La Jolla

El Cajon

San
Diego

Tijuana

Rosarito

Ensenada

To El
Centro

To
Mexicali

	Interstate
	U.S. Highway
	State Highway
	Other Roadway
	Boat Launch
	Fish Hatchery
	Campground

Northern Baja Coastline

by Jeff Solis

High, sloping cliffs and beautiful, uncrowded sandy beaches make this one of the most beautiful places in the West to saltwater fly fish. The Northern Baja California coast, just 20 minutes' drive from San Diego, is what Southern California looked like 100 years ago. Who knows how long it will stay this way, so sample this frontier for fly fishing adventures now. Be sure to enjoy the villages of Popotlá, Santa Marta, Puerto Nuevo, and Cantamar.

Access is easy along the well-maintained Mexican highways. Mex Highway 1-D, a toll road, is the main route. Generally high quality, it's worth the few extra dollars. To travel free, stay on the old Mexico Highway 1. Two-wheel-drive vehicles can negotiate most of the secondary surface roads. Contact the Mexico Tourism Board (in Los Angeles) for details and travel documents. See listing in the Resources section.

Don't let some hotel and condo expansion get you down. Heck, you might even find the amenities to your liking. Tijuana, Rosarito, and Ensenada offer a multitude of tourist activities but can be crowded. Ensenada is the hub for inshore, offshore, and shoreline access. The Bahía Todos Santos and local island structure are magnets for calico bass, rockfish, barracuda, white sea bass, yellowtail, tuna, and more! If you are south of Rosarito, make a point of stopping in Puerto Nuevo for a great lobster meal.

Offshore anglers should target pinnacles and sea stacks. Beach anglers should use sinking lines with short leaders and concentrate on the troughs and rips. Long casts are not necessary, as most fish are within 50 feet of the beach; corbina are even closer. Wade cautiously, because there are no lifeguards. Kelp beds are close, much to the kayakers' delight. Beach aficionados can do well from Rosarito south.

Remember, you're in another country and you must be courteous. Follow these basics: Keep your car in good condition and get Mexican auto insurance (available at the border, about $12 a day). Avoid driving at night and always travel with another person. Obey speed limits, and watch for drastic changes in posted speeds. U.S. dollars are welcome in Mexico. No tourist card, passport, or birth certificate is needed north of Ensenada, but take one of these documents if fishing south of Ensenada. As of now a Mexican fishing license is not required if fishing from shore, but contact a Southern California fly shop for updated information.

Editor's note: For more on fly fishing West Coast bays and shorelines, consult Ken's fine books, *Fly Fishing Afoot in the Surf Zone* and *Fly Fishing the Pacific Inshore*, and *Mexico Blue-Ribbon Fly Fishing Guide*.

Types of Fish
Calico bass, barracuda, corbina, croaker, halibut, and surfperch.

Known Baitfish
Anchovy, mackerel, smelt, squid, shrimp, Pacific mole crabs, and sardines.

Equipment to Use
Rods: 7–10 weight, 9–9½ feet in length.
Reels: I prefer an anodized large arbor with disk drag.
Lines: WF floating, intermediate, type-4 or type-6, sinking shooting heads, sink tip 200 to 500 grains.
Leaders: 1X to 5X, 4–7 feet in length.
Wading: Wet-wade or use lightweight waders and booties for sandy beaches. Use due caution.

Flies to Use
Streamers: ALF Baitfish, Deceiver #4–4/0, Popovic's Surf Candy, Popovic's Jiggy #2, Squid Fly #1/0, Rusty Squirrel Clouser, #1/0–4/0 Sandworm, Ruffy, Salt Bugger (bleeding anchovy), Abel Anchovy #4–2/0, Sea Habit Bucktail (White Knight) #2/0, Sar Mul Mac Anchovy #3/0, Clouser Minnows #2–6, Alf #3/0, Crazy Charlie, M.O.E. (mother of epoxy) patterns #6–2 and various Mole Crab patterns.
Topwater & Subsurface: Gurgler #2/0–2.

When to Fish
Fish year-round, but the prime times are as follows:
Bass: May through October, June and July.
Barracuda: Late July through September.
Corbina: May through September.
Croaker: Summer through fall.
Halibut: June through September.
Surfperch: May through September.

Seasons & Limits
No license is necessary for wade fishing the coast. A license is required to fish from any floating craft, including a surfboard. Contact the Mexico Department of Fisheries, 2550 Fifth Avenue, Suite 15, San Diego, CA 92104, phone 619-233-4324, fax 619-233-0344 for fishing and boating licenses, and regulations. Call to receive license applications via e-mail, fax, or mail. Licenses are also available from tourism offices in Tijuana, Rosarito, and Ensenada, but it's easiest to work with the office in San Diego.

Accommodations & Services
Lodging and supplies are available in Tijuana, Rosarito, and Ensenada. Rosarito has excellent hotels and restaurants, picturesque beaches, and shopping. Ensenada offers the same, and has a full-service marina. Campsites are plentiful along the coast.

Travel Information
Baja California Secretaria de Turismo
(Across from San Ysidro/Tijuana border entrance)
Viva Tijuana Commercial Center
Vía de la Juventud #8800-2523, Zona Río
011-52-664-973-0430
www.discoverbajacalifornia.com
Baja on the Fly: www.bajafly.com
BajaLinks: www.bajalinks.com

Rating
A solid 7 for most folks, higher for the adventurous.

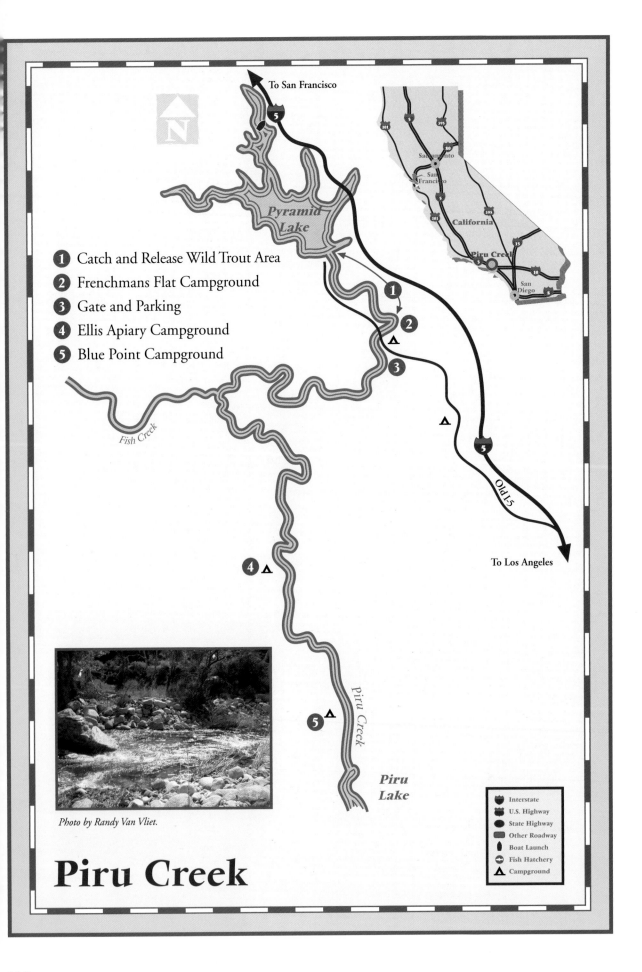

To San Francisco

N

Pyramid Lake

1 Catch and Release Wild Trout Area
2 Frenchmans Flat Campground
3 Gate and Parking
4 Ellis Apiary Campground
5 Blue Point Campground

1

2

3

Fish Creek

Old I5

To Los Angeles

4

5

Piru Creek

Piru Lake

Photo by Randy Van Vliet.

Piru Creek

Sacramento
San Francisco
California
Piru Creek
San Diego

Interstate
U.S. Highway
State Highway
Other Roadway
Boat Launch
Fish Hatchery
Campground

Piru Creek

by Jeff Solis

Thanks to the California Department of Fish & Game, as well as Cal-Trout, the Sierra Pacific Fly Fishers, and other conservation organizations, Piru Creek has developed into a great urban wild trout fishery, boasting approximately 6,000 trout per mile. Located only an hour north of Los Angeles, this wonderful little stream allows you to catch the morning blue-winged olive hatch and still be home by the afternoon.

Piru Creek contains many deep pools, slow-moving runs, riffles, and pocket waters. The best fly fishing is found on the 1.5-mile wild trout section, where short fly rods and long leaders are the norm.

To reach Piru Creek's wild trout section, exit on Templin Highway off Interstate 5. Go west and then north on old I-5 which will take you to the creek. When the road ends, you'll find a gate and parking area next to Frenchmans Flat and the campground. Walk 1.4 miles upstream on the paved road to the waterfalls. From the falls upstream to the Big Bridge is the catch and release section of the creek.

If you're looking for a way to treat an advanced case of cabin fever but don't have the time to trek up to the eastern Sierra, Piru Creek offers the opportunity to fish dry flies 365 days a year.

Springtime run off and recent rains affect the visibility of Piru Creek, this being a couple weeks after a good 3" rain.
Photo by Randy Van Vliet.

Types of Fish
Rainbow trout.

Known Hatches
Blue-winged olives, tricos, caddis, midges, ants, and hoppers.

Equipment to Use
Rods: 7½–8½ feet in length, 2–6 weight.
Reels: Standard click or disk.
Lines: WF or double-taper floating.
Leaders: 10–15 feet in length, 5X to 7X.
Wading: Because of heavy vegetation along the creek banks, wading is a must. Chest waders are highly recommended.

Flies to Use
Dries: Blue Dun #16–20, Blue-Winged Olive #16–20, Parachute Adams #16–20, Adams #16–20, Elk Hair Caddis #14–18, Caddis Emerger #14–18, Griffith's Gnat #20–24, Light and Dark Midge #20–24, and Hopper patterns.
Nymphs: Hare's Ear #12–18, Prince Nymph #12–18, PT #12–18, Brassie #18–22, Disco Midge #18–22, Candy Cane #18–22, Serendipity #14–18, and Latex Caddis Larva #14–18.

When to Fish
Mornings and evenings during the spring, summer, and fall. All day during the winter.

Seasons & Limits
Piru Creek and tributaries upstream of Pyramid Lake open year-round. Artificial lures and flies with barbless hooks only. Consult the California Department of Fish and Game regulations for other restrictions below Pyramid Lake.

Permits
You must obtain an Adventure Pass in advance to park your vehicle. Passes are currently $5 daily and are sold Forest Service offices and retailers throughout southern California including three in nearby Castaic. For vendors see www.fs.fed.us/r5/angeles/passes.

Accommodations & Services
Frenchmans Flat Campground. Call the Angeles National Forest (626-574-1613) with questions.

Rating
Piru Creek is a 5-7 in the winter and best with enough water. It rates less in the summertime.

The Arroyo toad, a native of the Piru Creek drainage.
Photo by Randy Van Vliet.

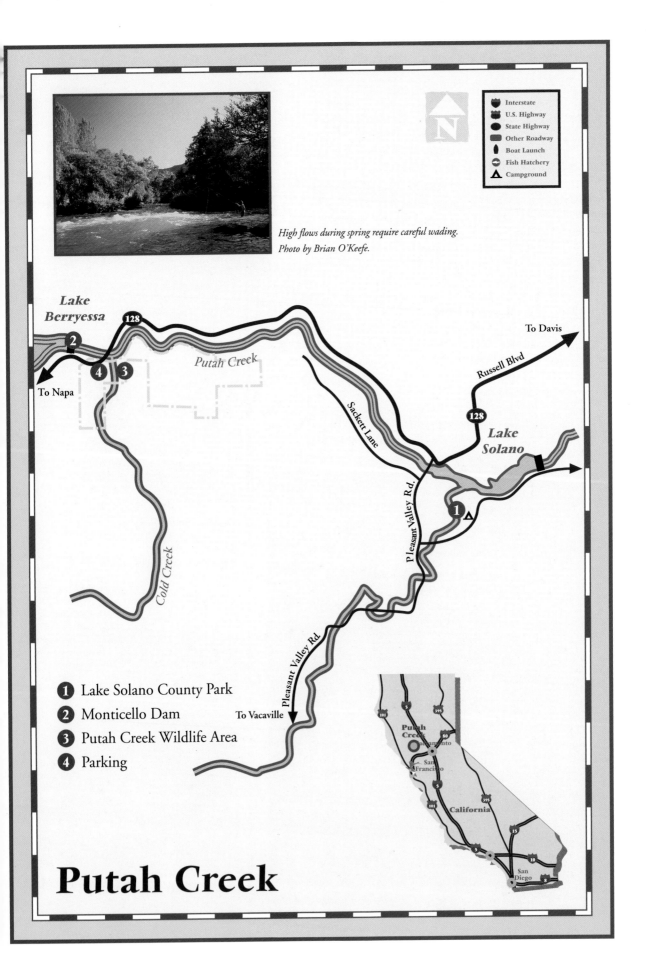

High flows during spring require careful wading.
Photo by Brian O'Keefe.

N

	Interstate
	U.S. Highway
	State Highway
	Other Roadway
	Boat Launch
	Fish Hatchery
	Campground

Lake Berryessa

128

To Napa

Putah Creek

Cold Creek

Sackett Lane

Pleasant Valley Rd.

Russell Blvd

To Davis

128

Lake Solano

1

Pleasant Valley Rd

To Vacaville

1 Lake Solano County Park
2 Monticello Dam
3 Putah Creek Wildlife Area
4 Parking

Putah Creek

Sacramento
San Francisco
California
San Diego

Putah Creek

Putah Creek

If you're looking for a stream to work when the rest of the state is closed, head to Putah Creek, one of the few stream corridors available all year long. It's close to just about everyone in the Bay Area, being less than two hours from most metropolitan areas. The main drawbacks are the shortness of the waterway and the fact that just a few miles of the stream are productive. The anglers can be elbow-to-elbow when the bite is hot.

Putah spills out of Lake Berryessa and is a classic tailwater fishery. More often than not it runs off-colored, and clarity is marginal. Its pools, riffles, and runs are paralleled by brushy banks.

There's a healthy population of wild fish in the river, and it's not unheard of to catch an 18- to 20-inch (or larger) fish here. Keep in mind that they're winter spawners, so tread lightly if you wade during the cold season. In addition to these wild fish, the Department of Fish & Game plants trout every year. Nymphing tactics are the most productive approach. The dry fly hatch is sporadic and light.

The Vacaville area is your southern approach to Putah from eastbound Interstate 80; take the Pleasant Valley Road exit directly to the river. Use Sackett Lane for streamside access. If you're coming from the north on Interstate 5, Dunnigan will be your gateway. Exit on to Interstate 505 and continue toward Winters. Highway 128 will take you to the water.

The best time for Putah Creek may be late fall and early winter when the fishing is catch and release with barbless hooks only.
Photo by Brian O'Keefe.

Types of Fish
Rainbow trout.

Known Hatches
All Year: Midge, caddis, small worms, and scuds.

Equipment to Use
Rods: 5–6 weight, 8–9 feet in length.
Reels: Mechanical or palm drag with at least 50 yards of backing.
Lines: Generally floating. Sink tips are helpful with faster flows or deeper presentations.
Leaders: 4X to 6X, 6–9 feet in length.
Wading: Chest-high waders and studded boots. A wading staff is required because of lots of mossy rocks!

Flies to Use
Dries: Parachute Adams #14–18, Parachute Hare's Ear #14–18, Elk Hair Caddis #12–16.
Nymphs: Bird's Nest or Hare's Ear #12–18, Prince #14–16, Poxyback PMD #16–18, Black AP #14–18, PT Nymph #12–18, Scud #16, Red San Juan Worm #14.
Streamers: Woolly Bugger #2–10.

When to Fish
All year.

Seasons & Limits
Special regulations apply. From the last Saturday in April through November 15 the limit is five trout. From November 16 through the last Friday in April, catch and release using artificial flies with barbless hooks only. Consult current California Department of Fish & Game regulations.

Nearby Fishing
Lakes Solano and Berryessa.

Accommodations & Services
Camping and supplies are available at Markley Cove Resort and Lake Solano County Park. Several nearby towns provide lodging and services.

Rating
An easily accessed creek that is a good location for developing nymphing techniques: a 6.5.

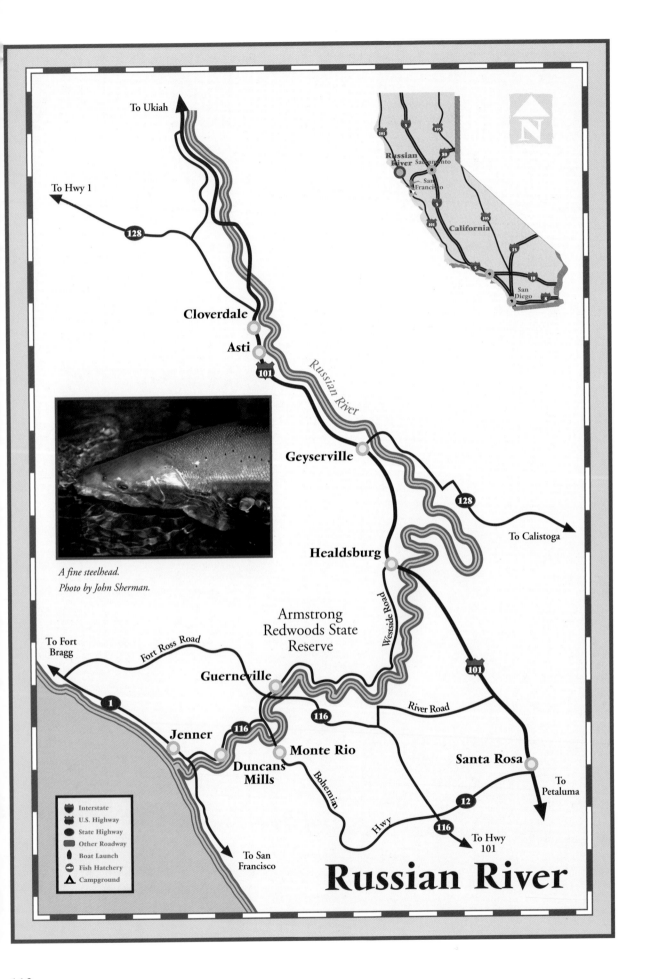

To Ukiah

To Hwy 1

128

Cloverdale

Asti

101

Russian River

Geyserville

128

To Calistoga

A fine steelhead.
Photo by John Sherman.

Healdsburg

Armstrong
Redwoods State
Reserve

Westside Road

To Fort
Bragg

Fort Ross Road

Guerneville

101

River Road

1

Jenner

116

116

Monte Rio

Duncans
Mills

Bohemia

Santa Rosa

To
Petaluma

12

Hwy

116

To Hwy
101

To San
Francisco

Interstate
U.S. Highway
State Highway
Other Roadway
Boat Launch
Fish Hatchery
Campground

Russian
River

Sacramento

San
Francisco

California

San
Diego

Russian River

Russian River

Of northern California's major coastal rivers, the Russian is closest to major population areas. It also runs through more civilization than most rivers of this type. Access is the biggest hurdle that anglers contend with, because private lands make getting to the water difficult for anyone on foot.

The flip side of this coin is the easy wading in much of the stream, once you do find passage to the water. Deeper pools and riffles exist along the lower stretch, while the upper reaches are a mix of rapids, undercut banks, flats, and pools. In the lower region, the Duncans Mills area provides classic fly fishing water. Foot access increases around and above the town of Healdsburg.

The upper and lower sections are easily navigated with a canoe or small craft. During the fall run, most fly fishers work from prams or skiffs and concentrate on fish in the tidal basin. This area is subject to low-flow closures. Your success depends on the sandbar opening at the river's mouth. Contact King's Sport & Tackle, (707) 869-2156, for daily fishing conditions.

If you're looking for a quiet bass stream, largemouth bass patrol the lower pools while smallmouth opportunities are best upstream in the Alexander Valley region north of Healdsburg. Since many consider the river's salmon and steelhead to be the "glory fish," the bass populations rarely receive as much pressure.

You can explore this historic waterway by driving Highway 1 along the coast to Jenner. Highway 116 east follows the river into Guerneville. For inland highway access, take 101 past Santa Rosa to Highway 12 which intersects Highway 116. Highway 116 west takes you directly to the lower reaches. Upper-river access is possible from Highway 101 in Healdsburg, Geyserville, Asti, or Cloverdale. Local surface roads take you to the river's edge.

Angler stalking on the Russian River.
Photo by Ken Hanley.

Types of Fish

King salmon (chinook), steelhead, shad, smallmouth and largemouth bass.

When to Fish

Salmon: September and October.
Steelhead: November on the lower river; November to February on the upper river.
Shad: May through June.
Bass: All year, prime time is from late spring to mid-fall.

Equipment to Use

Rods: 6–8 weight, 8–10 feet in length.
Reels: Mechanical or palm drag with 75 yards of backing.
Lines: Full floating or sink tip lines.
Leaders: 5X to 1X, 6–12 feet in length.
Wading: Use chest-high waders and felt-soled boots. Take a wading staff.

Flies to Use

Dries: Yellow Humpy #10–12, Dave's Hopper #8–10, Adams Irresistible #10–14, Yellow Gurgler #4, Ant #12, Olive Gaines Popper #8.
Nymphs: Olive or Prince Aggravator #6, Black AP #10–14, Gold Beaded Poopah #14, Dragonfly #6, Zug Bug #10, Prince Nymph #10–12, Rubber Legs #4–6.
Streamers: Polar Shrimp #6, Brindle Bug or Silver Hilton #6–10, Boss #4–10, Gold Comet #6, Glo Bug #4–8, Muddler Minnow #6, Softshell Crayfish #8, various hot colored Bead-Eye Shad patterns #6, Babine Special #6, Orange General Practitioner #2, Boss and Flame Boss #2–6, Copper Train #2, Poxyback Crayfish #8, Krystal Rubber Bugger #8.

Season & Limits

Special regulations apply. Generally Russian River main stem below the confluence of the east branch, open all year, barbless hooks, special limits of two hatchery fish only. Other restrictions include within 250 feet of the Healdsburg Memorial Dam closed all year. Consult the California Department of Fish & Game booklet.

Accommodations & Services

Lodging, gas, groceries, and some fly fishing supplies are available in Jenner, Duncan Mills, Monte Rio, Guerneville, Healdsburg, and Cloverdale. Camping is best at Armstrong Redwoods State Reserve.

Rating

For now, a 5.5, but if the rain and water flows are consistent and the fish get past the sea lions, the rating could improve.

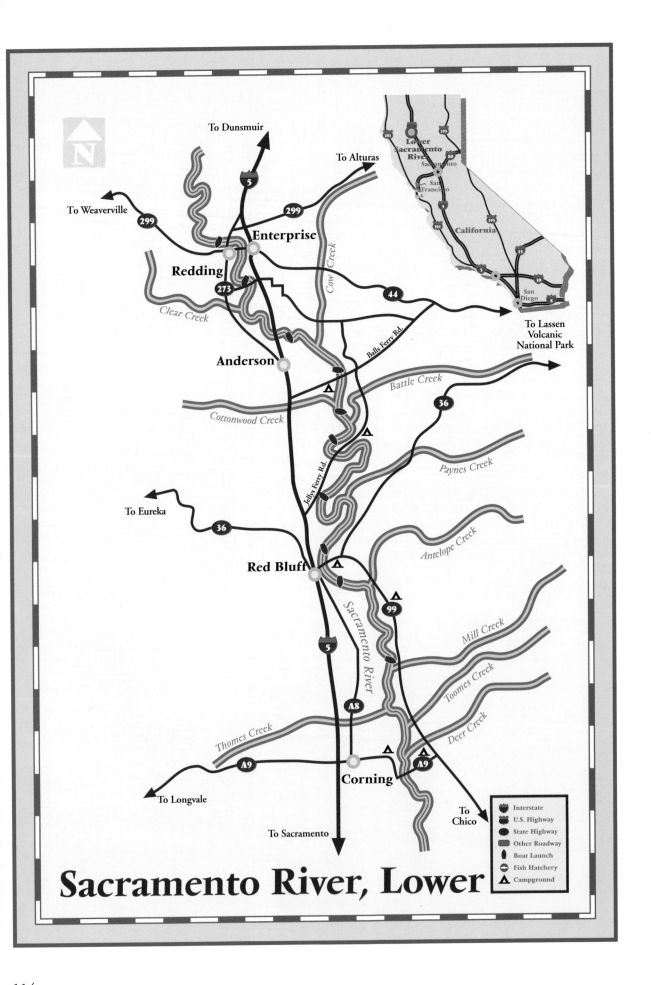

Sacramento River, Lower

Sacramento River
Lower

The fly fishing community recognizes "the Sac" from Lake Shasta to Sacramento as the "lower river." In this section, we target the prime territory from Redding to Red Bluff, a stretch offering big water and big fish. The wide and sweeping river runs over huge gravel bars and shallow riffles and through deep pools.

Flows are affected by weather and controlled releases. Typically, the water runs around 2,800 cfs (cubic feet per second) but can be boosted to well more than 10,000 cfs during the summer season. Call the Bureau of Reclamation's 24-hour recording, (530) 246-7594, to see if it's worth making the trip. High, roaring waters usually make the fly game a very tough proposition. Most guides say flows from 3,000 to 7,000 cfs are fishable.

Now for the good news: caddis hatches on this river are incredible. Clouds of insects take flight throughout the midday hours. Dry fly action can be tremendous. Nymphing the riffles is a solid approach during non-hatch periods. Salmon begin to run the river in the fall, and steelhead are right behind. For salmon, use bright-colored streamers. In fact, some of your shad flies will work just fine for this application. For steelies, try egg patterns and streamers.

Reach the Lower Sac by driving north or south on Interstate 5. At either Redding or Red Bluff, take surface roads directly to the river's edge. As a gauge for highway travel, from San Francisco to Redding is around 220 miles. From the Oregon border to Redding is approximately 120 miles.

Valley shad. Photo by Ken Hanley.

Types of Fish
King salmon (chinook), steelhead, rainbow trout, shad, and striped bass.

Known Hatches
March through May: Caddis (Hydropsyche & Brachycentrus) prime time.
Spring and Fall: Caddis.
Summer: Midge, little yellow stone, caddis.
September and October: Mayfly (Baetis), October caddis.

Equipment
Rods: 5–8 weight, 8–10 feet in length. Spey rods are popular here.
Reels: Standard drag systems with lots of backing.
Lines: WF Floating, sink tip type-4, modified sink tips from 130 to 250 grains, or sinking shooting heads type-4 and type-6.
Leaders: 0X to 7X, 6–12 feet in length.
Wading: Chest-high waders, studded boots, and a wading staff. The river is best fished from a boat if possible.

Flies to Use
Dries: Tan Elk Hair Caddis #12, Yellow Humpy #12–16, Black Ant #12–14, Parachute Adams #14, Burk's CDC Stone #14.
Nymphs: Bird's Nest #12, Pulsating Caddis #12–14, Fox's Poopah #14, Hare's Ear #10–16, Aggravator #12, Bead October Poopah #8, Z-Wing Caddis Emerger #12–16, Hunched Back Infrequens #18.
Streamers: Black and Olive Krystal Woolly Buggers #6, Muddler Minnow #2, Olive Clouser Minnow #6, Shad patterns #6, Single Egg #6, Mercer's Sac Fry #12, Hot Flash Minnow #6, Sea Habit Bucktail (White Knight) #2–1/0.

When to Fish
Rainbow Trout: March through November 15. Prime time is March to April and October.
Steelhead: September through March, the prime window is January through March.
Salmon: Fall.
Striped Bass: Summer.
American Shad: May through July.

Seasons & Limits
Fairly complicated restrictions on tackle and harvest apply throughout the river system. Refer to the current regulations booklet, and we recommend call a fly shop or the Department of Fish & Game to confirm conditions and restrictions.

Accommodations & Services
Lodging and supplies are available in Redding or Red Bluff. Camping is in the Red Bluff area. There are eight launch ramps, some of which charge a fee.

Rating
This is a world-class fishery to my mind. With great options and excellent game fish, overall it's nothing short of an 8.

Lower Sac anglers and steelhead.
Photos by John Sherman.

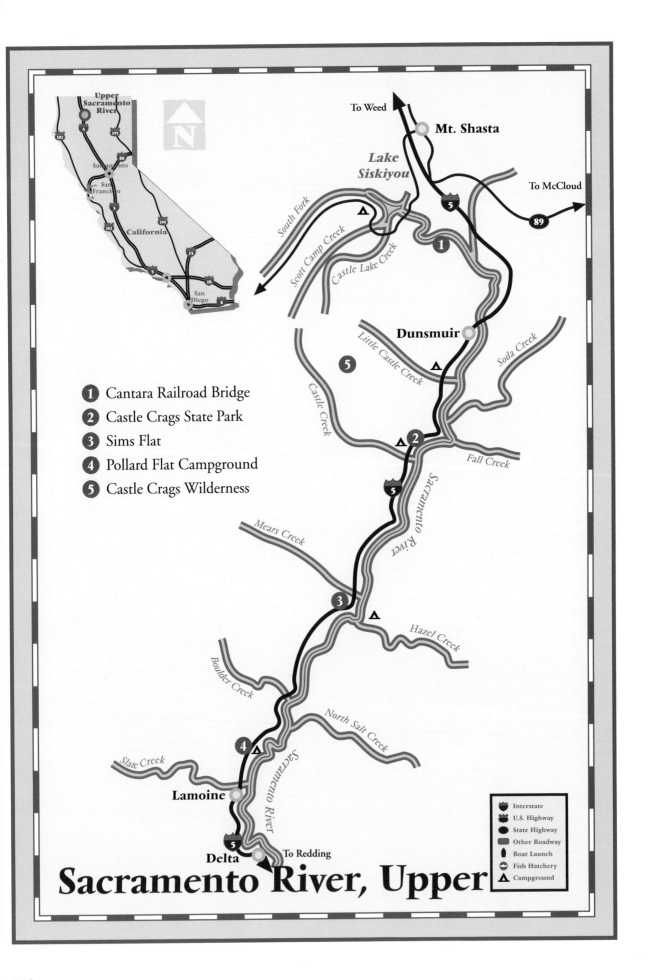

1 Cantara Railroad Bridge
2 Castle Crags State Park
3 Sims Flat
4 Pollard Flat Campground
5 Castle Crags Wilderness

Sacramento River, Upper

Interstate
U.S. Highway
State Highway
Other Roadway
Boat Launch
Fish Hatchery
Campground

To Weed
Mt. Shasta
Lake Siskiyou
To McCloud
89
South Fork
Scott Camp Creek
Castle Lake Creek
Dunsmuir
Soda Creek
Little Castle Creek
Castle Creek
Fall Creek
Sacramento River
Mears Creek
Hazel Creek
Boulder Creek
North Salt Creek
Slate Creek
Lamoine
Sacramento River
Delta
To Redding

Upper Sacramento River
California
Sacramento
San Francisco
San Diego

Sacramento River
Upper

This section, the granddaddy of northern California fly fishing rivers, is gorgeous in all respects. It provides a world-class experience almost every time. You must give this fishery a try. Believe me, it's worth it.

On July 14, 1991, a railroad tanker crashed and spilled 19,000 gallons of toxins into the river. Nearly all the fish and the supporting food chain died as a result. Don't be dismayed, however, time has been on our side. Nature's ability to recover and adapt has been nothing short of miraculous! Many in the fly fishing community believe that this fishery is actually better today than it was prior to the accident. Yes, it's a wonder, and you can now enjoy amazing, high-quality action for beautiful trout.

The uppermost section, above Sims Flat, has classic pocket water. The trout are consistently larger than before the spill. Ted Fay, a legend in these parts, was responsible for popularizing the "two-fly short-line nymphing technique" that's so successful along the river. Ask at a nearby shop if you have questions about this setup.

Walk the lower stretch, below Sims Flat to the Lamoine area, and you'll find a mixture of trout and aggressive smallmouth bass. I love this bass show! I stress walk, by the way. With little effort you'll find plenty of open water and casting room. Anywhere you fish the Upper Sac you'll find easy streamside access. The interstate and many surface roads run right next to or near the river.

Interstate 5 is the state's central artery and the way, north or south, to access this waterway. Nearly any exit provides access, but be prepared for some unimproved dirt roads. Parking areas are generally small, so be flexible.

The road follows this gorgeous river its entire distance.
Photo by Pete Chadwell.

Types of Fish
Rainbow and brown trout, smallmouth bass.

Known Hatches
May & June: Little yellow stone, green drake.
October & November: October caddis, midge.
All Year: Caddis (Hydropsyche, Rhyacophilia), PMD and pale evening dun mayflies.

Equipment to Use
Rods: 4–6 weight, 8–9½ feet in length.
Reels: Standard drag systems.
Lines: WF floating, sink tip type-2 or -4.
Leaders: 3X to 6X, 6–12 feet in length.
Wading: Chest-high waders, studded boots, and a wading staff.

Flies for Use
Dries: Light Cahill #14, Parachute Adams and Hare's Ear #14–16, Elk Hair Caddis #14–16, Royal Trude #14, Gold Stimulator #8, Dave's Hopper #8, Yellow or Orange Humpy #12, Black Ant #12–14.
Nymphs: Fox's Poopah #14, Olive or Tan Glasstail Caddis Pupa #14, October Poopah #8, Hunched Back Infrequens #14–18, Poxyback PMD #16, Black AP #12–14, Poxyquill #18–20, Poxyback Golden Stone #10, Poxyback Green Drake #12.
Streamers: Olive Matuka Sculpin #2, Bullet Head #6, Clouser Minnow #6, Poxyback Crayfish #4–8.

When to Fish
May and mid-September through mid-November are great, though the fishing continues all season.

Seasons & Limits
River management is constantly being reevaluated, and restrictions on tackle, access, and harvest exist. Stay in contact with local fly shops and the Department of Fish & Game to be sure what's in effect.

Accommodations & Services
Find lodging and supplies in Dunsmuir, Castella, Lakehead, and the town of Mt. Shasta. Camping is good at Castle Crags State Park, Railroad Park, and Sims Flat.

Rating
Absolutely one of the best in the West (or anywhere, for that matter)! Rates a solid 9.

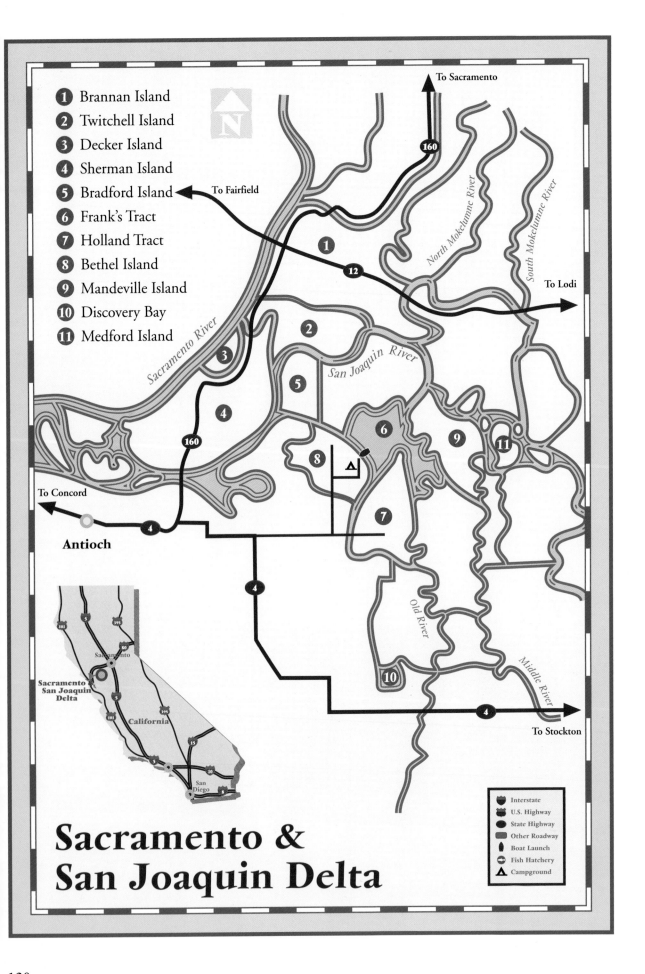

1. Brannan Island
2. Twitchell Island
3. Decker Island
4. Sherman Island
5. Bradford Island
6. Frank's Tract
7. Holland Tract
8. Bethel Island
9. Mandeville Island
10. Discovery Bay
11. Medford Island

To Sacramento

To Fairfield

North Mokelumne River

South Mokelumne River

To Lodi

Sacramento River

San Joaquin River

To Concord

Antioch

Old River

Middle River

To Stockton

Sacramento
San Joaquin
Delta

California

Sacramento

San Diego

Interstate
U.S. Highway
State Highway
Other Roadway
Boat Launch
Fish Hatchery
Campground

Sacramento &
San Joaquin Delta

Sacramento & San Joaquin Delta

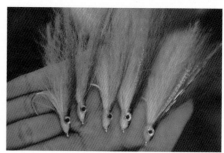
Delta flies. Photo by John Sherman.

During the last 10 years, the Sacramento and San Joaquin delta system has evolved into an amazing fishery for fly rodders. Deep within these braided waterways lies a fly fishing wonderland for the adventurous angler. An unbelievable number of cuts, sloughs, islands, and levees present a smorgasbord of angling locations. The structure and cover range from tule-lined banks to grassy flats and channels and mile after mile of riprap-style rocky banks. Much of the fly fishing game is played in waters from 1 to 25 feet deep. A boat or inflatable is key to finding working game fish. Though you could walk the levees and catch fish, being mobile on the water is a definite advantage.

Striped bass are the reigning champs of the region. Largemouth bass are also on tap, with the occasional king salmon spicing things up. The chance to sight-fish over surface-busting stripers is something everyone should experience at least once in his or her life. The southwest delta region, around Franks Tract in particular, is very consistent with a fly rod. Don't be afraid to explore, however—it pays off to cover lots of water on most outings.

To reach Franks Tract State Recreation Area, take Highway 4 to Antioch and continue past Oakley. Taking Cypress Road to Bethel Road will put you right at Bethel Island. Access from the east will be through Stockton on Highway 4 west past Discovery Bay and Brentwood, and onto Cypress Road.

Types of Fish
Striped and largemouth bass, king salmon, panfish.

Known Hatches & Baitfish
Shiner perch, smelt, sculpin, game fish fry, crayfish, mice, grass shrimp, damselflies, and dragonflies.

Equipment to Use
Rods: 5–10 weight, 8½–10 feet in length.
Reels: Standard drag systems; lots of backing helps.
Lines: Intermediate, sink tip type-4, modified sink tips of 200 to 400 grains, shooting heads type-4, and LC-13.
Leaders: 0X to 3X, 4–9 feet in length.
Wading: It's best to work from a boat or inflatable, yet walking the levees is possible.

Flies to Use
Nymphs: Putnam's Damsel #12, Kaufman's Dragonfly #8.
Streamers: Sea Habit Bucktail (White Knight) #1/0, Tan Flashtail Clouser #1/0–2, Blanton's Flash Tail Whistlers #3/0 (yellow, SPS, all black), Blanton's Sar Mul Mac (Mullet) #3/0, Purple Eelworm #6, Hot Flash Minnow #6, Whitlock Near Nuff Sculpin #6.
Topwater & Subsurface: Gurgler #1/0, Swimming Frog #6, Deer Hair Mouse #6, Loudmouth Shad #6, Gaines Bluegill Popper #12, Sponge Spider #10–12.

When to Fish
Stripers: October through December, prime months are October and November.
Largemouth Bass: All year, prime times are April to May and October to November.
Panfish: All year, prime in summer and early fall.

Seasons & Limits
All-year access. Harvest restrictions apply, so check with local fly shops or consult the Department of Fish & Game booklet.

Accommodations & Services
Camping, public launch ramps, marina, boat rentals, a store, and supplies are available around the delta. Skiffs can be rented at Russo's Marina (Bethel Island) and houseboats at Paradise Point Marina (Stockton).

Rating
I love the wilderness feeling of the Delta. I also love the quality and quantity of game fish. Overall, an easy 7.5 (some might even say a 9).

Delta anglers. Photo by John Sherman.

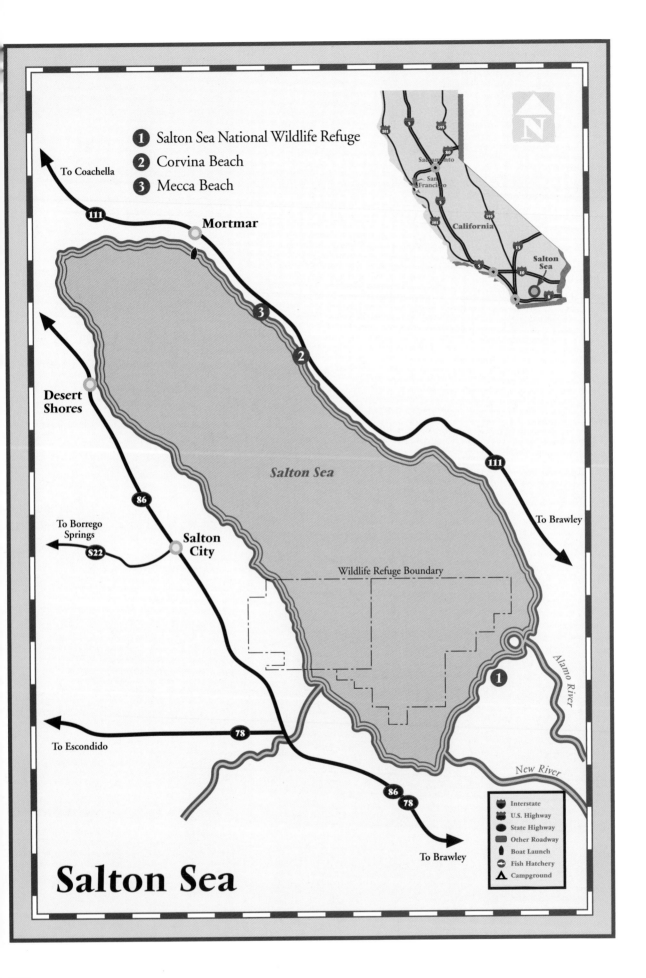

1 Salton Sea National Wildlife Refuge
2 Corvina Beach
3 Mecca Beach

To Coachella

111

Mortmar

N

Sacramento
San Francisco
California
Salton Sea

3

2

Desert Shores

Salton Sea

111

86

To Brawley

To Borrego Springs

Salton City

S22

Wildlife Refuge Boundary

1

Alamo River

To Escondido

78

New River

86
78

To Brawley

Interstate
U.S. Highway
State Highway
Other Roadway
Boat Launch
Fish Hatchery
Campground

Salton Sea

Salton Sea

The Salton Sea is a bizarre fishery, yet it's one you should know about. In fact, it just might end up being one of your favorites. If you're looking for a remote desert location, this is it. If you're looking for expansive flats fishing, you've found it here. Want a shot at catching a 5- to 15-pound corvina? You can do it here. Yes, the Salton Sea offers you a chance to catch saltwater fish in the desert! Bizarre—but a darn fine fly fishing experience nonetheless.

The Salton Sea is 35 miles long, and averages 15 miles wide. Most of the flats fishing occurs in waters of five feet or less in depth. Wade fishing is best around Mecca Beach and Corvina Beach. Boaters, of course, can explore anywhere they desire, particularly deeper waters. These areas can exceed 20 feet in depth and usually hold fish during extreme heat cycles. Electronics are a very useful tool for scouting the open water. The Salton Sea is typically off-colored; in fact, it's like French roast coffee! There isn't much chance of sight-fishing this location. It's to your advantage to watch for diving birds, explore any scum lines, look for color breaks, and be willing to cast, cast, cast.

Corvina like high water temperatures—the hotter the better in this case. Days when you find the surface temperature exceeding 90 degrees can produce aggressive feeding sessions. This isn't a fishery for the faint of heart. Exposure to extreme weather is a fact of life in the desert. Stay hydrated! Stay covered! Be well prepared to handle any emergency situation (particularly heat stroke or exhaustion).

To reach this unique fishery, head east out of Los Angeles on Interstate 10 to Indio. Then go south on Highway 111, which brings you to the east shoreline access. To explore the western shore you'll need to exit Highway 111 onto Highway 86 (heading south), which takes you directly to the lake.

Types of Fish
Orangemouth corvina, tilapia, croaker, and sargo.

Known Baitfish
Game fish fry and shrimp.

Equipment to Use
Rods: 7–9 weight, 8–10 feet in length.
Reels: Standard drag systems—having lots of backing is a plus around here.
Lines: Intermediate, sink tip type-4, modified sink tips 130 to 200 grains, shooting heads type-4 and type-6.
Leaders: 0X to 3X, 4–9 feet in length.
Wading: Best worked from a boat but wading is possible.

Flies to Use
Streamers: Chartreuse Flashtail Clouser #2/0–#2, Blanton's Flash Tail Whistler #3/0–4/0 (yellow/red), Llamahair Baitfish #1/0 (orange/yellow), ALF Baitfish #1/0–2, Red/Brown Woolly Bugger #2.
Topwater & Subsurface: Gurgler #1/0, Chartreuse Wiggle Bug #2.

When to Fish
All year, prime times are fall and spring.

Seasons & Limits
Twenty-four-hour access year-round. Harvest restrictions apply. Check the California Department of Fish & Game booklet.

Accommodations & Services
Camping and marinas are available around Indio. Lodging and supplies are in Niland and Westmorland. Find launch ramps at Bombay Beach Marina, Bob's Riviera, Desert Shores, Imperial County Park, Red Hill Marina, and Salton Sea State Recreation Area.

Rating
At least a 7. Keep in mind that the wind can be monstrous out here in any season.

The coastline surrounding the Salton Sea has little vegetation. Photo by Howard Fisher.

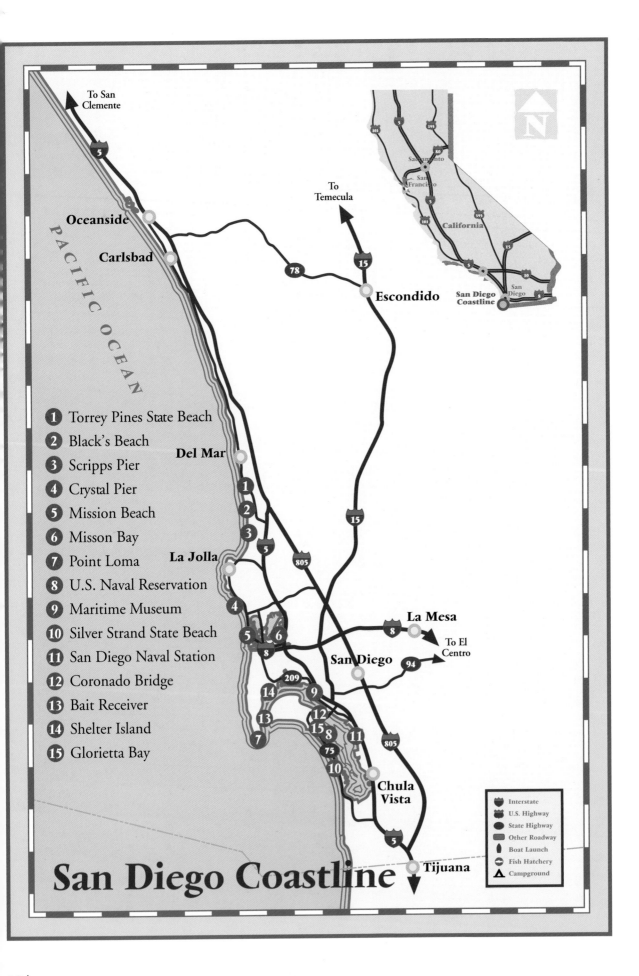

San Diego Coastline

1. Torrey Pines State Beach
2. Black's Beach
3. Scripps Pier
4. Crystal Pier
5. Mission Beach
6. Misson Bay
7. Point Loma
8. U.S. Naval Reservation
9. Maritime Museum
10. Silver Strand State Beach
11. San Diego Naval Station
12. Coronado Bridge
13. Bait Receiver
14. Shelter Island
15. Glorietta Bay

Oceanside
Carlsbad
Del Mar
La Jolla
Escondido
La Mesa
San Diego
Chula Vista
Tijuana

To San Clemente
To Temecula
To El Centro

PACIFIC OCEAN

California

Interstate
U.S. Highway
State Highway
Other Roadway
Boat Launch
Fish Hatchery
Campground

N

San Diego Coastline

by Jeff Solis

The San Diego coast stretches from Oceanside down to the Mexican border. For the surf-fishing enthusiast, the beaches of this gorgeous coastline offer numerous jetties, rock outcroppings, lagoons, and other fish-attracting places to cast a fly rod.

San Diego County beaches fish the best on an incoming tide, but you will probably be successful any time there is tidal movement. Most of these beaches are gradually sloping, so wading is not too tough. However, for your safety, do not wade in over your knees.

Generally, fish hold close to shore, but a relatively stiff nine-footer is still the rod of choice, especially when fighting coastal breezes. When sight casting to corbina, a floating line sometimes works, but generally stick to using subsurface lines such as shooting heads or full sink lines with a short leader tapered down to 3X or 4X. A multitude of specialty surf fly shops have recently opened in the area, so stop in for the latest information as well as several hot patterns.

Although a large city looms nearby, you can still find relatively low-traffic beaches all along the San Diego coast even during the summer. This is a great place to bring the family. They can enjoy the beach while you spend the day soaking flies with the long rod. Here are some highlighted areas to try.

San Diego Bay borders downtown and the airport. Photos by John Sherman.

Mission Bay

Located near downtown San Diego and not far from one of the city's most popular attractions, Sea World, Mission Bay has many access points, is not too deep and is easy to fish with a fly rod. Cast near boat docks, jetties, pilings, and drop-offs with sinking lines and Clouser-type minnows. Retrieves should be slow and animated. The slow-moving back bays have little boat traffic and are great places for wading and night float tubing (use streamers). Try fishing fast and steady retrieves at the unlikely looking Bait Receiver. This large raft in the basin is where sport fishing boats load live bait.

San Diego Bay

This is Southern California's number-one bay in terms of fly fishing availability and masses of quality game fish. There are many access points from the mainland, or you can cross the Coronado toll bridge and fish Silver Strand State Beach. Some weekends it seems like almost all of the two million San Diegans are on this bay. Weekday fly fishing tends to be more productive and quieter. Deep bottom channels create underwater ledges and drop-offs that are home to game fish. Concentrate on these cuts, which are mostly accessible by boat or float tube. Slow drifts with slow retrieves produce jolting strikes! Use sinking lines and weighted streamer patterns.

Imperial Beach & Coronado Island

You'll find quiet stretches of beach where you can do a little fishing without the usual clutter of anglers. The beaches tend to be flat during low tide, but steepen dramatically as the tide rises. Use care when wading and remember the rule of never wading deeper than your knees. Slowly walk these beaches and cast into likely looking spots such as rips, deep slots, holes, breakwaters, and pier pilings. Try eight to ten casts and then move on. Use a shooting head line with a bonefish or Clouser Minnow fly. Mornings often have the best fishing, though the wind comes on strong early. As compensation, croaker and corbina get chased less here than on other beaches.

Working the tides off Coronado Island.
Photo by John Sherman.

Types of Fish
Corbina, croaker, barred surfperch, halibut, and mackerel.

Known Baitfish
Mole crabs, shrimp, anchovies, sardines, and perch fry.

Equipment to Use
Rods: 9 feet in length, 5–9 weight.
Reels: Corrosion-resistant disk.
Lines: Sink tip or full sink lines and shooting heads.
Leaders: 4–9 feet in length, 0X to 5X.
Wading: Chest waders all year except July through September. Float tube/flats, booties or tennis shoes are adequate.

Flies to Use
Streamers & Poppers: Mole Crab #2–6, Clouser Minnow #1/0–6, Deceiver #2/0–4, Crazy Charlie #2–6, Alf #3/0–2, and Bonefish Biters #8.

When to Fish
Early or late, when the light is low, during an incoming tide is generally best, but specific beaches have their own optimal times. So get out and fish!

Seasons & Limits
Season is open year-round. Halibut must be 22 inches to keep, but check local regulations for other limits and restrictions.

Nearby Fly Fishing
Oceanside Harbor.

Accommodations & Services
Hotels, motels, launch ramps, stores, and restaurants abound up and down the San Diego coast.

Rating
The San Diego coast rates a solid 9 in my book.

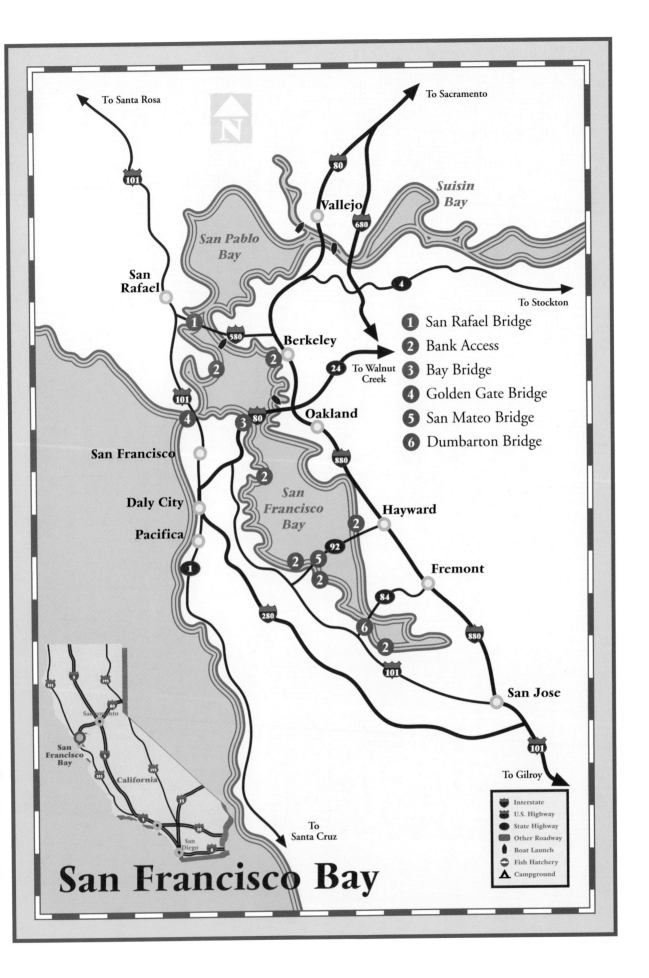

San Francisco Bay

To Santa Rosa

To Sacramento

N

Suisin Bay

San Pablo Bay

Vallejo

San Rafael

Berkeley

To Walnut Creek

To Stockton

1 San Rafael Bridge
2 Bank Access
3 Bay Bridge
4 Golden Gate Bridge
5 San Mateo Bridge
6 Dumbarton Bridge

Oakland

San Francisco

San Francisco Bay

Daly City

Pacifica

Hayward

Fremont

San Jose

To Gilroy

To Santa Cruz

Interstate
U.S. Highway
State Highway
Other Roadway
Boat Launch
Fish Hatchery
Campground

California

Sacramento

San Francisco Bay

San Diego

San Francisco Bay

Home, sweet home—an incredible place to explore. The good news is that San Francisco Bay is getting better for fly rods every year! This is the inland sea of northern California, and it's virtually untapped when it comes to our sport, though there has been an increase in the number of guides who diligently work on learning the intricacies of this vast habitat. A core group of dedicated fly fishers have expanded everyone's understanding of the striped bass and halibut fisheries around these parts. It's a great adventure with ample rewards.

One of the key successes to any outing is coordinating your outing with the tide cycle. The best potential occurs during periods of moving water. If you're working any shallow mudflats, the second half of the flooding tide is excellent. Positioning yourself on the outer edge, near deeper water, is always a good idea during outgoing tides. The tidal shifts and resulting currents stir the baitfish and food chain, creating a more aggressive feeding session for the top-end predators that patrol the bay.

Boating undoubtedly provides the most efficient access. Red Rock, The Sisters, China Camp Basin, and Candlestick Point are just a few of the favorite spots to hit. Bank anglers can have some great sessions during the night, particularly for surface-feeding stripers. Please note that it's illegal to fish at night from any floating device, such as a boat or raft. Check the foot access around the San Mateo, Burlingame, Berkeley, Sausalito, Milpitas, and Hayward areas.

San Francisco Bay has an average depth of about 20 feet, with large tracts of mudflats that average less than 10 feet deep. Most of the bay system is well within the limits of fly tackle, with a few exceptions, notably the shipping lanes. These deep waters aren't fly-fishing-friendly and should be avoided for boating safety as well.

Here Dan Blanton has a fish on. Photo by Ken Hanley.

Types of Fish
Striped bass, halibut, leopard shark, smelt, and perch.

Known Hatches & Baitfish
Shiner perch, smelt, anchovy, grass shrimp, crabs, marine worms.

Equipment to Use
Rods: 8–10 weight, 8½–10 feet in length.
Reels: I prefer large arbor and disk drag designs; lots of backing is helpful.
Lines: Intermediate, sink tip type-4, modified sink tips of 200 to 400 grains, shooting heads type-4 and LC-13.
Leaders: 0X to 3X, 4–9 feet in length.
Wading: The bay is best worked by boat, though walking the shoreline is possible.

Flies to Use
Streamers: Sea Habit Bucktail (White Knight) #1/0, Tan Flashtail Clouser #1/0–2, Blanton's Flash Tail Whistlers #3/0 (red/white, SPS, all black), Blanton's Sar Mul Mac Anchovy #3/0, Yellow Lefty's Deceiver #3/0, Popovic's Surf Candy #2, ALF Baitfish #2.
Topwater & Subsurface: Gurgler #1/0 –3/0, Crystal Popper #2/0.

When to Fish
Stripers: March through December, prime months are August through November.
Halibut: June through September, prime time is June through August.
Shark: All year, prime in spring/early fall.
Smelt & Perch: All year.

Seasons & Limits
Somewhat confusing access, tackle, and harvest restrictions apply. Be sure to consult a local tackle shop or current Department of Fish & Game regulations booklet.

Accommodations & Services
Supplies and lodging are available throughout the Bay Area. Public launch ramps and marinas are best in the San Rafael, Sausalito, Richmond, Berkeley, and San Mateo areas.

Rating
This place is the real deal. Great adventure, lots of fish, and a very convenient locationadd up to a solid 7.

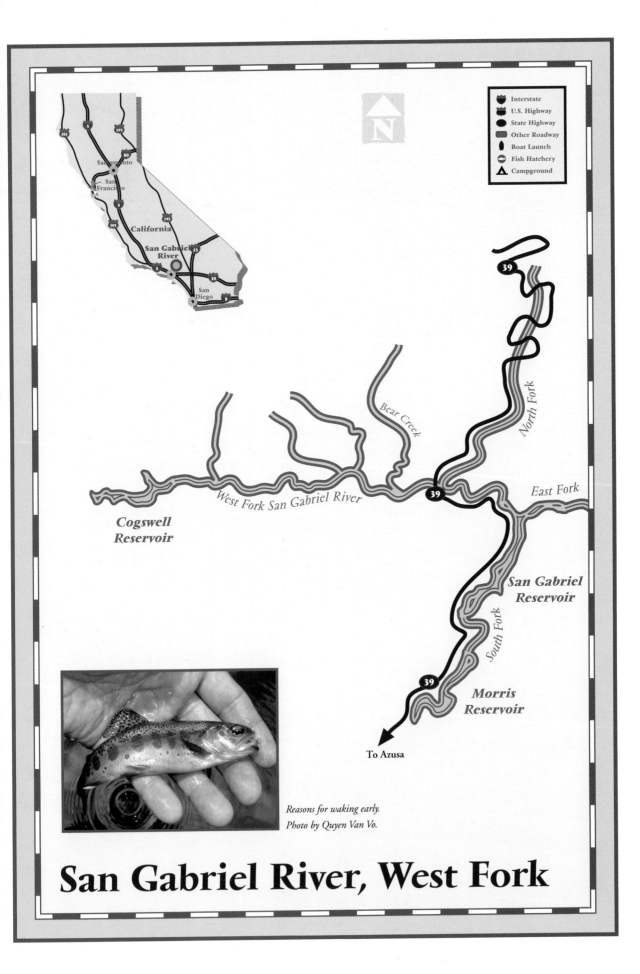

Interstate
U.S. Highway
State Highway
Other Roadway
Boat Launch
Fish Hatchery
Campground

California

San Gabriel
River

Sacramento

San
Francisco

San
Diego

39

Bear Creek

North Fork

East Fork

39

West Fork San Gabriel River

**Cogswell
Reservoir**

**San Gabriel
Reservoir**

South Fork

39

**Morris
Reservoir**

To Azusa

Reasons for waking early.
Photo by Quyen Van Vo.

San Gabriel River, West Fork

San Gabriel River
West Fork
by Jeff Solis

The West Fork of the San Gabriel River is a wonderful little trout stream located just 30 miles northeast of downtown Los Angeles. While it is not open to vehicles, a paved road paralleling the river offers anglers easy access by foot or mountain bike.

Flowing from Cogswell Reservoir, the San Gabriel is a tailwater fishery that boasts many trout per mile. Its narrow streambed consists of a succession of pools, riffles, runs, and pocket waters. In short, this is a classic Southern California trout stream.

Most anglers prefer to fish the San Gabriel with a dry fly or a dry fly with a nymph dropper, but a well-drifted nymph is also very effective, especially during the midday heat of summer when trout are holding deep.

To reach the San Gabriel, travel northeast out of Los Angeles on Interstate 210 to Azusa. Head north on Highway 39 past the Rincon Fire Station until you reach the parking area. Parking is available with a permit. There are not a lot of big trout in the San Gabriel, but it won't take you three days to get there either. What a great place to spend your day off!

Photo by Howard Fisher.

Types of Fish
Rainbow and brown trout.

Known Hatches
Blue-winged olives, tricos, caddis, and midges.

Equipment to Use
Rods: 7–9 feet in length, 2–6 weight.
Reels: Standard click or disk.
Lines: WF or double-taper floating.
Leaders: 7½–12 feet in length, 4X to 7X.
Wading: Waders are not needed here. Most people just wet-wade in their hiking boots.

Flies to Use
Dries: Parachute Baetis #16–20, BWO Comparadun #16–20, Parachute Adams #16–20, Adams #16–20, Elk Hair Caddis #16–18, Stimulator #16–18, Griffith's Gnat #20–24, and Black Midge #20–24.
Nymphs: Beadhead Hare's Ear #14–18, Beadhead Prince Nymph #14–18, Beadhead PT #14–18, Brassie #18–22, Disco Midge #18–22, and Miracle Nymph #18–22.

Seasons & Limits
Open year-round, one hour before sunrise until one hour after sunset. Catch and release only.

Nearby Fly Fishing
East and Main forks of the San Gabriel, and Bear Creek.

Accommodations & Services
Call the Mount Baldy Ranger Station (818) 335-1251 with questions.

Rating
The West Fork of the San Gabriel River rates a solid 8.

A tranquil day on the West Fork. Photo by Quyen Van Vo.

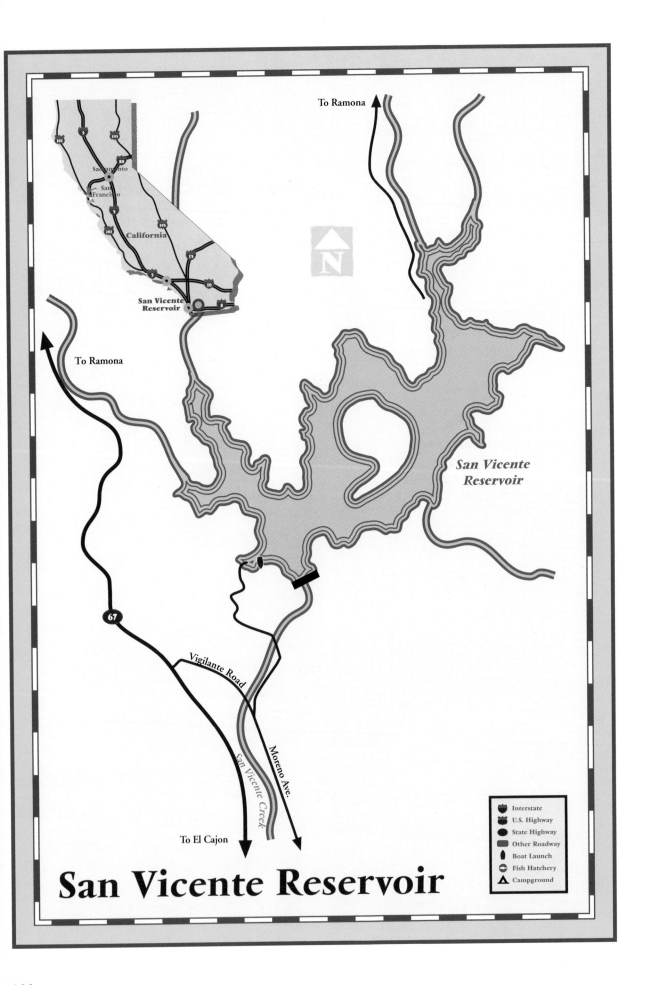

To Ramona

To Ramona

San Vicente
Reservoir

California

San Vicente
Reservoir

67

Vigilante Road

Moreno Ave.

San Vicente Creek

To El Cajon

Interstate
U.S. Highway
State Highway
Other Roadway
Boat Launch
Fish Hatchery
Campground

San Vicente Reservoir

San Vicente Reservoir

by Bob Zeller

I f you have the afternoon off after a morning meeting, check out the black bass fishing at San Vicente Reservoir. In the cool-weather months you can also fly fish for stocked trout. This 1,070-acre lake will challenge almost any angler and is one of nine the city of San Diego manages for freshwater fly fishing. San Vicente Reservoir is known primarily for its big 16-pound bass, two- to three-pound Florida bluegill, and crappie. A sample of records on a day in May when I was there included an 11.8-pound black bass, a 3.2-pound crappie, a 6.2-pound rainbow, and a 15-pound catfish. Not bad.

I had intended to rent a rowboat to exercise my airplane-weary muscles while fishing for bass near shore. The locals, however, recommended the deep water off Goat Island, in the middle of the lake. You might be able to row there and back before sundown, but I can't and still have fishing time. So, tight though I am, I shelled out an extra $12 and put a motor on my rental boat.

For San Vicente bass, a high-density, shooting head fly line and plastic grubs (the kinds the locals use) passes for well equipped. Leave most of your topwater bugs at home and use sinking lines and weighted nymphs and streamers to imitate crayfish, minnows, leeches, frogs, and shiners. For trout, match the callibaetis, midges, and damselflies during the put-and-take season.

I dropped anchor just off the island and cast. Soon the wind forced me to more secluded spots. You'd think the back side—or some side—of an island would be protected from the wind, but it blew everywhere, and fly fishing was not to be that day. I mention this to remind you that there will be days like this, so keep your expectations realistic and enjoy the outing. Windy days are good opportunities to scout for future fly fishing excursions.

Wind or not, you will like the drive to San Vicente Reservoir. To get to the reservoir, go east on Interstate 8 to El Cajon. Take Highway 67 north. Turn right on Vigilante Road, then take a left toward the reservoir.

Type of Fish
Largemouth bass, trout, bluegill, crappie, channel catfish.

Equipment to Use
Rods: 4–8 weight, 8½–9 feet in length.
Reels: Click or disk drag.
Lines: Floating, sink tip, or full weight.
Leaders: Bass 1X to 4X, 5–10 feet in length. Trout 5X to 7X, 7½–9 feet in length.
Wading: Some shore angling is possible, but it's best to rent a boat or bring a float tube. Look for rocky shoreline areas.

Flies to Use
Dries: Callibaetis #14–18, Adams #12–18, Midge Adult and Emerger #16–22.
Nymphs: Damsel #12–14, Prince #10–12, Pheasant Tail and Hare's Ear #10–18.
Streamers & Poppers: Krystal Buggers #4–10, Clouser Minnows #6–2/0, Alf #2–4/0, various Poppers #2/0–4/0, Wiggle Bugs #6–2/0.

When to Fish
Bass: Best April through September, A.M. and P.M.
Trout: November through May, January through April are prime.
Bluegill: June through September.
Crappie: Year-round.

Seasons & Limits
Days of operation and limits are subject to change. Consult San Diego City Lakes, (619) 465-3474.

Accommodations & Services
Ramp, boat rentals, snacks, and supplies are at the lake and in Lakeside. Hotels are all along Interstate 8. Everything you need is in El Cajon.

Rating
For all-around fishing, a 7.5.

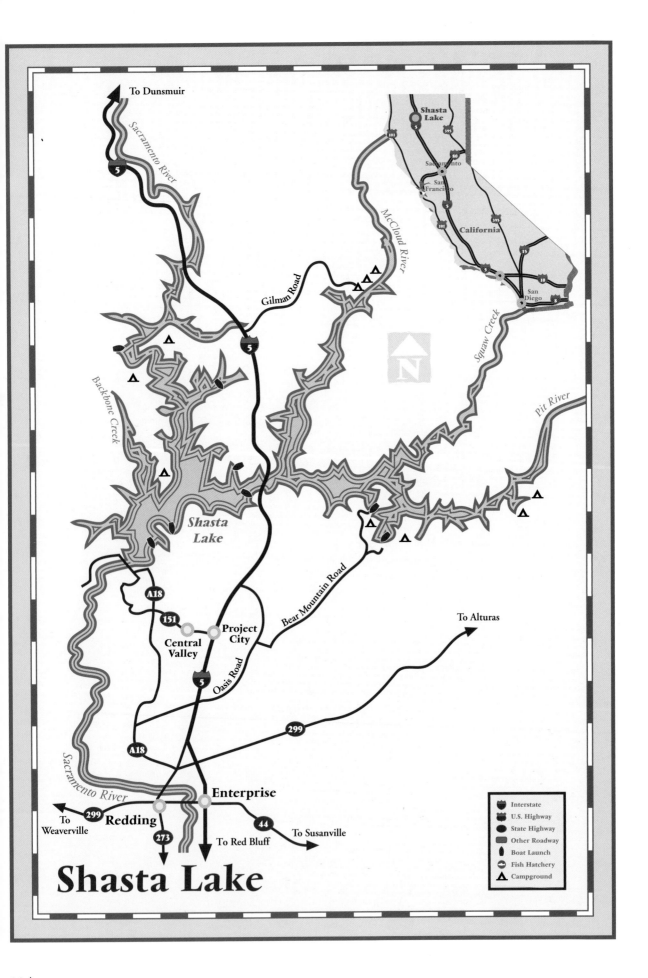

To Dunsmuir

Sacramento River

McCloud River

Shasta
Lake

Squaw Creek

California

San Diego

Gilman Road

Pit River

Backbone Creek

Shasta
Lake

A18

151

Central
Valley

Project
City

Bear Mountain Road

To Alturas

Oasis Road

299

A18

Sacramento River

Enterprise

299

To
Weaverville

Redding

273

To Red Bluff

44

To Susanville

Shasta Lake

Interstate	
U.S. Highway	
State Highway	
Other Roadway	
Boat Launch	
Fish Hatchery	
Campground	

Shasta Lake

This could be one of the best fisheries in the entire state! It's loaded with spotted and largemouth bass, trout, and crappie. The place is immense, with more than 365 miles of shoreline and 29,000 acres of surface water covering four huge river canyons. It's hard to imagine the magnitude of all this habitat for fly fishing but, hey, it works just fine!

Shasta is all about steep banks, deep banks, small coves, rocky points, and submerged timber. It's the perfect environment for healthy populations of bass and trout. Don't forget to work along the face of the dam as well. Upwelling provides consistent food supplies for aggressive game fish.

Be prepared to cover lots of water any time you fish Shasta. The main arms provide the best fly rod opportunities: The Backbone Creek, Pit, Sacramento, and McCloud Rivers and Squaw Creek areas can be fantastic. The central lake is more than 500 feet deep; it's just too vast to be a high-percentage zone for flies.

Early spring and early fall are the premier months for mixed-bag bass and trout. Fish are frequently found near the surface at this time. In the summer you'll find trout hanging around the mouths of tributaries. Large schools of crappie are around submerged timber, especially in the Pit River arm.

Houseboating is an awesome way to explore this super site. A floating base camp is perfect for launching a float tube or canoe to maximize your access to productive fishing grounds.

Shasta is located a few miles north of the city of Redding and is easily reached via Interstate 5.

Shasta Lake is a huge impoundment receiving flows from Sacramento, McCloud, and Pit rivers as well as major creeks. Photo by Brian Sak.

Types of Fish
Smallmouth, spotted, and largemouth bass; rainbow and brown trout, crappie, and panfish.

Known Hatches & Baitfish
Threadfin shad, game fish fry, crayfish, callibaetis mayflies, various caddis, damselflies, and dragonflies.

Equipment to Use
Rods: 5–8 weight, 8½–10 feet in length.
Reels: Standard drag systems.
Lines: Intermediate, sink tip type-4, modified sink tips of 130 to 200 grains, shooting heads type-4 or type-6, LC-13.
Leaders: 1X to 4X, 6–12 feet in length.
Wading: It's best to work from a boat or inflatable, though wading is possible almost everywhere.

Flies to Use
Nymphs: Putnam's Damsel #12, Kaufman's Dragonfly #8, Poxyback Callibaetis #16, Black Ant #14, Black AP #12, Prince #14.
Streamers: Sea Habit Bucktail #1/0, Flashtail Clouser #1/0–2, Purple Eelworm #6, Burk's V-Worm #10, Hot Flash Minnow #6, Whitlock Near Nuff Sculpin #6, Black Woolly Bugger #4.
Topwater & Subsurface: Gurgler #2, Loudmouth Shad #6, Gaines Bluegill Popper #12, Sponge Spider #10–12, Callibaetis Spinner #16, Elk Hair Caddis #10.

When to Fish
Bass: March through October, prime times are April-May, and September-October.
Trout: Late winter through fall, early spring and early fall are prime.
Crappie & Panfish: April through October, prime in summer.

Seasons & Limits
All-year access. Harvest restrictions apply so check with local fly shops or in the Department of Fish & Game regulations booklet for more exact information.

Accommodations & Services
Supplies, lodging, camping, boat rentals, launches—everything is available lakeside.

Rating
Overall an 8.5!

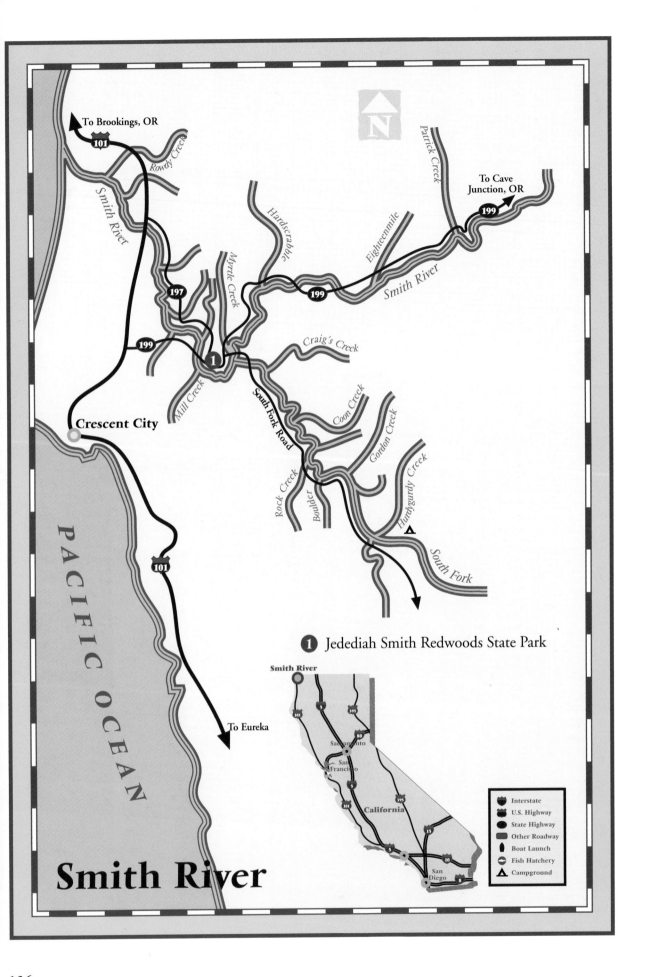

To Brookings, OR

101

Rowdy Creek

Smith River

Hardscrabble

Patrick Creek

To Cave
Junction, OR

199

Eightenmile

197

Myrtle Creek

199

Smith River

199

1

Craig's Creek

Mill Creek

Crescent City

South Fork Road

Coon Creek

Gordon Creek

Hardygurdy Creek

Rock Creek

Boulder

South Fork

101

To Eureka

PACIFIC OCEAN

1 Jedediah Smith Redwoods State Park

Smith River

California

Sacramento
San Francisco
San Diego

Interstate
U.S. Highway
State Highway
Other Roadway
Boat Launch
Fish Hatchery
Campground

Smith River

Smith River

When I think of steelhead rivers, I think of the Smith. I believe it is the single most beautiful coastal river corridor in the West. It certainly rivals the great waterways of the Pacific Northwest and British Columbia. The lush, wild setting is home to wonderful salmon and steelhead populations.

The Smith holds the distinction of being the home of California's record steelhead, a fish that tipped the scales at more than 27 pounds. Large steelies averaging 12 to 18 pounds are found every year in this watershed. If salmon is your game, look no further. The Smith has a world-class run of kings. These terrific beauties weigh in the range of 20 to 50 pounds. Keep in mind, however, nothing comes easily on this river. Expect to make many presentations. Expect to go fishless more often than not. Yet, when everything comes together, expect a very high-quality steelhead and salmon experience. The place is wild and magical indeed.

Given that the Smith is the northernmost coastal fishery of the state, weather—including wind, rain, and mud—can be a determining factor in stream access. One of the pluses of this fishery is its ability to recover rapidly after storm conditions, though.

The river is best explored from a drift boat. Bank access is somewhat limited, and the wading is generally pretty demanding. Studded boots and a staff are a must. Chinook action is best during the early fall season, while steelhead enter the system later in the fall. The winter months definitely offer the strongest population densities for presenting your fly.

Often overlooked but also lots of fun is the local cutthroat fishery. It's the perfect pursuit for light-line aficionados. Sea-run cuts are found throughout the tidal basin and are catchable during the summer season. In addition, the tidal basin harbors surfperch, smelt, and flounder.

The drive is long but worth it. Directions to the region are simple. Take Highway 101 to Crescent City, then take Highway 199 (east) straight to the river. If you prefer to work the estuary environs, take 101 to Fort Dick and follow Morehead Road to Lower Lake Road.

There are many tributaries to the Smith. Photo by Scott Harding.

Types of Fish
King salmon (chinook), steelhead, cutthroat trout.

Known Hatches & Baitfish
The tidal basin is loaded with baitfish, isopods, and shrimp. Upstream, use dark nymphs or spawn-style and attractor patterns.

Equipment to Use
Rods: 7–9 weight, 9–10 feet in length. Spey rods are also showing up.
Reels: I prefer a disk drag and large arbor design for these game fish; be sure to have plenty of backing.
Lines: Primarily sinking styles of 130 to 300 grains, or shooting heads type-4 and type-6, WF floating on occasion.
Leaders: 1X to 3X, 6–9 feet in length.
Wading: Chest-high neoprene waders (or Gore-Tex with appropriate insulating undergarments), studded boots, and wading staff are required. Beware of cold, fast flows and slippery footing.

Flies to Use
Tidewater Area: Screaming Shad Shrimp #6, Joe's Prawn #2, Hot Flash Minnow #6, Olive and White Clouser Minnow #2–6, Gurgler #2.
Main Stream Area: Burlap #4, Silver Hilton #6, Mossback #10, Skunk #4, Copper Train #2, Boss #4–8, Single Egg #6, Mercer's Sac Fry #12, Steelhead Skating Muddler #2.

When to Fish
King Salmon: September to January, prime time is late October through December.
Steelhead: November through April, prime time is November through March.
Cutthroat Trout: Summer months.

Seasons & Limits
This river is subject to low-flow closures and complex restrictions on tackle and harvest also exist. Contact the Department of Fish & Game, or check the regulations for details.

Accommodations & Services
This area is remote. The best camping is at Jedediah Smith Redwoods State Park. There are also a couple of Forest Service campgrounds on Highway 199. Lodging is available near the town of Gasquet, and in Crescent City.

Rating
The Smith is truly a first-rate experience. Outstanding game fish and quality water demand that you handle your gear skillfully. Not for the faint of heart, it rates a big 9 for adventure and rewards!

Spey casting on the Smith River.
Photo by John Sherman.

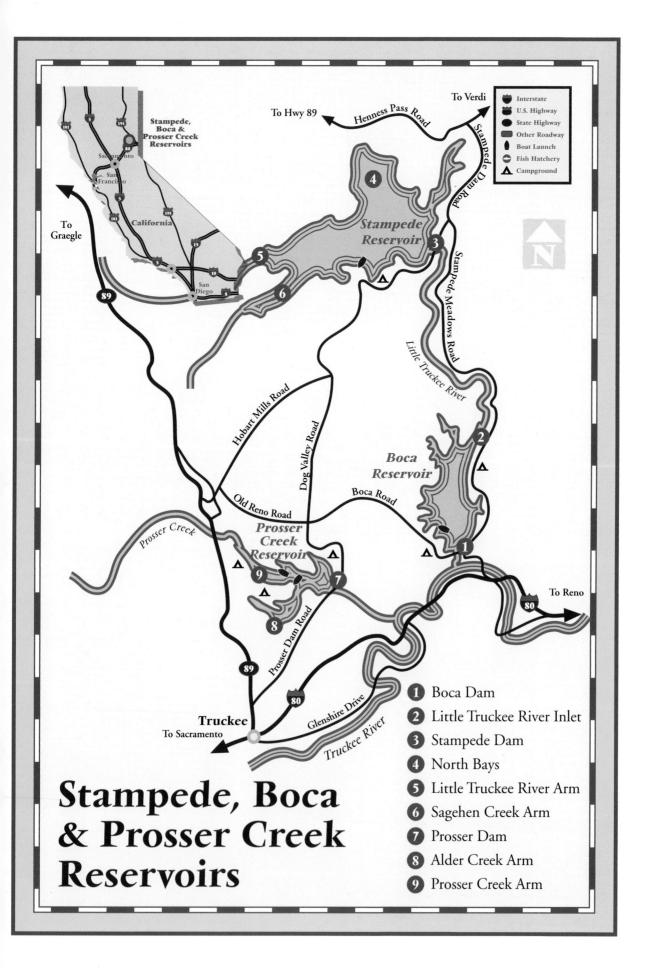

Stampede, Boca & Prosser Creek Reservoirs

Legend:
- Interstate
- U.S. Highway
- State Highway
- Other Roadway
- Boat Launch
- Fish Hatchery
- Campground

1. Boca Dam
2. Little Truckee River Inlet
3. Stampede Dam
4. North Bays
5. Little Truckee River Arm
6. Sagehen Creek Arm
7. Prosser Dam
8. Alder Creek Arm
9. Prosser Creek Arm

Stampede, Boca, & Prosser Creek Reservoirs

by Dave Stanley

These three reservoirs, at 5,800 to 6,000 feet in elevation, were built for water storage on the Truckee River drainage system. They offer more bite-sized alternatives to the nearby giant, Lake Tahoe. Yearly fluctuating water levels, however, can change the fishing conditions. It's not a bad idea to phone the Truckee Ranger District in advance for water levels and conditions: (530) 587-3558. All three reservoirs hold some very large trout and are stocked by the California Department of Fish & Game each year.

The inlets of the streams flowing into these impoundments are by far the most productive areas to fly fish, especially early and late in the season. Shallow flats and weed beds provide trout with food and cover, and should be stalked and probed. Another productive area at each reservoir is along the bases of the dams, especially early in the morning. Big fish cruise these areas looking for baitfish and other prey.

Stampede has a good population of kokanee. These landlocked sockeye salmon offer good sport on a fly rod. In late April and May they can often be found in shallow water (less than 15 feet) and will take a well-presented Blood Midge Larva, small nymph, or leech pattern. In late September the kokanee and brown trout in both Boca and Stampede congregate at the feeder stream mouths in preparation for their spawning runs. This is another good opportunity to take them on a fly. The largest brown trout I have ever seen in this area was taken during the fall spawning period. If you are lucky enough to catch one, take a picture and let it go. It has important work to do upstream.

This fishery is easily accessed from Interstate 80 or off Highway 89 north of Truckee. Because the waters are readily accessible to the Reno/Tahoe populace, solitude can be hard to come by.

Types of Fish
All three lakes hold healthy populations of rainbow and brown trout. Boca and Stampede contain kokanee salmon. Stampede produces an occasional lake trout.

Known Hatches
Midges, callibaetis, and damselflies.

Equipment to Use
Rods: 5–7 weight, 8½–9 feet in length.
Reels: Click or disk drag.
Lines: Floating, intermediate sink, and II and IV full sink lines matched to the rod.
Leaders: Sinking lines, 6–7½ feet in length, 3X to 4X. Floating lines, 9–12 feet in length, 5X to 7X.
Wading: All reservoirs have many areas to wade. Float tubing is popular, though 3,400-acre Stampede is a bit intimidating. Boats are helpful.

Flies to Use
Dries: Midge patterns (particularly the Blood Midge), Callibaetis, Elk Hair Caddis, Parachute Adams, Parachute Hare's Ears, Adult Damsels.
Nymphs: Damsel, Pheasant Tail, Zug Bug, Hare's Ear, Sheep Creek Special, Black Bird's Nest, Blood Midge Larva.
Streamers: Various big streamers, Woolly Buggers, Leeches.

When to Fish
The best times are from ice-out to late June, then from mid-September to the winter freeze.

Seasons & Limits
Open all year with general limits. Consult the California Sport Fishing Regulations or visit a local fly shop for more details.

Accommodations & Services
Everything you could need is about 20 miles away in downtown Reno, Nevada, or 10 miles away in Truckee. There are improved Forest Service campgrounds at all three reservoirs, and a full-service RV park and general store at the United Trails Campground. Take the Boca exit off Interstate 80 for these services.

Rating
Early in the season Prosser Creek and Boca can be a strong 7 or an 8 for the fly fisher. Boca, with all its windsurfers and jet skiers, barely rates a 5 during summer months. Stampede, just after ice-out then in late spring and again in late September and October, earns a solid 8.

An expansive, high-mountain impoundment, Stampede Reservoir drains a vast backcountry. Photo by Don Vachini.

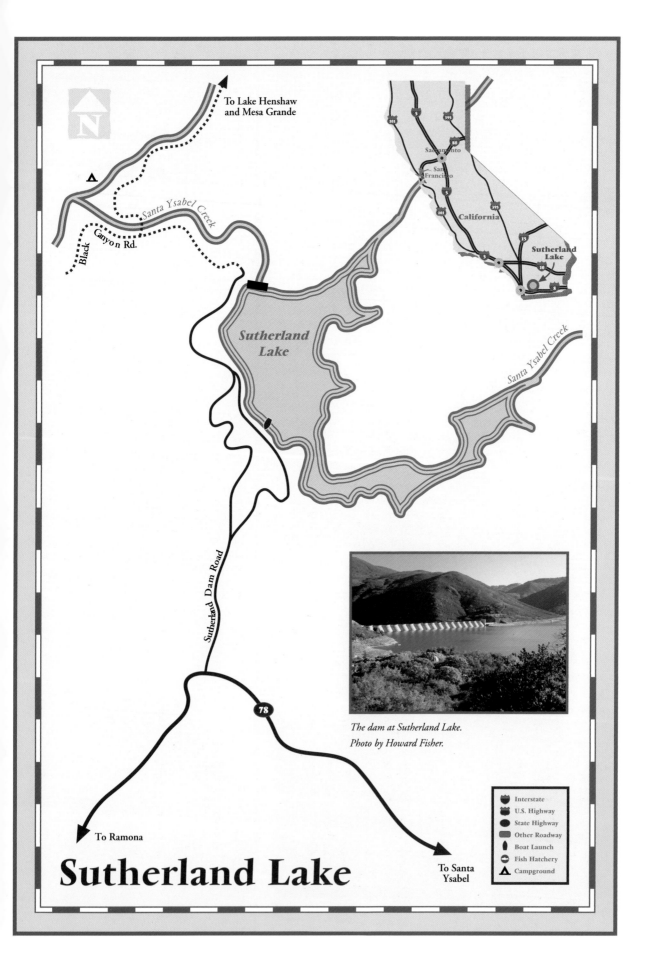

To Lake Henshaw
and Mesa Grande

Santa Ysabel Creek

Black Canyon Rd.

Sutherland Lake

Santa Ysabel Creek

Sutherland Dam Road

78

To Ramona

To Santa Ysabel

Sacramento

San Francisco

California

Sutherland Lake

The dam at Sutherland Lake.
Photo by Howard Fisher.

⬡	Interstate
⬡	U.S. Highway
⬤	State Highway
▭	Other Roadway
⬮	Boat Launch
⬡	Fish Hatchery
△	Campground

Sutherland Lake

Sutherland Lake

by Jeff Solis

R elatively isolated for San Diego County, Sutherland Lake offers anglers good numbers of bass on a decent day, big crappie, and the chance to catch a red-ear sunfish in the three-plus-pound range, all with no traffic noise or housing developments to block the view. If you want good numbers of bass and the chance to cast to three-pound panfish, Lake Sutherland is your spot.

Surrounded by oak- and chaparral-covered hills, Sutherland Lake is a beautiful two-armed lake with lots of points and coves. The water level here can fluctuate from year to year, but the reservoir is usually chock-full of bassy-looking submerged structure along the shoreline.

Like most warmwater lakes, the preferred way to fish Sutherland Lake is by staying close to shore and keeping your casts tight to brush, boulders, and other shoreline structure. A slowly worked leech, minnow, or streamer pattern that matches the lake's golden shiners or shad usually produces lots of strikes.

To reach the reservoir, take Interstate 15 north from San Diego about 25 miles to the Highway 78 exit. Head east on 78 through Ramona, then take the Sutherland Lake turnoff (Sutherland Dam Road) seven miles east of town.

At 2,074 feet in elevation, Sutherland offers 11 miles of shoreline when full. Photo by Howard Fisher.

Types of Fish
Largemouth bass, crappie, bluegill, and red-ear sunfish.

Known Hatches & Baitfish
Santa Ysabel Arm: golden shiners.
Mesa Grande Arm: threadfin shad.

Equipment to Use
Rods: 9 feet in length, 7–8 weight.
Reels: Standard click or disk.
Lines: WF or double-taper floating is all you'll need.
Leaders: 6–9 feet in length, 1X to 3X.
Wading: You can, but this lake is better tubed than waded.

Flies to Use
Nymphs: Carey Special and other dragonfly patterns.
Streamers & Poppers: Dahlberg Diver, Lefty's Deceiver, and an assortment of Clouser Minnows.

When to Fish
Bass seem to wake up early in the day. Surface action is often an afternoon thing.

Seasons & Limits
Closed November through February. The limit for bass is five, and crappie and other panfish have a 25-fish limit. Days and hours of operation may be limited and subject to closure. Consult the City of San Diego Reservoirs and Recreation Program phone (619) 465-3474 for current schedule, or check their web site.

Nearby Fly Fishing
There are green sunfish, bluegill, and bass in the tailwater if you can find a way to get to it. Don't try to reach it from the lake!!!

Accommodations & Services
There is a bait, tackle, and snack shop at the lake, as well as boat rentals (rowboat and motorboat, half and full day) and a launch ramp.

Rating
Sutherland Lake is a solid 7.

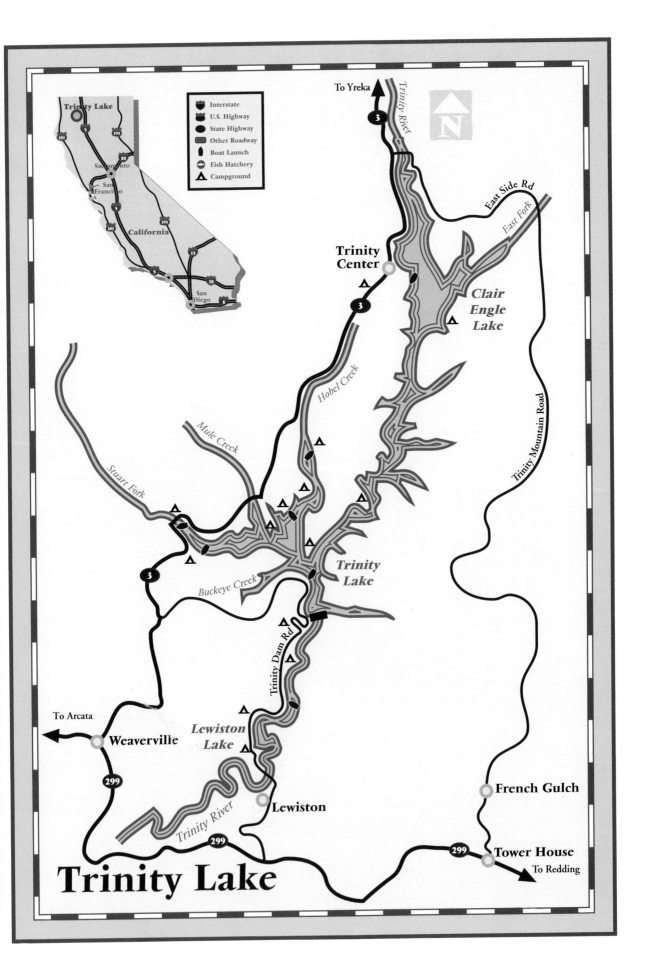

To Yreka

Trinity River

3

Interstate
U.S. Highway
State Highway
Other Roadway
Boat Launch
Fish Hatchery
Campground

N

Trinity Lake

Trinity Lake

101 5 395

Sacramento
San Francisco
5
101
California
395
15
10
San Diego
8

East Side Rd
East Fork

Trinity Center

3

Clair Engle Lake

Hobel Creek

Mule Creek

Stuart Fork

Trinity Mountain Road

Buckeye Creek

3

Trinity Lake

Trinity Dam Rd

To Arcata

Weaverville

299

Lewiston Lake

French Gulch

Trinity River

Lewiston

299

Tower House

299

To Redding

Trinity Lake

Trinity Lake
& Clair Engle Lake

Here's a wonderful foothills fishery. The waters are generally clear, cold, and home to high-quality game fish—smallmouth bass in particular. The reservoir has an amazing number of coves and arms that present you with sheltered habitat perfect for fly rodding adventures. With more than 150 miles of intricate shoreline, you'll be busy learning all the productive spots. Trinity is arguably one of the premier still-water locations in California. Remember, however, it's at mid-elevation and can get pretty cold even on clear days.

This fishery lays claim to the state record smallmouth bass, a nine-pound, one-ounce brute. In addition, Trinity has tons of aggressive smallies. The abundance of rocky structure and cover make this a haven for the bass. The most productive of these regions are the dredge piles in the northern part of the lake. If you want to tangle with a largemouth bass, seek the vegetative cover instead. Submerged willows and stump-studded flats are prime territory around here.

Fly fishing for trout can be solid around the streams that enter the lake. Key trout environs include the Buckeye and Mule Creek areas, plus the Stuart Fork and East Fork Trinity River arms. As the summer progresses, the trout will leave these shallower habitats and cruise the depths, making them tough to connect with.

Interstate 5 is the central corridor for access to the reservoir. At Redding, take Highway 299 west. If you wish to explore the lake's western shore, travel into Weaverville then follow Highway 3 to the lake. An alternate route follows 299 west to Lewiston, eventually connecting with Highway 3 via Rush Creek Road. If you've a little extra time and can appreciate back-road travel, take Trinity Mountain Road out of French Gulch. You'll connect with East Side Road and ultimately with Highway 3 at the northernmost point of the lake. If you choose to take this route, however, be sure to have plenty of gas in your tank first!

A great aerial view of the dam looking north.
Photo by U.S. Fish & Wildlife Service.

Types of Fish
Smallmouth and largemouth bass, rainbow trout, and panfish.

Known Hatches & Baitfish
Threadfin shad, game fish fry, crayfish, callibaetis mayflies, various caddis, hoppers, damselflies, and dragonflies.

Equipment to Use
Rods: 5–8 weight, 8½–10 feet in length.
Reels: Standard drag systems.
Lines: Intermediate, sink tip type-4, modified sink tips of 130 to 200 grains, shooting head type-4.
Leaders: 1X to 4X, 6–12 feet in length.
Wading: Bank angling is best around the western shoreline. Overall, the fishery is best worked from a boat or inflatable.

Flies to Use
Nymphs: Putnam's Damsel #12, Kaufman's Dragonfly #8, Poxyback Callibaetis #16, Black Ant #14, Black AP #12, Prince #14.
Streamers: Flashtail Clouser #2, Purple Eelworm #6, Burk's V-Worm #10, Hot Flash Minnow #6, Whitlock Near Nuff Sculpin #6, Black Woolly bugger #4, Poxybou Crayfish #4.
Topwater & Subsurface: Gurgler #2, Loudmouth Shad #6, Gaines Bluegill Popper #12, Sponge Spider #10–12, Callibaetis Spinner #16, Elk Hair Caddis #10.

When to Fish
Bass: March through October, prime times are April-May and September-October.
Trout: Late winter through fall, prime time is May and June.
Panfish: All summer.

Seasons & Limits
All-year access. Harvest restrictions apply, so check with local fly shops in or the Department of Fish & Game booklet.

Accommodations & Services
There are some 400 campsites at the lake. Lodging and supplies are available in Lewiston and around the lake. Launch ramps and boat rentals are at Fairview, Stuart Fork, Cedar Stock, and Estrellita. Cabins are available at Cedar Stock Resort, Trinity Center Inn (Airporter Inn) and Trinity Alps Resort.

Rating
Overall a solid 7, though bass angling can get red-hot at times.

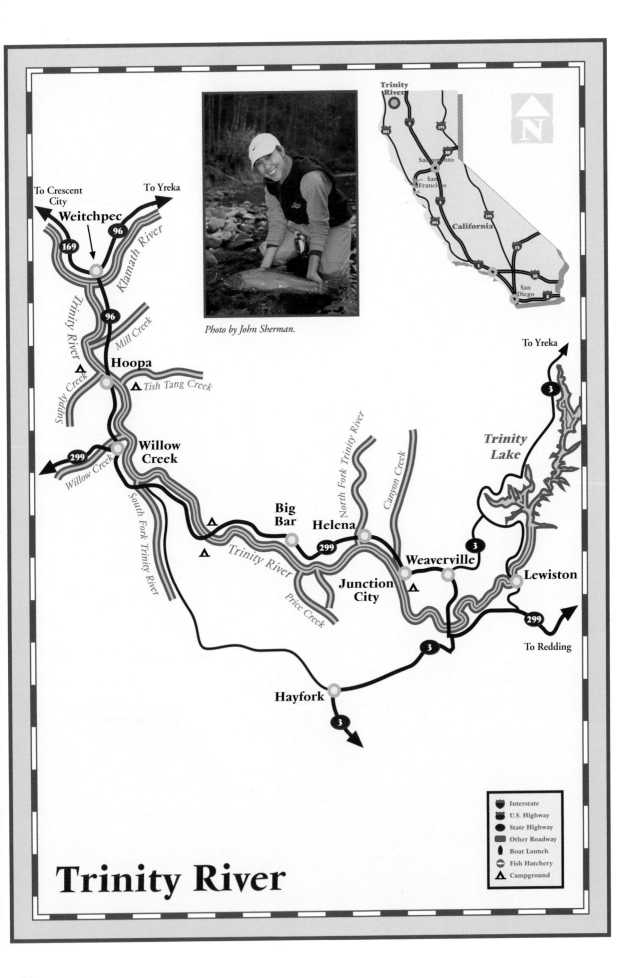

To Crescent City

To Yreka

Weitchpec

169

96

Klamath River

Trinity River

96

Mill Creek

Supply Creek

Hoopa

Tish Tang Creek

Willow Creek

299

Willow Creek

South Fork Trinity River

Photo by John Sherman.

Trinity River

California

To Yreka

3

Trinity Lake

North Fork Trinity River

Canyon Creek

Big Bar

Helena

299

Weaverville

3

Lewiston

Trinity River

Junction City

Price Creek

3

299

To Redding

Hayfork

3

| Interstate |
| U.S. Highway |
| State Highway |
| Other Roadway |
| Boat Launch |
| Fish Hatchery |
| Campground |

Trinity River

Trinity River

The Trinity watershed is an amazing place, seemingly made for the fly fisher. It offers great trout opportunities, superb steelhead action, and a nearly pristine setting in most cases. Each section of the river is completely different, so I separate it like this: The lower region, from Weitchpec to Hoopa Valley, is wide-open tidal waters. The middle section, from Willow Creek to Junction City, presents deep pools in a canyon. Finally, the upper reach, from Weaverville to Lewiston Dam, is a small mountain stream.

This highly productive salmon and steelhead fishery is definitely fly-fishing-friendly. Roads parallel many sections of the river, and turnouts aren't a problem. Bank access is almost unlimited, so wading anglers enjoy all kinds of water. Hike-in fly fishers find excellent conditions with less-pressured game fish. The river's manageable size permits casting to most pools, riffles, and runs.

The river's three sections provide a thorough workout of your field techniques. The variety of habitat and feisty fish demand everything from short-line nymphing to skating big flies on greased-line swings. Subtly drifting egg patterns can also produce well.

The fish are typically in the 2- to 12-pound range. Kings might average 6 to 12 pounds, while the steelhead run around 4 to 8 pounds. Brown trout offer you another terrific target. They tend to weigh around 2 to 4 pounds. Any silver salmon (coho) you come across is currently off-limits to angling.

Most fly fishers get to the river from Redding via Highway 299 west. To work the lower stretch, near the confluence of the Klamath River, follow Highway 96 past Hoopa and on to Weitchpec. North-coast anglers can take Highway 101 south to Arcata, then 299 east to Willow Creek; this is the major steelhead section.

The Trinity is a great river for targeting steelhead and salmon. Photo by John Sherman.

Types of Fish
King salmon (chinook), steelhead, brown trout, silver salmon (off-limits).

Known Hatches
Fall: Isonychia mayflies, October caddis, blue-winged olive mayflies.
Winter: Baetis mayflies, PMDs, golden stones.
Salmon & Fresh-Run Steelies: Use streamers.
Tidal Basin: Baitfish, game fish fry, isopods, shrimp.
Upper River: Dark nymphs, spawn, and fry.

Equipment to Use
Rods: 6–8 weight, 9–10 feet in length. Spey rods are popular here.
Reels: Disk drag and large arbor preferred.
Lines: WF floating, sink tip type-2.
Leaders: 5X to 2X, 6–12 feet in length.
Wading: Chest-high waders, felt-soled or studded boots, and staff recommended.

Flies to Use
Dries: Madam X #6–8, Orange Stimulator #8, PMD Sparkle Dun #16–18, Burk's Crystal Waker #4–8, Waller Waker #4, Paradun Sulfur #16–20.
Nymphs: Poxyback Isonychia #10–16, PMD #16, Poxyback Golden Stone #6, Black AP #10–14, Black Rubber Legs #4, October Poopah #8.
Streamers: Gold Comet #6, Burlap #6, Brindle Bug #6–10, Chappie #2–8, Boss #4, Copper Train #2, Babine Special #4–8.

When to Fish
Salmon
Lower River: Summer.
Middle River: July through September.

Steelhead
Lower River: September and October.
Middle River: November and January.
Upper River: Late winter.

Brown Trout
Primarily Upper River Access: November through March.

Seasons & Limits
Rules along the Trinity are complicated and subject to change. Restrictions on access, tackle, and harvest are in effect. Check with local fly shops or the Department of Fish & Game for the latest news and conditions. See the special regulations supplement for the Klamath River System published in May each year by the Department of Fish and Game.

Accommodations & Services
Lodging and supplies are in Hoopa, Willow Creek, Junction City, and Weaverville. Camping areas and sites abound throughout the region. See the special regulations supplement for the Klamath River System published in May each year by the Department of Fish and Game.

Rating
Without a doubt one of my favorite stream corridors. Overall a solid 7.5.

Trinity River.
Photo by John Sherman.

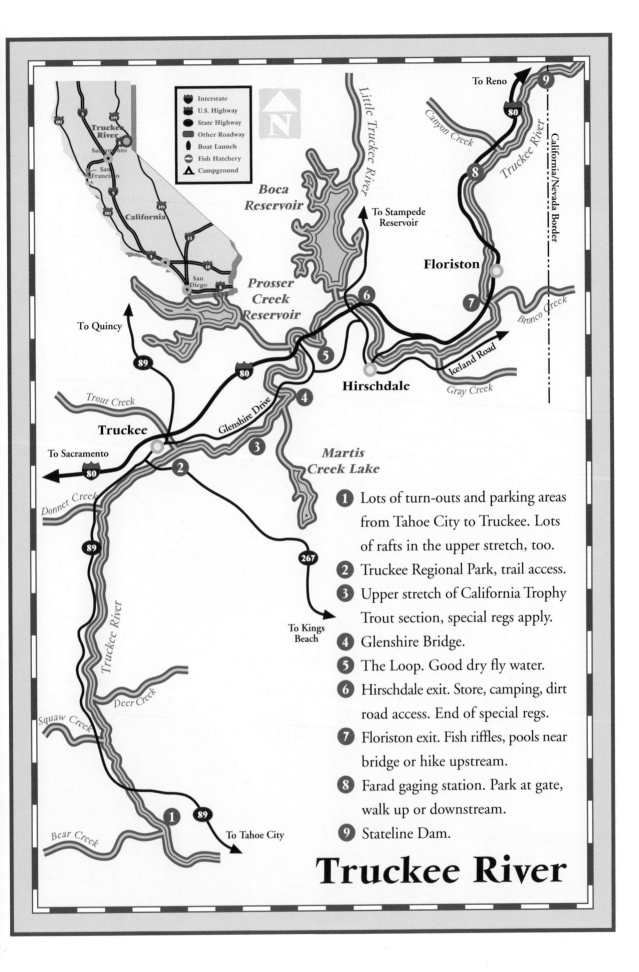

Legend:
- Interstate
- U.S. Highway
- State Highway
- Other Roadway
- Boat Launch
- Fish Hatchery
- Campground

N

Boca Reservoir

Little Truckee River

To Stampede Reservoir

To Reno

Canyon Creek

Truckee River

California/Nevada Border

Floriston

Prosser Creek Reservoir

To Quincy

Bronco Creek

Iceland Road

Gray Creek

Hirschdale

Trout Creek

Glenshire Drive

Truckee

To Sacramento

Donner Creek

Martis Creek Lake

Truckee River

Deer Creek

Squaw Creek

267

To Kings Beach

Bear Creek

To Tahoe City

1 Lots of turn-outs and parking areas from Tahoe City to Truckee. Lots of rafts in the upper stretch, too.

2 Truckee Regional Park, trail access.

3 Upper stretch of California Trophy Trout section, special regs apply.

4 Glenshire Bridge.

5 The Loop. Good dry fly water.

6 Hirschdale exit. Store, camping, dirt road access. End of special regs.

7 Floriston exit. Fish riffles, pools near bridge or hike upstream.

8 Farad gaging station. Park at gate, walk up or downstream.

9 Stateline Dam.

Truckee River

Truckee River (inset)

Sacramento

San Francisco

California

San Diego

Truckee River

by Dave Stanley

The Truckee, the largest of the three major rivers in the Reno area, provides year-round fly fishing. Easy access, beautiful canyon scenery, and feisty wild trout earn the Truckee an easy 8 on the quality-of-fly-fishing scale. The truth though is that the Truckee is a tough river to fly fish.

Wide and fast in some areas, this freestone stream can be very tricky to wade. Proper presentations are difficult to make in the pocket water, big riffles, and deep runs. Success here requires skill in getting the right flies in front of the fish. When nymphing, use long leaders of nine feet or more, and a split shot and indicator setup to reach the bottom. Bring lots of flies and be prepared to match prevailing hatches. Try streamers in the spring and fall in the deeper runs and pools. Use them elsewhere all year.

The Truckee drains huge Lake Tahoe, flowing north and east from the lake through the town of Truckee, where the better fishing begins. It then tumbles through a steep forested canyon down the eastern slope of the Sierra Nevada and through the city of Reno. From Reno it flows 35 miles to the north, into the desert and into one of Nevada's famous fisheries, Pyramid Lake.

Access to the Truckee is great. From the town of Truckee to the state border, the canyon stretch of the river is accessible off Interstate 80. The fly fishing is reasonably unaffected by the river's proximity to a major, all-weather freeway, however. The best fly fishing water is between Truckee and the town of Verdi, Nevada, a small community west of Reno.

When the river enters Nevada, it slows down and provides more opportunities to fish flatwater. In the late summer, however, the water temperature rises, and the best fishing is in the cooler canyon area upstream. Tributaries to the Truckee are also productive, particularly the Little Truckee River. Here there are excellent hatches and large populations of trout as well.

The Truckee River possesses ideal trout habitat as it tumbles toward Nevada. Photo by Brian O'Keefe.

Types of Fish

Rainbow and brown trout, with isolated populations of cutthroat and brookies. Average fish are 10 to 12 inches, but trout of 18 inches plus are not uncommon. A fish over 20 inches would be considered a trophy. Whitefish also populate the Truckee and can provide good sport, especially during winter months.

Known Hatches

A variety of caddisflies hatch regularly on the river from late May through October. Green rockworm is the most prevalent caddis. Golden stone and little yellow stone nymphs are found almost everywhere. Sporadic mayfly hatches also occur throughout the warmer months, including a fair-to-good green drake hatch in early June. The most reliable hatch for summer dry fly fishing is the little yellow stone hatch from mid-June into late August and early September. Midge hatches are consistent throughout the year, including winter, when fishing during warm spells is highly recommended.

Equipment to Use

Rods: 5–6 weight, 9 feet in length.
Reels: Mechanical or palm drag.
Lines: Floating. Sink tip for deep holes or runs.
Leaders: 9–10 feet in length, 4X to 6X.
Wading: The Truckee is a difficult stream to wade. Felt-soled boots are a must. A wading staff is recommended.

Flies to Use

Dries: Adams, Humpy, Royal Wulff, Stimulators, Elk Hair Caddis, Parachute Hare's Ear and other parachute patterns in various colors, Little Yellow Stone patterns, Ants, and Hoppers.
Nymphs: Bird's Nest, Gold Ribbed Hare's Ear, Prince, Zug Bug, and any of these with a beadhead. Also use a variety of Soft Hackles and Caddis Larva Emergers, as well as the Western Coachman.
Streamers: Muddler Minnow, Woolly Bugger, Zonker and Matuka. Sculpins are common in the Truckee.

When to Fish

Very reliable evening and some morning dry fly action from late May to mid-October. Nymphs are productive year-round.

Seasons & Limits

California: Last Saturday in April to November 15. Barbless hooks in most sections.
Nevada: Open all year, barbless hooks. There are a variety of special regulations on both the California and Nevada sections of the Truckee. Make sure you check the appropriate regulations!

Accommodations & Services

All services are readily available in the Reno, Tahoe, and Truckee areas.

Rating

During the summer months, the Truckee rates an 8. Year-round nymph fishing also deserves an 8.

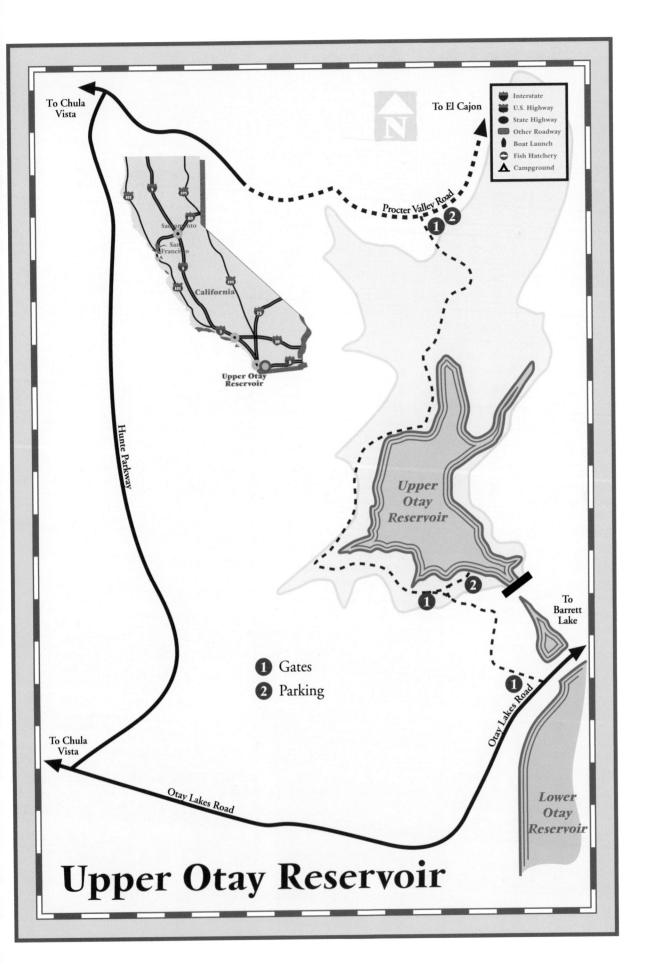

Upper Otay Reservoir

To Chula Vista

To El Cajon

Procter Valley Road

① ②

N

Interstate
U.S. Highway
State Highway
Other Roadway
Boat Launch
Fish Hatchery
Campground

California

Sacramento

San Francisco

Upper Otay Reservoir

Hunte Parkway

Upper Otay Reservoir

① ②

To Barrett Lake

① Gates

② Parking

Otay Lakes Road

①

To Chula Vista

Otay Lakes Road

Lower Otay Reservoir

Upper Otay Reservoir

by Jeff Solis

Upper Otay Reservoir was chosen as the original site in the western United States to receive Florida largemouth bass and has since become the source of virtually all Florida bass found west of the Mississippi River. In addition to bass, the California Department of Fish & Game has recently stocked trout in the reservoir, and rainbows over five pounds have already been caught.

There are a lot of trees along the western shore of Upper Otay, while numerous grassy flats and a steep-sided, deep arm breaks up the eastern side of the reservoir. You can feel really secluded here. On most days, seeing six other anglers would be considered fishing in a crowd.

Upper Otay is custom-made for float tubing, but you'll want to have two rods rigged up when you launch. A floating line allows you to fish the top of the water column with a streamer, and a full sink or sink tip line will take a dark Clouser Minnow or Leech pattern down to dredge the bottom.

To reach the reservoir, take Interstate 5 south to H Street. Go east on H Street and cross I-805, continuing east on East H Street. Turn right on Otay Lakes Road, left on Telegraphic Canyon Road, which then becomes Otay Lakes Road again and passes by this small impoundment. Here you will find the purest population of Florida bass in the West and, maybe best of all, no crowds!

Upper Otay is a very small impoundment adjacent to some big water at Lower Otay. Photo by Howard Fisher.

Types of Fish
Pure-strain Florida largemouth bass. Rainbow trout are stocked in the winter.

Known Hatches & Baitfish
Midges, mayflies, damselflies, shad, and crayfish.

Equipment to Use
Rods: 9 feet in length, 5–6 weight for trout; 9 feet in length, 6–9 weight for bass.
Reels: Standard click or disk.
Lines: WF or double-taper floating and a full sink or sink tip.
Leaders: 7½–10 feet in length, 4X to 6X for trout; 5–8 feet in length, 2X or 3X for bass.
Wading: Float tubing is the best way to chase trout and bass. Be careful if you wade, and stay off spawning beds in the spring!

Flies to Use
Dries: Parachute Adams #14–20, Callibaetis pattern #14–18, and Foam-Bodied Midge #18–22.
Nymphs: Beadhead Hare's Ear #10–16, Beadhead PT #10–16, Large Dragonfly or Damselfly Nymph, and Nygeri's Nymph.
Streamers & Poppers: Brown Woolly Bugger, shad Deceiver, pink/white Clouser Minnow, and Foam or Deer Hair Frog.

When to Fish
From midmorning until dark. Spring produces the most numbers, but fall is when larger fish are caught.

Seasons & Limits
Barbless flies only. Catch and release only. Days and hours of operation may be limited and subject to change and closure. Consult the City of San Diego Reservoirs and Recreation Program phone (619) 465-3474 for current schedule. At time of publication open on Wednesdays, Saturdays, and Sundays.

Nearby Fly Fishing
Lower Otay Lake is big water with great early-summer fishing for trophy panfish.

Accommodations & Services
There is a concession stand at Lower Otay Reservoir. All services available in nearby Eastlake.

Rating
Upper Otay is a strong 8.

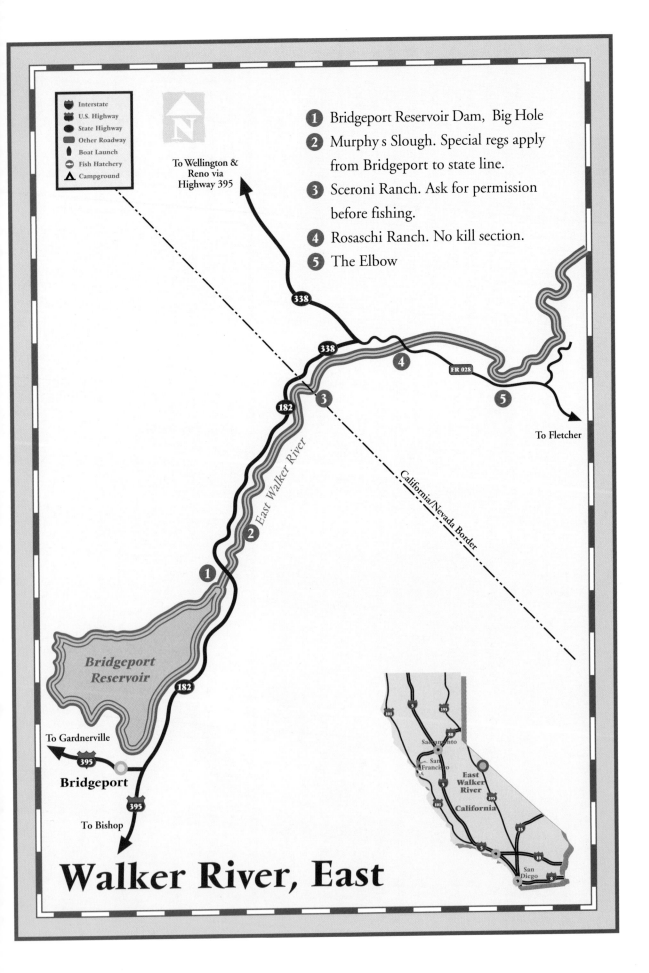

Legend

- Interstate
- U.S. Highway
- State Highway
- Other Roadway
- Boat Launch
- Fish Hatchery
- Campground

N

To Wellington & Reno via Highway 395

1. Bridgeport Reservoir Dam, Big Hole
2. Murphy's Slough. Special regs apply from Bridgeport to state line.
3. Sceroni Ranch. Ask for permission before fishing.
4. Rosaschi Ranch. No kill section.
5. The Elbow

338

338

182

4

FR 028

3

5

To Fletcher

East Walker River

California/Nevada Border

2

1

Bridgeport Reservoir

182

To Gardnerville

395

Bridgeport

395

To Bishop

Walker River, East

101
395
80
Sacramento
San Francisco
5
East Walker River
101
395
California
15
5
10
San Diego
8

Walker River, East

by Dave Stanley

The East Walker River, below Bridgeport Reservoir, has long been a popular destination for the avid fly angler. In years past, the fast riffles and deep, powerful runs of this section were rated, in terms of fish per mile, one of California's top trout streams.

Easily accessible as it flows alongside Highway 182, from Bridgeport to the Nevada state line, this section offers serious nymph and streamer anglers opportunities to catch trophy rainbow or brown trout, especially if they avoid the weekend crowds. Twenty-inch fish are common in this stretch of the river. In the spring or fall, stripping a Woolly Bugger or Zonker tempts any rod-bender within chomping distance.

The East Walker River features the famed "Big Hole," where Bridgeport Reservoir waters pour into a basin before entering the stream channel. This pool and the stretch below it are, for the fly fisher, some of the most difficult and potentially rewarding spots on the river.

In Nevada, the East Walker flows through sagebrush flats and is known for consistent insect hatches and large fish. That's why it's considered by many the best trout stream in that state. Summer irrigation demands, however, can cause water levels to fluctuate. While some of the river flows through private land, public access is readily available on the significant portion of the river that runs through land controlled by the Bureau of Land Management and the U.S. Forest Service. The summer snake season also bears mention: Be careful!

Open year-round, the Nevada section of the East Walker offers the winter fly fisher excellent stream angling. Large populations of stoneflies provide exceptional year-round nymph fishing. If you like to fish streamers, large browns and rainbows can be taken using big flies and sink tip lines.

Changing flies on the East Walker.
Photo by Jim Levison.

Types of Fish

Rainbow and brown trout and mountain whitefish.

Known Hatches

Golden stoneflies hatch prior to or just at the beginning of runoff, usually in March or April. Mayflies also begin to appear in March, coming off sporadically throughout the warmer months and into late September and early October. As is true of the Truckee and Carson rivers, caddis is the most prolific insect in the Walker drainage: Huge hatches occur in the summer. In summer also look for little yellow stones. Baitfish to consider are sculpin, chubs, dace, and trout fry.

Equipment to Use

Rods: 5–6 weight, 9 feet in length.
Reels: Palm or disk drag.
Lines: Floating, use sink tips for deep holes or runs.
Leaders: 7½–10 feet in length, 3X to 6X.
Wading: Wading is moderately difficult. Wear felt-soled boots and use a wading staff in the gnarlier sections.

Flies to Use

Dries: Adams, Humpy, Royal Wulff, Blue-Winged Olive, Elk Hair Caddis, Parachute Hare's Ear, other parachute patterns in various colors, Little Yellow Stone patterns, Ants, and Hoppers.
Nymphs: Bird's Nest, Gold Ribbed Hare's Ear, Prince, Zug Bug, and any of these with beadheads; Green Rockworm patterns to imitate the prevalent caddis, Golden Stone and Little Yellow Stone, various Soft Hackles, Caddis Larva, Pupa, and Emergers, Western Coachman.
Streamers: Muddler Minnow, Woolly Bugger, Hornberg, Zonker, Matuka.

When to Fish

March, when the water is low and the stonefly hatch is on, is the best fly fishing. June through July, when caddis are hatching is also good. September and October offer good hopper dry fly action. Nymphs and streamers are productive year-round. On the East Walker in Nevada, late fall through March can be outstanding when low, clear water conditions prevail.

Seasons & Limits

California: Last Saturday April to November 15. Minimum size limit: 18 inches total length. Only artificial lures with barbless hooks.
Nevada: Open all year. Catch and release and barbless hooks in areas.
Special regulations apply on the California and Nevada sections. Check the appropriate state regulations.

Accommodations & Services

All services are available in larger towns like Gardnerville, NV, and Bridgeport, CA. Limited services exist in Wellington, NV, and at Topaz Lake.

Rating

Productive dry and nymph fishing and outstanding streamer action for large trout—a solid 9.

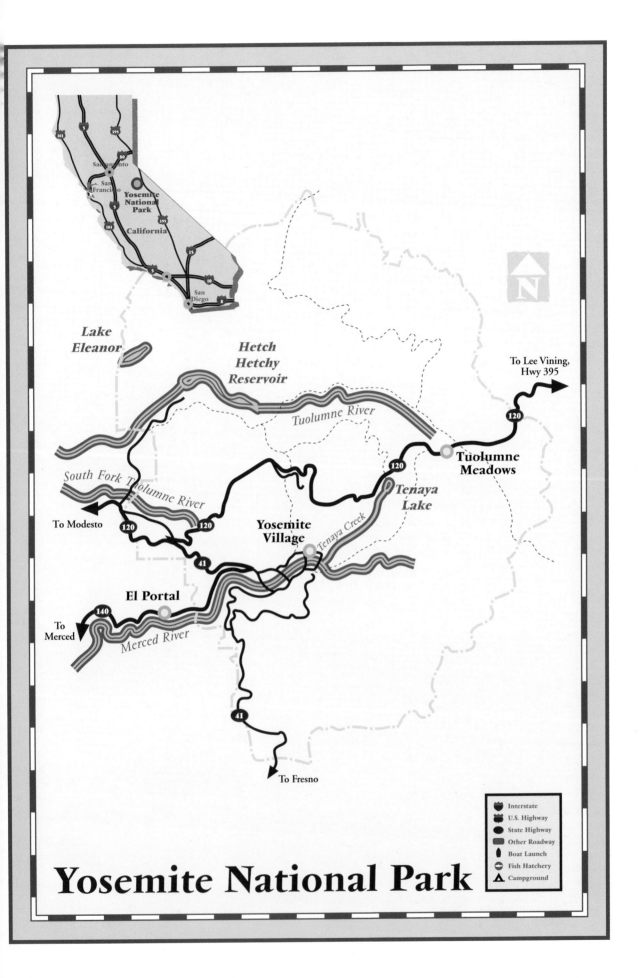

Yosemite National Park

Lake Eleanor

Hetch Hetchy Reservoir

To Lee Vining, Hwy 395

Tuolumne River

South Fork Tuolumne River

Tuolumne Meadows

Tenaya Lake

To Modesto

Tenaya Creek

Yosemite Village

El Portal

To Merced

Merced River

To Fresno

Interstate
U.S. Highway
State Highway
Other Roadway
Boat Launch
Fish Hatchery
Campground

California

Sacramento
San Francisco
Yosemite National Park
San Diego

Yosemite National Park

Whether you live in California or are visiting this great state, Yosemite is a must-do. This park is a magnificent example of high-altitude wilderness terrain. Glaciers, waterfalls, alpine tarns, forested stream corridors, and abundant wildlife combine for a terrific wilderness experience. And, yes, there are beautiful mountain trout as well.

The backpacking explosion of the 1960s and '70s has dwindled, and the backcountry has been far less populated with hikers over the last 10 years. Take the extra time to walk just a bit farther than most, and you'll be rewarded with tremendous views, uncrowded conditions, and intimate waters to explore. Use the map in this guide for general reference; do not use it for hiking directions. Acquire and study a good topographical map of the area before you head out.

The High Sierra isn't a place to catch huge fish. Harsh winters and short growing seasons mean only the hardiest trout survive; average sizes are 6 to 12 inches in length. But don't let the small fish keep you away. They are exquisite examples of high mountain trout—gems to behold and a real treasure for all to enjoy.

"Intimate" is the key word to describe Yosemite's waters. Most of the lakes and streams are small, while the creeks are tiny. The challenges are varied, with short-cast scenarios being frequent. If you want to air out a line, then the park's many lakes are your best venue. Favorite still waters for fly rodding include Tilden, Smedberg, Minnow, Wilmer, Virginia, Mattie, Edyth, and Benson lakes. There are more than 100 still waters to explore within Yosemite's boundaries.

The early explorer and champion of the area, John Muir, had it right when he called the Sierra Nevada the "Range of Light." This portion of the range is perfect for sunrises and sunsets. There's something magical in the mountains and forests of this vast country. Get out to the park and revel in the glory!

There are four main entrances to Yosemite. From the east, turn off Highway 395 onto Highway 120 at Lee Vining. From the south, Fresno, take Highway 41 to Fish Camp. From the west, take Highway 120 at the Big Oak Flat entrance for the direct route to Tuolumne Meadows. Travel on Highway 140, from Highway 99, to El Portal to get right into Yosemite Valley. All roads into the park are well paved and easy to negotiate.

Types of Fish
Rainbow, brown, and brook trout.

Known Hatches
May through July: Callibaetis, PMD, spotted sedge, alderfly, and midge.
July through September: Callibaetis, blue-winged olive, trico, PMD, American grannon, spotted sedge, midge, and damselfly.

Equipment to Use
Rods: 4–6 weight, 7–9 feet in length.
Reels: Standard click and pawl or disk drag systems.
Lines: WF Floating, type-2 sink tip.
Leaders: 3X to 6X, 6–12 feet in length.
Wading: Use chest-high waders, felt-soled boots, and a wading staff. Bank angling is no problem. Float tubes are a bonus for still waters.

Flies to Use
Dries: Trico #18–20, Quigley Loopwing Callibaetis #16, Quigley Loopwing Paradun Baetis #20, Trico Poly Spinner #22, Foam Back Spinner Callibaetis #16, Little Yellow Stone #14, Henryville Special #16, Adams #14–16, Black Ant #10–16, Hopper #8.
Nymphs: Olive Bird's Nest #12–14, Hunched Back Infrequens #16, Olive Fox Poopah #14, Mercer Z-Wing Caddis #12–18, Burk's Damsel #12, Marabou Damsel #12, Ultra Scud #14, Poxyback Callibaetis #14–16, Hare's Ear #12–16.
Streamers: Olive or Brown Woolly Buggers #8–10.

When to Fish
April through November 15. Prime time is from late June through October.

Seasons & Limits
Last Saturday in April to November 15. Check the California Department of Fish & Game regulations booklet or call a local fly shop for current regulations.

Accommodations & Services
Lodging, camping, and supplies are abundant in Yosemite Valley and Tuolumne Meadows. Phone the park headquarters for reservations and information (209) 372-0200. An entry fee is charged and special permits are necessary for travel in the backcountry.

Rating
Great high country, pretty little trout, beautiful waters. Overall, an 8.5.

Merced River, Yosemite National Park.
Photo by Brian Sak.

Resources

This listing of resources is provided as a courtesy to help you enjoy your travels and fishing experience and is not intended to imply an endorsement of services either by the publisher or author. These listings are as accurate as possible as of the time of publication and are subject to change.

Resources by Zip

Reno Fly Shop
294 E. Moana Ln. #14
Reno, NV 89502
775-825-3474
www.renoflyshop.com

Just Fishing by Pete
2427 190th St.
Redondo Beach, CA 90278
310-376-7035

Sport Chalet Sporting Goods
920 Foothill Blvd.
La Canada, CA 91012
818-790-9800
www.sportchalet.com

Orvis
346 S. Lake Ave. #102
Pasadena, CA 91101
626-356-8000
www.orvis.com

Malibu Fish'n Tackle
3166 E. Thousand Oaks Blvd.
Thousand Oaks, CA 91362
805-496-7332
www.malibufishntackle.com

Fishermen's Spot
14411 Burbank Blvd.
Van Nuys, CA 91401
818-785-7306
www.fsflyfishing.com

Baja on the Fly
P.O. Box 300189
Escondido, CA 92030
800-919-2252
www.bajaonthefly.com

San Diego Fly Shop
124 Lomas Santa Fe Dr. #208
Solana Beach, CA 92075
858-350-3111
www.sandiegoflyshop.com

Stroud Tackle
1457 Morena Blvd.
San Diego, CA 92110
619-276-4822
www.stroudtackle.com

Andy Montana's Surfside Fly Fisher
957 Orange Ave.
Coronado, CA 92118
619-435-9992
www.andymontanas.com

Riverside Ski and Sport
6744 Brockton Ave.
Riverside, CA 92506
951-784-0205
www.riversideskiandsport.com

His and Her Fly Fishing
1566 Old Newport Blvd.
Costa Mesa, CA 92627
949-548-9449
www.hisherflyfishing.com

Salty Fly Guide Service
8451 Northport Dr.
Huntington Beach, CA 92646
714-235-7715
saltyflyhb@yahoo.com

Bob Marriott's Fly Fishing Store
2700 W. Orangethorpe Ave.
Fullerton, CA 92833
800-535-6633
www.bobmarriotts.net

The Artful Angler
3817 Santa Claus Lane
Carpinteria, CA 93013
866-787-3359
www.artfulangler.com

Kern River Troutfitters
11301 Kernville Rd.
Kernville, CA 93238
866-347-4876
www.kernrivertroutfitters.com
www.kernriverflyfishing.com

The Buz's Buszek Fly Shop
110 W. Main St. #D
Visalia, CA 93291
559-734-1151
buzsflyshop@clearwire.net

Buz's Fly Shop Too!
1220 Oak St. Suite D
Bakersfield, CA 93304
661-395-0032

Four Seasons Outfitters
432 Higuera St.
San Luis Obispo, CA 93401
805-544-5171

Hole in the Wall Fly Shop
570 Higuera St. #115
San Luis Obispo, CA 93401
805-595-3359

Barrett's Outfitters
482 Cottonwood Dr.
Bishop, CA 93514
760-872-3830
www.barrettsoutfitters.com

Brock's Fly Fishing Specialists
100 N. Main St.
Bishop, CA 93514
760-872-3581
www.brocksflyfish.com

Trout Scouts of Sierra Guide Group
637 Grove St.
Bishop, CA 93514
760-872-9836
www.sierraguidegroup.com

Ken's Alpine Shop & Sporting Goods
258 Main St.
Bridgeport, CA 93517
760-932-7707
www.kenssport.com

Bell's Sporting Goods & Hardware
Highway 395
Lee Vining, CA 93541
760-647-6406

Kittredge Sports
3218 Main St.
Mammoth Lakes, CA 93546
760-934-7566
www.kittredgesports.com

Rick's Sport Center
3241 Main St.
Mammoth Lakes, CA 93546
760-934-3416

The Trout Fly
Shell Mart Center #3
Mammoth Lakes, CA 93546
760-934-2517
www.thetroutfly.com

The Troutfitter
Shell Mart Center #3
Mammoth Lakes, CA 93546
800-637-6912
www.thetroutfitter.com

Resources by Zip (continued)

Wilderness Outfitters
#2 Minaret Rd.
Mammoth Lakes, CA 93546
760-924-7335
www.mammothmountain.com/around_mammoth/fly_fish/

Herb Bauer Sporting Goods
6264 N. Blackstone Ave.
Fresno, CA 93710
559-435-8600
www.herbbauersportinggoods.com

Central Coast Fly Fishing
7172 Carmel Valley Rd.
Carmel, CA 93923
831-626-6586
www.centralcoastflyfishing.com

California Fly Shop
1538-D El Camino Real
Belmont, CA 94002
650-508-0727
www.californiaflyshop.com

The Midge Fly Shop
271 State St.
Los Altos, CA 94022
650-941-8871

Leland Fly Fishing Outfitters
463 Bush St. (at Grant)
San Francisco, CA 94108
415-781-3474
www.flyfishingoutfitters.com

Orvis
248 Sutter St.
San Francisco, CA 94108
415-392-1600
www.orvis.com

Orvis
63 Town and Country Village
855 El Camino Real
Palo Alto, CA 94301
540-983-4204
www.orvis.com

Creative Sports Flyshop
1924-C Oak Park Blvd.
Pleasant Hill, CA 94523
925-938-2255
www.creativeflyshop.com

Ken Hanley's Adventures Beyond
P.O. Box 3239
Fremont, CA 94539
www.pacificextremes.com
kenpacx@yahoo.com

Rod Rack
1029 B Street
Hayward, CA 94541
510-881-1775
www.rodrack.net

Sweeney's Sport Store
1537 Imola Ave. West
Napa, CA 94559
707-255-5544
www.sweeneyssports.com

Walton's Pond
14837 Washington Avenue
San Leandro, CA 94578
510-352-3932

Pacific Coast Anglers
5677-A Gibraltar Dr.
Pleasanton, CA 94588
925-734-0110
www.pacificcoastanglers.com

Outdoor Pro Shop
1822 Embarcadero
Oakland, CA 94606
510-332-2824
www.outdoorproshop.com

A-1 Fly Fishing
517 8th St.
Oakland, CA 94607
510-832-0731
www.a1flyfishing.com

Fish First!
1404 Solano Ave.
Albany, CA 94706
510-526-1937
www.fishfirst.com

Western Sport Shop
902 Third St.
San Rafael, CA 94901
415-456-5454
www.westernsportshop.com

Outdoor Pro Shop
6315 Commerce Blvd.
Rohnert Park, CA 94928
707-588-8033
www.outdoorproshop.com

Sea Level Flyfishing
1010 Line St.
Hollister, CA 95023
510-908-1809
www.sealevelflyfish.com

Upstream Flyfishing
54 N. Santa Cruz Ave.
Los Gatos, CA 95030
408-354-4935
www.upstreamflyfish.com

San Jose Fly Shop
15569 Union Ave.
Los Gatos, CA 95032
877-626-7621
www.sjflyshop.com

Capitola Wharf - Boat Rentals
15 Municipal Wharf
Santa Cruz, CA 95060
831-462-2208
http://bonita.mbnms.nos.noaa.gov/visitor/Access/capitola.html

Santa Cruz Wharf
15 Santa Cruz Municipal Wharf
Santa Cruz, CA 95060
831-423-1739
www.santacruzwharf.com

Ernie's Casting Pond
4845 Soquel Dr.
Soquel, CA 95073
831-462-4665
www.ernies.com

Mel Cotton's Sporting Goods
1266 W. San Carlos St.
San Jose, CA 95126
408-287-5994
www.melcottons.com

Herman & Helen's Marina
15135 W. Eight Mile Rd.
Stockton, CA 95219
877-468-7326
www.houseboats.com/hermanandhelens

High Sierra Rod Company
1163 South Main Street
Angels Camp, CA 95222
209-736-9197
www.highsierrarods.com

White Pines Outdoors
2182 Highway 4 B-140
Arnold, CA 95223
209-795-1054
wpineso@sbcglobal.net

Sierra Anglers Fly Shop
700 McHenry Ave.
Modesto, CA 95350
209-572-2212
www.sierraanglers.com

Valley Sporting Goods
1700 McHenry Ave. #D-50
Modesto, CA 95350
209-523-5681
www.valleysg.com

E. Crosby Tobacco/ Outfitters
2625 Coffee Rd. Suite T
Modesto, CA 95355
209-529-6200

Mother Lode Fly Shop
14841 Mono Way
Sonora, CA 95370
209-532-8600
www.motherlodefly.com

Village Sport Shop
Yosemite Village
Yosemite Park, CA 95389
209-372-1286

Western Sport Shop
2790 Santa Rosa Ave.
Santa Rosa, CA 95407
707-542-4432
www.westernsportshop.com

Resources by Zip (continued)

King's Sport & Tackle
16258 Main St.
Guerneville, CA 95446
707-869-2156

Eureka Fly Shop
1632 Broadway
Eureka, CA 95501
707-444-2000
www.eurekaflyshop.com

Sierra Fly Fishers
13396 Lincoln Way
Auburn, CA 95603
530-823-6968
www.sierraflyfishers.com

Fly Fishing Specialties
6412-C Tupelo Dr.
Citrus Heights, CA 95610
916-722-1055
www.flyfishingspecialties.com

Kiene's Fly Shop
2654 Marconi Ave.
Sacramento, CA 95821
916-486-9958
www.kiene.com

American Fly Fishing Company
3523 Fair Oaks Blvd.
Sacramento, CA 95864
916-483-1222
www.americanflyfishing.com

Chico Fly Shop
1154 W. 8th Ave.
Chico, CA 95926
530-345-9983
www.chicoflyshopinc.com

Fish First!
167 E. Third St.
Chico, CA 95928
530-343-8300
www.fishfirst.com

Sierra Stream Fly Shop
847 W. 5th St.
Chico, CA 95928
530-345-4261
www.sierrastreamflyshop.com

Hot Creek. Photo by John Sherman

Nevada City Anglers
417-C Broad St.
Nevada City, CA 95959
530-478-9301
www.nevadacityanglers.com

The Fly Shop
4140 Churn Creek Rd.
Redding, CA 96002
800-669-3474
www.theflyshop.com

Vaughn's Sport & Fly Shop
37307 Main St.
Burney, CA 96013
530-335-2381
www.vaughnfly.com

Dunsmuir Rod Company
5210 Florence Loop
Dunsmuir, CA 96025
530-235-4058
www.dunsmuirrodcompany.com

Ted Fay Fly Shop at Acorn Inn
4310 Dunsmuir Ave.
Dunsmuir, CA 96025
530-235-2969
www.tedfay.com

Clearwater Lodge on the Pit River
24500 Pit One Powerhouse Rd.
Fall River Mills, CA 96028
530-336-5005
www.clearwaterlodge.com

Shasta Angler
43503 Highway 299 East
Fall River Mills, CA 96028
530-336-6600
shastaangler@frontiernet.net

Spinner Fall Lodge Circle 7 Guest Ranch
P.O. Box 931
Fall River Mills, CA 96028
530-336-5300
530-336-5827
www.spinnerfalllodge.com
www.circle7guestranch.com
Open during trout season

Trinity Canyon Lodge & Resort
27025 Highway 299 West
Junction City, CA 96048
800-354-9297
www.trinitycanyonlodge.com

Trinity Fly Shop
P.O. Box 176
4440 Old Lewiston Rd.
Lewiston, CA 96052
530-623-6757
www.trinityflyshop.com
trinflyguy@shasta.com

McCloud River Inn
325 Lawndale Ct.
P.O. Box 1560
McCloud, CA 96057
800-261-7831
www.mccloudriverinn.com

McCloud Fly Fishing Adventures
Box 388
McCloud, CA 96057
530-964-2533
www.mccloudflyfishing.com
ricmcfly@mccloudflyfishing.com

McCloud Fly Fishing Ranch
P.O. Box 68
McCloud, CA 96057
530-964-2878

Three Rivers Guide Service
16725 Friar Pl.
Weed, CA 96094
530-938-1514
www.threeriversguideservice.com
alan@threeriversguideservice.com

The Tackle Shop
614 S. Main St.
Yreka, CA 96097
530-841-1901
www.thetackleshop.cc

Sorensen's Inn
Hope Valley, CA 96120
800-423-9949

Gold Rush Sporting Goods
196 East Sierra St.
Portola, CA 96122
530-832-5724

Johnson's Guide Service
P.O. Box 26
Tahoma, CA 96142
415-453-9831
www.flyfishingtahoe.com

Four Seasons Fly Fishing
P.O. Box 5122
Tahoe City, CA 96145
530-550-9780
www.flyfishingtruckee-tahoe.com

Mother Nature's Inn
551 N. Lake Blvd.
Tahoe City, CA 96145
530-581-4278

Tahoe Fly Fishing Outfitters
2705 Lake Tahoe Blvd.
South Lake Tahoe, CA 96150
530-541-8208
www.tahoeflyfishing.com

Alpine Fly Fishing
P.O. Box 10465
South Lake Tahoe, CA 96158
530-542-0759
www.worldwideflyfishing.com/california/b487

Resources by Zip (continued)

Mountain Hardware and Sports
11320 Donner Pass Rd.
Truckee, CA 96161
530-587-4844
www.mountainhardwareandsports.com

Truckee River Outfitters
10200 Donner Pass Rd.
Truckee, CA 96161
530-582-0900
www.renoflyshop.com
Summer only

Ralph & Lisa Cutter's California School of Fly Fishing
P.O. Box 8212
Truckee, CA 96162
530-470-9005
www.flyline.com

Thy Rod & Staff Guide Services
P.O. Box 10038
Truckee, CA 96162
530-587-7333
www.cyberfly.com

Clubs & Organizations

California Fly Fishers Unlimited
Sacramento, CA
www.cffu.org

California Striped Bass Association
Several Chapters
www.striper-csba.com

California Trout
870 Market St. #528
San Francisco, CA 94102
415-392-8887
www.caltrout.org

Federation of Fly Fishers National Headquarters
215 E. Lewis St.
Livingston, MT 59047
406-222-9369
www.fedflyfishers.org
Call for local Club

International Game Fish Association
300 Gulf Stream Way
Dania Beach, FL 33004
954-927-2628
www.igfa.org

National Fresh Water Fishing Hall of Fame
P.O. Box 690
Hayward, WI 54843
715-634-4440
www.freshwater-fishing.org

Northern California Bass Fishing
www.westernbass.com/ncalifornia

Northern California Council Federation of Fly Fishers
www.nccfff.org

United Anglers of California
15572 Woodard Rd.
San Jose, CA 95124
408-371-0331
www.unitedanglers.org

Government Resources

California Bureau of Land Management
2800 Cottage Way Suite W-1834
Sacramento, CA 95825
916-978-4400
www.blm.gov/ca

California Department of Water Resources Current River Conditions
http://cdec.water.ca.gov/river/rivcond.html

California Dept. of Boating & Waterways
2000 Evergreen St. Suite 100
Sacramento, CA 95815
888-326-2822
www.dbw.ca.gov

California Dept. of Fish & Game
1416 Ninth St.
Sacramento, CA 95814
916-445-0411
www.dfg.ca.gov

California Dept. of Fish & Game Licensed Guides Listing
www.dfg.ca.gov/licensing/pdffiles/licensefishingguidelist.pdf

California Dept. of Parks & Recreation
1416 9th St.
Sacramento, CA 95814
800-777-0369
www.parks.ca.gov

California Office of Tourism
www.gocalif.ca.gov

Eastern Sierra Stream Flows & Reservoir Levels
http://wsoweb.ladwp.com/Aqueduct/realtime/realtimeindex.htm

Mexico Tourism Board
1880 Century Park East
Suite 511
Los Angeles, CA 90067
310-282-9112

National Park Service
www.nps.gov

U.S. Fish & Wildlife Service
2800 Cottage Way
Sacramento, CA 95825
916-414-6464
www.fws.gov/cno

United States Forest Service Pacific Southwest
1323 Club Dr.
Vallejo, CA 94592
707-562-8737
www.fs.fed.us/r5

USDA Forest Service Maps
1400 Independence Ave. SW
Washington, DC 20250
202-205-8333
www.fs.fed.us/maps

Tides

Worldwide & U.S. Tide Predictor
http://tbone.biol.sc.edu/tide
http://tidesonline.nos.noaa.gov

Websites

Dan Blanton
Guide and Internet resource
www.danblanton.com

California Fly Fisher
Message board
www.calflyfisher.com/msgboard

Fliflicker
Salt water fly fishing in Southern and Central California
www.fliflicker.com

Fly Fish Norcal
Articles, maps, resources, photos
www.flyfishnorcal.org

Gary Bulla's Fly Fishing Adventures
Salt water fishing in Southern California and Baja
www.garybullas.com

Northern California Fly Fishing Board
www.ncffb.org

SC Surf Fishing
All about surf fishing in Southern California
www.scsurffishing.com

Custom Flies and Field Instruction
Jay Murakoshi
Fresno, CA 93720
www.fliesunlimited.com
jaysflies@sbcglobal.net

Conservation

No Nonsense Fly Fishing Guidebooks believes that, in addition to local information and gear, fly fishers need clean water and healthy fish. We encourage preservation, improvement, conservation, enjoyment and understanding of our waters and their inhabitants. While fly fishing, take care of the place, practice catch and release and try to avoid spawning fish.

When you aren't fly fishing, a good way to help all things wild and aquatic is to support organizations dedicated to these ideas. We encourage you to get involved, learn more and to join such organizations.

American Fly Fishing Trade Association ....(360) 636-0708
American Rivers...(202) 347-7550
California Trout..(415) 392-8887
Deschutes Basin Land Trust ....(541) 330-0017
Federation of Fly Fishers ....(406) 585-7592
International Game Fish Association..(954) 927-2628
International Women Fly Fishers ....(925) 934-2461
New Mexico Trout...(505) 884-5262
Oregon Trout...(503) 222-9091
Outdoor Writers Association of America..(406) 728-7434
Recreational Fishing Alliance ....(888) JOIN-RFA
Rails-to-Trails Conservancy...(202) 331-9696
Theodore Roosevelt Conservation Partnership..(877) 770-8722
Trout Unlimited ....(800) 834-2419

Find Your Way with These No Nonsense Guides

Fly Fishing Colorado
Jackson Streit

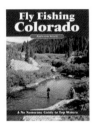

Your experienced guide gives you the quick, clear understanding of the essential information you'll need to fly fish Colorado's most outstanding waters. Use this book to plan your Colorado fly fishing trip, and take this guide along for ready reference. This popular guide has been updated, redesigned and is in its third printing. ISBN #1-892469-13-8..........$19.95

Fly Fishing New Mexico
Taylor Streit

Since 1970, Mr. Streit has been New Mexico's foremost fly fishing authority and professional guide. He's developed many fly patterns used throughout the region. Taylor owned the Taos Fly Shop for ten years and managed a bone fishing lodge in the Bahamas. He makes winter fly fishing pilgrimages to Argentina where he escorts fly fishers and explorers. Newly revised. ISBN #1-892469-04-9..........$18.95

Fly Fishing Arizona
Glenn Tinnin

Desert, forest, lava fields, red rocks and canyons. Here is where to go and how to fish 32 cold water and warm water streams, lakes, and reservoirs in Arizona. Newly revised. ISBN #1-892469-02-2..........$18.95

Fly Fishing Southern Baja
Gary Graham

With this book you can fly to Baja, rent a car and go out on your own to find exciting saltwater fly fishing! Mexico's Baja Peninsula is now one of the premier destinations for saltwater fly anglers. Newly revised. ISBN #1-892469-00-6..........$18.95

Fly Fishing Central & Southeastern Oregon
Harry Teel

New waters, maps, hatch charts and illustrations. The best fly fishing in this popular region. ISBN #1-892469-09-X..........$19.95

Fly Fishing Nevada
Dave Stanley

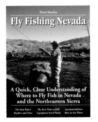

The Truckee, Walker, Carson, Eagle, Davis, Ruby, mountain lakes and more. Mr. Stanley is recognized nationwide as the most knowledgeable fly fisher and outdoorsman in the state of Nevada. He owns and operates the Reno Fly Shop and Truckee River Outfitters in Truckee, California. Newly revised. ISBN #0-9637256-2-9..........$18.95

Fly Fishing Utah
Steve Schmidt

Utah yields extraordinary, uncrowded and little known fishing. Steve Schmidt, outfitter and owner of Western Rivers Fly Shop in Salt Lake City has explored these waters for over 28 years. Covers mountain streams and lakes, tailwaters, and reservoirs. Newly revised. ISBN #0-9637256-8-8..........$19.95

Fly Fishing Idaho
Bill Mason

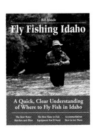

The Henry's Fork, Salmon, Snake and Silver Creek plus 24 other waters. Mr. Mason shares his 30 plus years of Idaho fly fishing. Newly revised. ISBN #1-892469-17-0..........$18.95

A Woman's Guide To Fly Fishing Favorite Waters
Yvonne Graham

Forty-five of the top women fly fishing experts reveal their favorite waters. From scenic spring creeks in the East, big trout waters in the Rockies to exciting Baja: all described from the female perspective.
ISBN #1-892469-03-0..........$19.95

Business Traveler's Guide To Fly Fishing The Western States
Bob Zeller

A seasoned road warrior reveals where one can fly fish within a two-hour drive of every major airport in thirteen western states. Don't miss another day fishing!
ISBN #1-892469-01-4..........$18.95

Fly Fishing Magdalena Bay
Gary Graham

Guide and excursion leader Gary Graham (Baja On The Fly) lays out the truth about fly fishing for snook in mangroves, and off-shore marlin. Photos, illustrations, maps, and travel information, this is "the Bible" for this unique region.
ISBN #1-892469-08-1........$24.95

Fly Fishing Pyramid Lake Nevada
Terry Barron

The Gem of the Desert is full of huge Lahontan Cutthroat trout. Terry has recorded everything you need to fly fish the most outstanding trophy cutthroat fishery in the U.S. Where else can you get tired of catching 18-25" trout?
ISBN #0-9637256-3-7.......... $15.95

Fly Fishing Lees Ferry
Dave Foster

This guide provides a clear understanding of the complex and fascinating 15 miles of river that can provide fly anglers 40-fish days. Detailed maps direct fly and spin fishing access. Learn about history, boating and geology, the area's beauty. Indispensable for the angler and intrepid visitor to the Marble Canyon. Newly revised.
ISBN #1-892469-15-4.......... $18.95

Seasons of the Metolius
John Judy

This book describes how a beautiful riparian environment both changes and stays the same over the years. This look at nature comes from a man who makes his living working in nature and chronicles John Judy's 30 years of study, writing and fly fishing his beloved home water, the crystal clear Metolius River in central Oregon.
ISBN #1-892469-11-1..........$20.95

About Us

No Nonsense Fly Fishing Guidebooks give you a quick, clear understanding of the essential information needed to fly fish a region's most outstanding waters. The authors are highly experienced and qualified local fly fishers. Maps are tidy versions of the author's sketchess. These guides are produced by the fly fishers, their friends, and spouses of fly fishers, at No Nonsense Fly Fishing Guidebooks.

All who produce these books believe in providing top quality products at a reasonable price. We also believe all information should be verified. We never hesitate to go out, fly rod in hand, to verify the facts and figures that appear in the pages of these guides. The staff is committed to this research.

It's hard work, but we're glad to do it for you.

Fly Fishing Knots

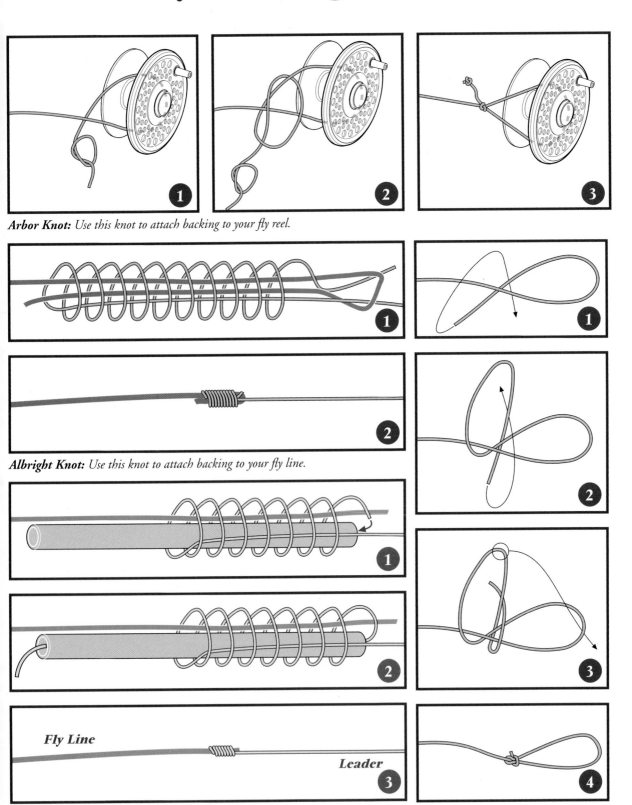

Arbor Knot: Use this knot to attach backing to your fly reel.

Albright Knot: Use this knot to attach backing to your fly line.

Fly Line

Leader

Nail Knot: Use a nail, needle or a tube to tie this knot, which connects the forward end of the fly line to the butt end of the leader. Follow this with a Perfection Loop and you've got a permanent end loop that allows easy leader changes.

Perfection Loop: Use this knot to create a loop in the butt end of the leader for loop-to-loop connections.

166

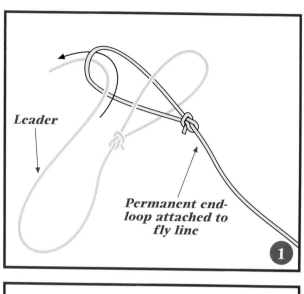

Leader

Permanent end-loop attached to fly line

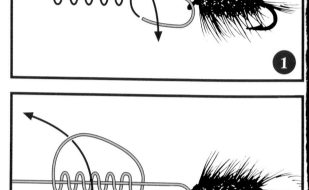

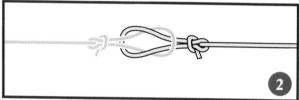

Loop-to-Loop: *Easy connection of leader to a permanent monofilament end loop added to the tip of the fly line.*

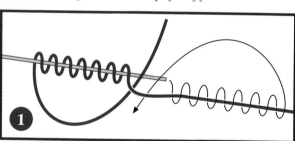

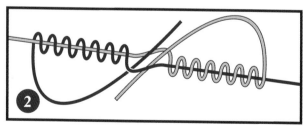

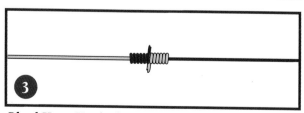

Blood Knot: *Use this knot to connect sections of leader tippet material. Hard to tie, but worth the effort.*

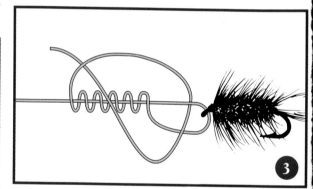

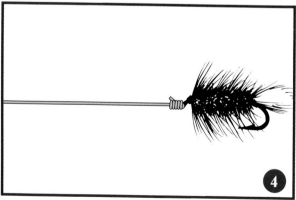

Improved Clinch Knot: *Use this knot to attach the fly to the end of the tippet. Remember to moisten the knot before pulling it up tight.*

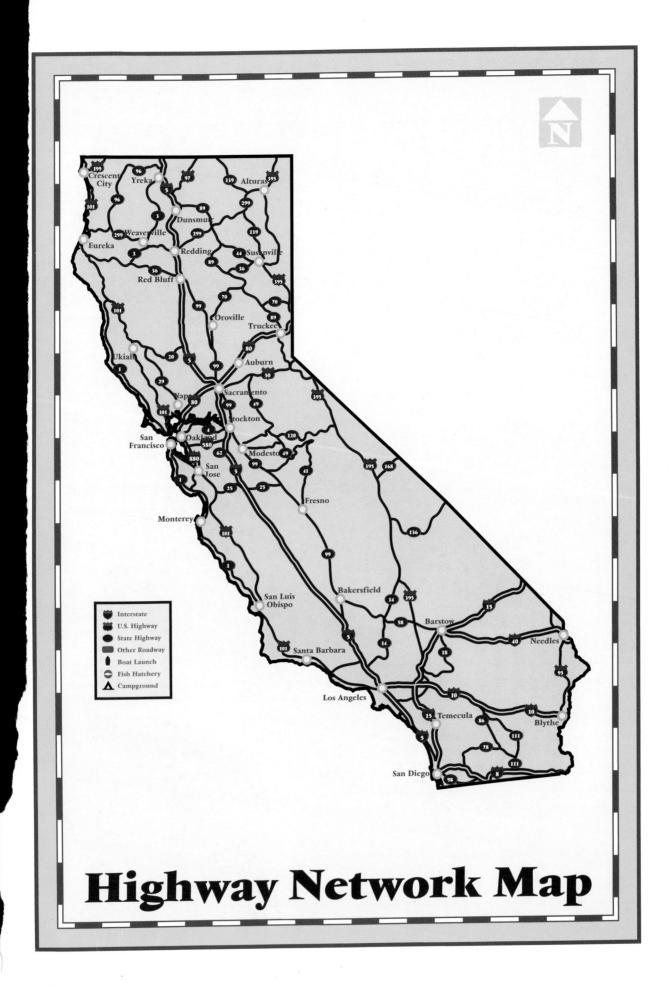

Highway Network Map